YOUTH JUSTICE: CONTEMPORARY POLICY AND PRACTICE

W9-BQJ-982

Youth Justice: Contemporary Policy and Practice

Edited by
BARRY GOLDSON
Department of Sociology, Social Policy and Social Work Studies
The University of Liverpool

Ashgate

Aldershot • Burlington USA • Singapore • Sydney

Ashgate Publishing Limited
Gower House
Croft Road
Aldershot
Hants GU11 3HR
England

Ashgate Publishing Company
131 Main Street
Burlington,
Vermont 05401-5600
USA

Ashgate website:http://www.ashgate.com

Reprinted 2000

British Library Cataloguing in Publication Data
Youth justice : contemporary policy and practice
1. Juvenile delinquency - Great Britain 2. Juvenile
delinquents - Great Britain - Social conditions 3. Juvenile
justice, Administration of - Great Britain 4. Juvenile
delinquency - Government policy - Great Britain
I. Goldson, Barry
364.3´6´0941

Library of Congress Catalog Card Number: 98-074514

ISBN 1 84014 381 9

Printed and bound in Great Britain by Biddles Limited,
Guildford and King's Lynn.

Contents

V
?145
?S
'68
999

Notes on Contributors

Barry Anderson is the Chief Executive of Communities that Care (UK), a recently established organisation sponsored by the Joseph Rowntree Foundation. CtC is pioneering the development of community-based long-term preventive approaches to problems such as youth crime, drug misuse and school failure in various locations throughout the UK. A former Head of NACRO's Youth Crime Section he initially qualified as a social worker and has substantial experience of youth justice practice and management. He has written widely on youth crime and youth justice topics, was a member of the steering group in respect of the Audit Commission *Misspent Youth* report, and spent three years as a visiting lecturer at the South Bank University in London where he developed and taught courses on crime and delinquency.

Justine Ashton qualified as a solicitor in 1994 after completing an LLM in the International Law of Human Rights. She worked with the Howard League for Penal Reform on the Troubleshooter Project before being appointed by the Children's Society as Senior Practitioner working on the National Remand Rescue Initiative. Having established the Initiative's base in HM Young Offender Institution and Remand Centre Feltham she is now located at HM Prison and Young Offender Institution Doncaster.

Adrian Bell is the Director of the Northamptonshire Diversion Unit. He is a qualified teacher and social worker with extensive practice and management experience of social work and criminal justice services. Before taking up his current post in 1993 he managed an Intermediate Treatment Centre in Birmingham and the Juvenile Liaison Bureau in Dudley. He has served as a member of the National Committee of the Intermediate Treatment Federation and he will shortly be assuming full management responsibility for piloting the youth offender team in Northamptonshire.

Charles Bell has been a lead figure in youth justice at a national level for many years and has an authoritative knowledge of contemporary policy and practice developments. He worked closely with both government and opposition in relation to the Criminal Justice Act 1991 and he is a key commentator on the Crime and Disorder Bill 1998 and its associated guidance and regulations. He was a manager of a local authority youth justice team for over 10 years, was active in the Association for Juvenile Justice and is currently active with the National Association for Youth Justice. In 1993 he established *VisionQuest* which provides training and consultancy on youth justice policy and practice and has published the *Youth Justice Newsletter* since June 1996. More recently he has been commissioned to publish and edit *Juvenile Justice Worldwide,* a quarterly journal produced on behalf of *Defence for Children International,* a Geneva-based NGO which promotes the rights of children and young people and the development of best practice in accordance with the United Nations Convention on the Rights of the Child.

Ruth Chigwada-Bailey teaches criminology at Birkbeck College, University of London. She has published widely particularly in relation to Black girls and women and their experiences of the criminal justice process. Her latest book *Black Women and Criminal Justice* was published by Waterside Press in 1997. She has served on a number of editorial boards including *Gender and Education Journal* and *Criminal Justice Matters* and has worked closely with the Mental Health Foundation in developing research.

Helen Davies is a Policy Development Officer with NACRO Cymru and leads on many aspects of youth justice training, consultancy and best practice advice to local authorities in Wales. She has 10 years experience of working with young people in community development and youth justice work. Immediately prior to joining NACRO Cymru she was employed by Barnardos as a Systems Development Officer where she implemented computerised client systems and monitoring and evaluation packages.

Barry Goldson has lectured at the Department of Sociology, Social Policy and Social Work Studies at the University of Liverpool since 1993, prior to which he spent over 10 years working as a practitioner and as a manager with children and young people in both the voluntary and statutory sectors. His primary teaching and research interests include social policy and social welfare law, criminal justice and criminology, children and young people in public care, youth justice and state institutions, the sociology of childhood and youth, and the contemporary children's rights debates. He has researched and published in all of these areas. He retains a keen interest in youth social work and allied practice and has worked closely with the National Children's

Bureau's Practice Development Department since 1994. He is a committee member of the National Association for Youth Justice and has extensive experience of management committee membership and service development in the non-statutory sector.

Mark Grindrod is a Policy Officer and member of the policy coordinating group at the Howard League for Penal Reform. He qualified as a barrister in 1987 and spent six years in practice on the South Eastern Circuit specialising in criminal legal aid work. In 1993 he was appointed by the Howard League to establish, manage and develop their Troubleshooter Project with the expressed aim of 'rescuing' 15 year-old children from prison custody. Following the conclusion of the project in 1997 he went on to conduct research on the quality of through-care and aftercare provided for children in the prison system which has recently been published by the Howard League entitled *Sentenced to Fail – Out of sight, out of mind: Compounding the problems of children in prison.*

Mike Hodgson has managed a regional Diversion Unit in Northamptonshire since 1996. He is a qualified social worker with previous experience as a Juvenile Justice Manager in Birmingham and as a Probation Officer in Northamptonshire.

Shirley E. Jackson lectures at the Department of Social Work Studies at the University of Southampton where her primary teaching and research interests are service user empowerment and rights particularly regarding children, young people and their families. She has nearly 20 years experience of social work and has worked in generic, mental health and youth justice settings. Immediately prior to taking up her academic post at Southampton in 1994 she was the Advice and Policy Worker for the Family Rights Group in London. She is particularly interested in Family Group Conferencing as a means of empowering users of public services and has recently completed a substantial research project evaluating the application of family group conferences within youth justice services and has contributed to the contemporary debates in this field through a number of publications.

Sandy Pragnell has managed a regional Diversion Unit in Northamptonshire since 1993 when youth and adult diversion services were combined. She is a qualified teacher and youth and community worker with previous experience of residential social work. She was appointed as a youth worker in

Northamptonshire in 1984 and as Director of the Juvenile Liaison Bureau in 1985, a post that she occupied until taking up her current position.

David Smith has been Professor of Social Work at the University of Lancaster since 1993, having taught there since 1976. He has researched and published extensively on youth justice, probation policy and practice, inter-agency working in criminal justice, crime prevention, witness support, and victim-offender mediation. His current research activity includes an evaluation of community-based projects for persistent juvenile offenders in Scotland and a study, funded by the ESRC, of perpetrators of racist violence in Greater Manchester.

Anne Worrall is a Senior Lecturer in the Department of Criminology at Keele University prior to which she was Director of the MA/Diploma in Social Work programme. She has been a social work lecturer at Manchester University and a probation officer in Staffordshire. She has researched and published in the areas of women and crime, prisons and alternatives to prison. She is author of *Offending Women* published by Routledge (1990) and co-editor (with Pat Carlen) of *Gender, Crime and Justice* published by the Open University Press (1987). She is a member of the Board of Visitors at Drake Hall a women's open prison in Staffordshire, and is author of *Have you got a minute? The changing role of prison Boards of Visitors* published by the Prison Reform Trust (1994). Her latest book *Punishment in the Community* was published by Addison Wesley Longman (1997). She has recently been appointed Honorary Research Fellow at the University of Western Australia, Perth, where she will be researching Community Corrections for six months in 1998.

Preface

The problem of children breaking the law is one of the great preoccupations of our time. In recent years, juvenile crime has attracted unprecedented levels of attention from politicians, child welfare and criminal justice professionals, the media and the public: it has comprised a central site of legislative, policy and practice development. Indeed, crime, and the fear of crime – within which the behaviour of a small minority of children and young people has been prominent – is a dominant human concern as the twentieth century draws to its close.

Over the last two decades the UK has been witness to quite extraordinary developments which have had a profound impact upon its social and economic landscapes. The conditions within which increasing numbers of children and young people live and grow up have been scarred by the emergence and consolidation of patterns of entrenched poverty and associated forms of misery and disadvantage. Simultaneously, the practices of state agencies have manifested distinct signs of compassion fatigue: worn down, constantly responding to policy changes, under-resourced and operating under the permanent glare of critical government. Nowhere has the uneasy relationship between worsening material conditions and hardening policy and practice responses been more apparent than in the field of 'youth justice'. The sentiment behind John Major's words in February 1993, when he proclaimed that 'society needs to condemn a little more and understand a little less', was unmistakable. Moreover, the significance of the prime minister's statement was profound in signalling the shape that subsequent developments in policy and legislation have taken. A mood of unforgiving 'toughness' has forged such developments, and it is a mood which has seemingly survived the potentially disrupting influences of a change of government with the election of 'New Labour' in May 1997. Indeed, the very title of the incoming government's White Paper, *No More Excuses – A new Approach to Tackling Youth Crime in England and Wales*, published in November 1997, was ominous.

What does all of this mean for children and young people in trouble, for the practitioners and agencies who work with them, and for the kind of society in which we live? Why is it that the UK locks up more children than most other countries in the European Union? Why, in the 1990s, have we witnessed such dramatic changes and departures from the 'youth justice' policies and practices that were developed and applied successfully in the 1980s? The Children Act 1989 is often hailed as a progressive piece of child welfare legislation, and the UK formally ratified the adoption of the United Nations Convention on the Rights of the Child in December 1991. What can we deduce from the tensions and contradictions that are lodged between the provisions of child welfare law and the conventional obligations of European instruments on the one hand, and the harsh, retributive and punitive direction of 'youth justice' law, policy and practice on the other? How can we refer to policies, practices and processes as comprising a 'justice system' when they so evidently combine to produce and reproduce such blatant forms of injustice? Have the conditions which have been set by the policy context become so antagonistic and suffocating that effective practice has no room to 'breathe' and manoeuvre, or can 'agency' find sufficient space within 'structure' to develop and deliver creative and effective services to children in trouble despite such impediments and obstacles? At a time of monumental change, within which the 'youth justice' system is being restructured, it is these questions, and others, that this book addresses.

In the opening chapter I attempt to examine some of the core issues in the politics of 'youth justice': the structural location of children and young people, the political imperatives that have driven the principal policy shifts in recent years, and the implications of such shifts. I argue that the (re)politicisation of juvenile crime has ushered in a new irrationality, as policy has been energised more by political posturing and 'get tough' rhetoric than it has by a concern for effectiveness and responsibility. The chapter explores the specific provisions of the Crime and Disorder Act 1998 which will impact upon younger children, and it sets out a critique of the priorities of retribution and punishment by incarceration.

In chapter 1 much of the emphasis is placed upon social class. The 'youth justice' system is conceived in terms of an aggregate of state responses to the regulation of poor and structurally disadvantaged children and young people. Chapters 2 and 3 continue to develop structural analyses. In chapter 2, **Anne Worrall** locates the 'place' (both conceptually and institutionally) ascribed for girls and young women in the 'youth justice' system and critically examines gendered constructions of, and responses to, 'offending' adolescent females. Despite the plethora of 'equal opportunity' statements, policies, and procedures and training initiatives, and, moreover, the anti-discriminatory provisions contained within Section 95 of the Criminal Justice Act 1991, institutionalised forms of 'injustice' continue to affect identifiable groups of children and young people. In addition to class and gender, 'race' comprises a further determining context through which injustice is routinely dispensed. In chapter 3, myself and **Ruth Chigwada-Bailey** interrogate the research literature in relation to the multiple forms of social and criminal injustice endured by black children and young people. Despite the methodological complexities in explicitly identifying and measuring the 'race effect' within the 'youth justice' system, we gather ample evidence to confirm the endemic nature of racism and the appalling over-representation of black children and young people within the most negative domains of social and 'justice' systems.

From the (mis)management of children and young people *within* the 'youth justice' system, **Barry Anderson** shifts the emphasis in chapter 4 to crime prevention and efforts to reduce the likelihood of child criminality and criminalisation. Anderson argues that there are fundamental inconsistencies between policy and practice developments in relation to crime prevention and those which focus on 'youth justice'. He traces the 'rise of prevention' alongside the 'fall of youth justice' and proposes a 'third way', within which dynamic and evidence-based practice initiatives might be developed from within *the community in order to address the holistic needs of children and young people.* Prevention is also a theme of chapter 5, where **Adrian Bell**, **Mike Hodgson** and **Sandy Pragnell** set out an analysis of diversionary strategies, policies and practices which aim to offset the formalised criminalisation of children and young people. By drawing upon their extensive experience with the Northamptonshire Diversion Unit (widely regarded as being in the vanguard of this area of policy and practice), Bell, Hodgson and Pragnell examine the origins and development of effective policy and practice and consider the challenges and opportunities for diversion with respect to the most recent legislation.

Strategic policy and practice development is a key theme of chapter 6, where **Helen Davies** considers the management of juvenile remands and the provision of community-based alternatives to secure accommodation and prison custody in Wales. If we ever needed a reminder of the particular vulnerability of children on remand and the utterly inappropriate nature of many institutional 'placements', it came in July 1990 when Philip Knight, a 15 year-old boy, took his own life whilst being held on remand in Swansea prison. By drawing on an influential Welsh Office report and a major NACRO survey of juvenile remands in Wales, Davies examines the challenges before, and progress towards, the development of community-based services for children and young people on remand.

Social work in the community underlies chapters 7 and 8. In chapter 7,

Shirley Jackson critically examines the development of family group conferencing – a practice initiative with its origins in Maori culture in New Zealand – and its application within the 'youth justice' system. Jackson argues that family group conferences can have quite different forms of application and their underpinning principles are at risk of being corrupted. However, by engaging the imperatives of 'child-centredness' and 'family empowerment' she sets out a considered analysis of the actual and potential contribution of family group conferencing to effective 'youth justice' practice. This is followed by **David Smith**'s analysis of community supervision. Further developing some of the key issues that feature in earlier chapters, Smith provides an analytical overview of policy and practice in this area against a backdrop of changing political priorities. By drawing upon the various traditions which have informed and influenced the 'movement' for restorative justice, he optimistically explores the potential for the re-emergence and redevelopment of community supervision as an integral feature of an improved and more humane 'youth justice'.

In chapter 9, **Justine Ashton** and **Mark Grindrod** provide a powerful account of policy and practice developments in 'rescuing' children from prison custody. The Howard League for Penal Reform and the Children's Society have pioneered progressive interventionist initiatives in this area and by combining their respective experiences Ashton and Grindrod identify and assess the lessons for 'youth justice' which amount to a searing indictment of child incarceration.

From a searing indictment of child incarceration, **Charles Bell** provides a penetrating critique of the most contemporary changes in 'youth justice' law and policy in chapter 10. This concluding chapter reconnects with a number of issues raised in chapter 1 and elsewhere in the book and serves to complete the circle. Bell sets out the means by which the policies of diversion, decriminalisation and decarceration which so effectively guided policy and practice through the 1980s and into the 1990s have been supplanted with the most recent legislative developments by the promotion of prosecution, expanded forms of criminalisation and the intensification of incarceration.

Inevitably there are different emphases in analysis and interpretation running across this book. However, there is also a striking commonality which is consolidated around the consistent call for justice for children and young people. The vulgar politics of 'toughness' and the shrill demands for ever-increasing forms of punishment and retribution betray any notion of rationality and fundamental justice and children and young people simply deserve better.

Barry Goldson, Liverpool

1 Youth (In)Justice: Contemporary Developments in Policy and Practice

BARRY GOLDSON

> But those were the halcyon days of conservatism in the saddle at last, when it
> was national policy to believe we had finally turned from the bleeding-heart
> and mollycoddling theories and practices of the past and entered a new more
> disciplined approach to law and order ... Important studies, theories, and research
> findings from the past were not known, were selectively ignored, or were cast
> aside. Everyone seemed to be starting from scratch in this brave new world
> (Jerome G. Miller, *Last One Over the Wall*).

> *No More Excuses – A New Approach to Tackling Youth Crime in England and
> Wales* (the title of the White Paper presented to Parliament by the Secretary of
> State for the Home Department by Command of Her Majesty, November 1997).

Welfare, Justice and Children: Virtuous Rhetoric – Vicious Reality

September 1990 marked an historic occasion. The World Summit for Children,
which was held in the United Nations headquarters in New York, comprised
the largest gathering of world leaders ever. Seventy-one heads of state and
government – approximately half of the world's presidents and prime ministers
– met to formally adopt a set of principles intended to improve the life
circumstances of children. They observed that 'the well-being of children
requires political action at the highest level' and they pledged 'to take that
action [by making] a solemn commitment to give high priority to the rights of
children' (cited in Children's Rights Development Unit, 1994, p. xi). Margaret
Thatcher attended the summit and the UK government formally ratified the
United Nations Convention on the Rights of the Child in December 1991.

    The Convention sets out principles and detailed standards for the treatment
of children, for laws, policies and practices which affect children, and for

both formal and informal relationships with children. In many senses the adoption of the UN Convention was consistent with the provisions of the Children Act 1989 which came into force in October 1991. The Lord Chancellor described the Act as the 'most comprehensive and far-reaching reform of child law ... in living memory' (Lord Mackay, Hansard, H.L, Vol. 502, Col. 488), and a central thrust of the legislation (stated in its very first section) is that the welfare of children should be of 'paramount concern' in legal proceedings and professional practice.

The United Nations Convention on the Rights of the Child provides that 'a child means every human being below the age of eighteen years' (United Nations, 1989, Article 1) and the Children Act states that 'it shall be the general duty of every local authority ... to safeguard and promote the welfare of children within their area who are in need', that is, those 'who are unlikely to achieve or maintain, or have the opportunity of achieving or maintaining, a reasonable standard of health and development' (Children Act 1989, Sections 17(1) and 17(10) (a)). In England and Wales therefore, the state has both a legal and conventional obligation to 'safeguard and promote' the general health and welfare of its youngest citizens up to their eighteenth birthdays.

Taken together, ratification of the United Nations Convention on the Rights of the Child and the implementation of the Children Act 1989 apparently represented, and were certainly accompanied by, grand statements of political intent. However, as Hewlett (1993, p. 1) has observed, 'despite such impressive initiatives, a large gap between rhetoric and reality remains', and the Children's Rights Development Unit (1994, p. xiii) has added that 'in relation to the social and economic rights in the Convention, there is a very clear dissonance between a professed commitment to children's welfare, and the effective implementation of that commitment. There is evidence that in some very fundamental ways things are getting worse, not better for children'. Indeed, the 1980s and 1990s have been marked by an intensification of socioeconomic stratification and the consolidation of deeper and wider forms of polarisation and structural inequality (Department of Social Security, 1993; Commission on Social Justice, 1994; Joseph Rowntree Foundation, 1995; Hutton, 1996; Walker and Walker, 1997). Such economic patterns have inevitably impacted upon children, with 31 per cent living in poverty and a further 10 per cent held at 'the margins of poverty' (Kumar, 1993). Judged against other industrialised resource-rich countries, the UK invests comparatively little in services which affect the quality of children's lives. In 1989, the UK ranked seventeenth out of the 21 Organisation for Economic Cooperation and Development (OECD) countries with regard to investment in fundamental public services and in 1991, in terms of health spending alone, the UK was ranked twenty-second amongst the 24 OECD countries (Children's Rights Development Unit, 1994, p. xiii). Indeed, the combined effect of contemporary social and economic policies in relation to family support and social security, health care, housing, education and youth and community provision has been to subject substantial numbers of children and young people to the miseries of poverty and structural disadvantage which limit their opportunities and stunt their potential (Goldson, 1997a).

The disjuncture between rhetoric and reality is transparent and it is those children who live at the sharp end of socioeconomic reality who are at greatest risk of becoming the 'fodder' of the youth justice system. It is well established that the social circumstances of children in trouble, 'young offenders', are invariably scarred by complex configurations and multiple interrelated forms of disadvantage (Stewart and Stewart, 1993; Hagell and Newburn, 1994; Bottoms, 1995; Crowley, 1998; Goldson, 1998). However, too often in contemporary youth crime discourse (particularly at the levels of government and media) the formidable and adversarial social circumstances endured by children and young people in trouble are peripheral to the analysis (such as it is). Indeed, the processes of 'dematerialisation and decontextualisation' (Goldson, 1997b) obfuscate aetiological complexities and impose instead a vulgar reductionism underpinned by crude constructions of morality and individual responsibility. In this way, as Gelsthorpe and Morris have observed (1994, p. 982) an 'emphasis on parental and individual responsibility masks wider structural causes of crime (which are) ... explained away as a symbol of moral decay and reprehensible anti-authority attitudes rather than a sign of alienation, hopelessness, the decline in physical surroundings, unemployment, recession, and depression'.

Constructions and conceptualisations of individual and parental responsibility have become central elements within both contemporary youth justice discourse, and policy formation, and I shall return to these issues shortly. For now the point is that the virtuous proclamations from senior politicians in relation to child welfare and social justice have not been translated and expressed through policy, practice and the provision of tangible resources. It was of little surprise therefore, that in January 1995 the United Nations Committee found fundamental violations of children's rights in the UK following its examination of the Government's report to Geneva with respect to its implementation of the UN Convention on the Rights of the Child:

Policy after policy 'has broken the terms of the UN Convention' ... a report of the UN monitoring committee adds up to a devastating indictment of ministers' failure to meet the human rights of Britain's children ... the report is not all bad ... however, the 'positive aspects' cover only four paragraphs, and the remaining 39 are either critical or are recommendations for action (*The Guardian*, 28 January 1995).

Of particular concern to the United Nations Committee was the government's harsh policies in relation to juvenile crime, which were underpinned by retributive and punitive imperatives. Such developments represented a radical departure from the policy trajectory that had evolved during the previous decade as a new mood of 'toughness' emerged and began to eclipse the more measured and considered responses that had guided practice with children in trouble through the 1980s and into the 1990s.

Political Pragmatism Meets Rationality: A Period of Effective Policy and Practice

It is a curious paradox of the 1980s and early 1990s – a time when 'Thatcherism' was at its most commanding and a period which witnessed the most determined and ruthless affronts to social justice – that criminal law provided the space within which progressive, effective and humane policy and practice initiatives in relation to youth crime developed (Goldson, 1994, 1997b, 1997c). The principles of diversion, decriminalisation and decarceration comprised the cornerstones of a dynamic new practice with children in trouble constructed around minimum necessary intervention, systems management, effective monitoring, intra- and inter-agency strategies, systematic and targeted diversionary approaches, community supervision and alternatives to custody (Pitts, 1990; Rutherford, 1992). The formulation and application of such practice was directed and informed by a coalescence of academic research, professional practice developments within 'juvenile justice' and specific policy objectives and political imperatives of successive Conservative administrations. It was a delicately balanced consensus forged around an improbable coincidence of interests, but it was sufficiently robust to steer policy and practice responses to children in trouble for the best part of a decade.

Academic research and practice experience combined to affirm that for the overwhelming majority of 'offending' children their criminal transgressions were petty, opportunistic and transitory. Pitts (1988, p. 133) described juvenile crime as 'usually episodic and unplanned and often a complete shambles' and Dunkel (1991, p. 23 and 1996, p. 37) refers to its 'relative insignificance', little more than a 'ubiquitous and passing phenomenon linked to age'. Added to this was the contribution from the 'labelling theorists' who emphasised the negative impact that premature and overzealous welfare and justice interventions can have in creating or sustaining 'delinquent' identities and behaviour (see, for example, Blackmore, 1984). Perhaps of greatest significance however, was the consistent stream of research and inquiries, independent and state funded, which provided unequivocal evidence of the counterproductive and damaging impact of custodial interventions which left Pitts (1990, p. 8) concluding:

> In as much as social scientific research can ever 'prove' anything it has proved that locking up children and young people in an attempt to change their delinquent behaviour has been an expensive failure ... more and more studies have demonstrated the tendency of these institutions to increase the reconviction rates of their ex-inmates, to evoke violence from previously non-violent people, to render ex-inmates virtually unemployable, to destroy family relationships and to put a potentially victimised citizenry at greater risk.

The positive interrelation between research and practice during this period was bolstered by its paradoxical compatibility with discrete government policy objectives. Throughout the 1980s successive administrations presided over by Margaret Thatcher were resolute in their determination to relieve the Treasury of public spending commitments and to impose swingeing cuts and, as Pratt (1987, p. 429) observed, 'to reduce the custodial population on the grounds of cost effectiveness ... led to general support for alternatives to custody initiatives'. The government was able to exploit the research findings and establish political legitimacy for reducing the numbers of children being sent to custody: a master stroke of expedience and political pragmatism. In this way the 1988 Green Paper contained an explicit and rational policy commitment drawing heavily on the very language of academic research:

> ... most young offenders grow out of crime as they become more mature and responsible. They need encouragement and help to become law-abiding. Even a short period of custody is quite likely to confirm them as criminals, particularly as they acquire new criminal skills from more sophisticated offenders. They see themselves labelled as criminals and behave accordingly (Home Office, 1988, paras. 2.17–2.19).

David Faulkner, the Head of the Home Office Crime Department between 1982 and 1990 (who worked particularly closely and constructively with Douglas Hurd, Home Secretary 1985–89), commenting reflectively during a television interview, captured the emphasis of government policy in recalling that:

> The guiding principle of much of the policy in relation to juvenile offenders was one of the minimum use of custody and that policy was considered ... to have been successful in the visible reduction in known juvenile offending during that period (*Panorama*, 1 November 1993).

Indeed, the statistical data supports Faulkner's assertion. The number of 'juveniles' sentenced to custody between 1981 and 1990 fell from 7,900 to 1,700 (Home Office, 1991). Most compelling, however, was the apparent success of policy and practice, with the increased emphasis on diversion and decarceration producing a corresponding decrease in the incidence of juvenile crime. The Children's Society Advisory Committee noted that:

> Home Office statistics suggest that there has been a 37 per cent decline in the number of known juvenile offenders since 1985. This is partly attributable to demographic changes – the juvenile population has fallen by 25%. However, the number of known juvenile offenders per 100 000 of the population has also fallen, from 3,130 in 1980 to 2,616 in 1990, a drop of 16 per cent. It remains true that juveniles commit a high proportion of all detected offences but this also appears to be declining. In 1980 juvenile crime represented 32 per cent of all crime; in 1991 that figure has dropped to 20 per cent (Children's Society Advisory Committee on Juvenile Custody and its Alternatives, 1993, p. 21).

It would be misleading to describe the developments in policy and practice during this period in terms of unqualified success; not least because the 'justice' which prevailed was permeated with institutional injustices. Girls and young women remained enmeshed within the vagaries of 'welfarism' and black children and young people encountered racism at each discrete stage of the criminal justice process (see Worrall and Goldson and Chigwada-Bailey, this volume). Notwithstanding this important qualification however, significant progress was made in pursuit of a rational and effective decarcerative policy and practice agenda. The significance of political pragmatism in fortifying the consensus which underpinned such progress was crucial however. If political priorities were to shift, as they did in the 1990s, rationality alone would be hard-pressed to sustain diversionary and decarcerative policy and practice developments. Herein lies a familiar theme within the political history of criminal justice policy in which government can be seen 'imputing credibility to those (policies and practices) that fit current ideology and disregarding those that don't' (Miller, 1991, p. 240). Indeed, youth justice politics has proven to be a cynical business within which 'nothing fails like success or succeeds like failure' (ibid., p. xi) and so it was to be.

Ascendant Irrationality: Punishment, Retribution and the (Re)Politicisation of Youth Crime

By early 1993 there was already a fermenting body of opinion – manufactured and/or sustained by the tabloid and middle market press – that penal liberalism in general, and policy and practice regarding 'young offenders' in particular, had gone 'too far'. Media coverage of car crime, outbreaks of civil unrest within which children and young people appeared to be prominent players, and the construction of the 'bail bandit' and 'persistent young offender' (children apparently beyond the reach of the law) fuelled moral panic and the 'folk devilling of children and young people' (Carlen, 1996, p. 48). There was little, if any, considered and dispassionate analysis during this period and no attempt was made to provide separate accounts for the different strands of 'youth deviance'. A crude, reductionist assimilation of disparate behaviours was assembled and, in virtually no time, the rational youth justice policies and practices that had developed over the previous decade were renounced. The conditions which would serve to legitimise a complete repudiation of the principles of diversion, decriminalisation and decarceration emerged at a furious pace (Goldson, 1997b). Bottoms and Stevenson (1992, pp. 23–4) observe that:

> It is a fact well known to students of social policy that reforms of the system often take place not so much because of careful routine analysis by ministers and civil servants in the relevant Department of State ... but because one or more individual incident(s) occurs, drawing public attention to ... policy in a dramatic way which seems to demand change ... the reforms would not have taken place without the public attention created by the original incident.

The tragic death of James Bulger in February 1993 and the arrest of two 10 year-old boys who were later charged with his murder became one such 'individual incident'. The atypical nature of the 'incident' was corrupted to symbolise an unprecedented outbreak of child lawlessness; to trigger a moral panic in which children in trouble were 'described in terms reserved for hated enemies' (Stern, 1998, pp. 169–70). 'Young offenders' became the new 'enemy within', the language of punishment and retribution became ascendant and youth crime was effectively (re)politicised.

Indeed, the Conservative government did not hesitate in its attempts to seize political capital from the James Bulger tragedy. Days after the toddler's death the prime minister, John Major, proclaimed that 'society needs to condemn a little more and understand a little less' and the Home Secretary, Kenneth Clarke, referred to 'really persistent nasty little juveniles' (*Daily Mail*, 22 February 1993). Three months later, and after a Cabinet reshuffle, Michael Howard made his first public pronouncement as the new Home Secretary, referring to a 'self centred arrogant group of young hoodlums ... who are adult in everything except years [and who] will no longer be able to use age as an excuse for immunity from effective punishment ... they will find themselves behind bars' (*Daily Mail*, 3 June 1993). In October of the same year, to rapturous applause at the Conservative Party conference, Howard declared that he was speaking for the nation: 'we are all sick and tired of young hooligans who terrorise communities'. He promised a 'clamp down' and offered assurances that 'prison works'. The reactionary and authoritarian tone of the statements made by the country's most senior politicians was unmistakable. Moreover, it amounted to more than routine political posturing. The sentiments that were being expressed marked a radical new direction in policy responses to juvenile crime as Rutherford (1995, p. 58) notes:

> Rapidly drafted legislation during 1993 shot great holes in the Criminal Justice Act 1991, which was shortly followed by the Criminal Justice and Public Order Act 1994. Where the 1991 Act had removed 14-year-olds from the prison system, the 1994 Act seeks to create a new generation of child prisons for 12–14-year-olds. This is not a return to the 1970s but to the period preceding the Children Act 1908.

Although the 'clamp down' that Howard promised belied all previous experience and knowledge in relation to effective policy and practice with children in trouble, the new irrationality gathered a seemingly unabated momentum as the language of punishment and retribution was manipulated to justify the unjustifiable. Moreover, despite the fact that Howard's policy formulations were criticised from almost all quarters (child welfare organisations, penal reform groups, the probation service, academia, Home Office officials, the judiciary, the House of Lords, the United Nations Children's Rights Committee – see Goldson, 1997b, pp. 138–43) they were bulldozed on relentlessly.

Tonry (1996, p. 179) has observed that:

> Crime is an emotional subject and visceral appeals by politicians to people's

fears and resentments are difficult to counter. It is easy to seize the low ground in political debates about crime policy. When one candidate campaigns with pictures of clanging prison gates ... and disingenuous promises that newer, tougher policies will work, it is difficult for an opponent to explain that crime is a complicated problem, that real solutions must be long term, and that simplistic toughness does not reduce crime rates. This is why, as a result, candidates often compete to establish which is tougher in his views about crime. It is also why less conservative candidates often try to preempt their more conservative opponents by adopting a tough stance early in the campaign.

The extent to which New Labour is 'less conservative' than the Conservative party is a subject for debate. What is clearer, however, is that the former has done little to 'explain that crime is a complicated problem, that real solutions must be long term, and that simplistic toughness does not reduce crime rates'. Indeed, both in opposition and in government Tony Blair's restyled party has offered little that is different in either analysis, or policy formulation, to the Conservative party: the distinctions in relation to youth justice policy and practice – if they exist at all – are infinitesimal. Howard argued that to take account of children's disadvantaged backgrounds in analyses of juvenile crime was to 'take the criminals' side' and to succumb to 'excuses' from 'bleeding heart' social workers and probation officers who are a 'relic from the 1970s' (*Independent on Sunday*, 4 August 1996; *The Guardian*, 16 October 1997). New Labour, whilst still in Opposition, observed that:

> nobody really knows how many persistent young offenders there are because the government has chosen not to find out ... preferring to pretend that juvenile offending is falling ... only making a bad situation worse ... punishment is important as a means of expressing society's condemnation of misbehaviour ... first and foremost youth crime represents acts against other members of the community. Young offenders need to be held to account for their actions ... all this is common sense ... ultimately the welfare needs of the young offender cannot outweigh the needs of the community to be protected from the adverse consequences of his or her offending behaviour. The government seems to have lost sight of this guiding principle. We intend to restore it, changing the law if necessary ... Labour is not going to stand by watching things get even worse (Straw and Michael, 1996, *passim*).

The (re)politicisation of youth crime has ushered in a new agenda moulded and fixed around the imperatives of punishment, retribution and re-moralisation within which two issues have assumed particular importance: the responsibilities of parents and child incarceration.

The role of the family and 'responsible parenting' has taken centre stage in new (albeit simplistic) aetiological analyses of youth crime:

> You can argue forever about the causes of crime. My approach is based on some simple principles. That children – at home and at school – must be taught the difference between right and wrong (Michael Howard, Conservative Home Secretary, October 1993, cited in Cook, 1997, p. 2).

> We will uphold family life as the most secure means of bringing up our children. Families are the core of our society. They should teach right from wrong. They should be the first defence against anti-social behaviour (Tony Blair, Leader of the Labour Party, April 1997, cited ibid.).

Indeed, the notions of re-moralisation and parental responsibility are now central features of youth justice policy. Parenting and the family is conceived as the principal site for socialisation and securing social control: differentiating 'right' from 'wrong', instilling 'decency' and regulating the behaviour of children and young people. However such conceptualisations are promulgated and simplistically popularised in a way which would suggest that families live in a material vacuum. Demands are being made, and social duties piously imposed, 'despite the manifest erosion in the family's ability to shoulder these responsibilities' and seemingly oblivious to 'the earthquake that has shuddered through the family in the last 20 years' (Hewlett, 1993, p. 15). The virtuous rhetoric takes no account of the vicious economic realities and social complexities that many families endure. Whilst Tony Blair, now speaking as prime minister to the Labour Party conference, may refer to the desirability of creating a 'compassionate society' he is quick to add that it must be 'compassion with a hard edge [as] a strong society cannot be built on soft choices' (*The Guardian*, 1 October 1997). Such semantic riddles might invite interpretive conjecture but the introduction of Parenting Orders, Child Safety Orders and child curfews, to which I shall return shortly, require no such decoding.

The stubborn vulgarity that underpins the emphasis on re-moralisation and family responsibility has been accompanied by a restored faith in incarceration and 'the closing shades of the prison house around children' (Rutherford, 1998, p. 8). Here, too, Michael Howard's policy bequest has been left largely undisturbed by New Labour. The Howard League (1995a, p. 12) observed in 1995 that:

> Despite the fact that levels of offending have remained relatively stable over

the past five years there has been a 25 per cent increase in the use of imprisonment in the past two years. Young people constitute a disproportionate percentage of this increase.

There has been no relief in this pattern of child incarceration. The numbers of young people held in prison custody increased by 11 per cent in the first six months of 1997, and current projections indicate that 11,700 young males will be in prison custody by March 1999 (Lee, 1998, p. 12). Although the available statistics are incomplete they suggest, nevertheless, that the UK condemns a 'vastly greater proportion of young people to prison than any other state in the European Union' (Ruxton, 1996, p. 313). This not only flies in the face of all of the research evidence in relation to the rehabilitative failure of incarcerative practice, but also ignores all that we know of the corrosive and brutalising inhumanity of custodial institutions for children and young people (see, for example, Kuper and Williamson, 1993; Calouste Gulbenkian Foundation, 1993; Howard League, 1995a; Her Majesty's Inspectorate of Prisons for England and Wales, 1997). Furthermore, the intensification and diversification of custodial institutions for children, and their pre-eminence within contemporary state responses to juvenile crime, places the UK at loggerheads with the overall spirit of the United Nations Convention on the Rights of the Child, and, more specifically, some of its principal articles, most notably Article 37 which states that the 'arrest, detention or imprisonment of the child ... shall be used only as a measure of last resort and for the shortest appropriate time' (United Nations, 1989). This is consistent with three related international instruments to which the UK is also formally committed: The United Nations Standard Minimum Rules for the Administration of Juvenile Justice – The Beijing Rules – (United Nations, 1985); The United Nations Guidelines for the Prevention of Juvenile Delinquency – The Riyadh Guidelines – (United Nations, 1990a); and The United Nations Rules for the Protection of Juveniles Deprived of their Liberty 1990 – The Havana Rules – (United Nations, 1990b). Despite all of this however, Stern (1998, p. 169) observes that the imprisonment of children continues:

> The British Conservative government, in power from 1979 to 1997, decided to set up a number of new prisons for children aged twelve to fourteen, to be called secure training centres and to be run by private contractors. The incoming Labour administration, after initial hesitation, adopted the idea. A new intolerance and brutality in attitudes is widespread.

Undermining Child Welfare: Denying Youth Justice

The new agenda for youth justice policy and practice (established by the Conservative administration with the Criminal Justice Act 1993 and the Criminal Justice and Public Order Act 1994 (Goldson, 1997b and 1997c) and subsequently tailored, fashioned and applied by New Labour) draws its most recent statutory authority from the Crime and Disorder Act which received Royal Assent on 31 July 1998. The Act provides that 'the purpose of the youth justice system is to cut offending [and] action must be taken quickly to nip youth offending in the bud' (Home Office, 1998, p. 1). Little or no reference is made to the welfare of children and the provisions of the Act particularly target young children, including those below the age of criminal responsibility. In this adversarial spirit the new legislation provides for Parenting Orders; Child Safety Orders; local child curfews and the abolition of the rebuttable presumption that a child is *doli incapax* and, taken together with the implementation of the Secure Training Order in March 1998 (as provided by the Criminal Justice and Public Order Act 1994) and the operationalisation of the first Secure Training Centre in April 1998, it consolidates a sequence of policy and practice developments which will only serve to undermine child welfare and deny youth justice.

Targeting Parents: Criminalisation and Punishment

The Crime and Disorder Act promotes a punitive vision of parental responsibility rooted in constructions of family pathology, 'problem families' and 'crime-prone families' which reach back into the previous century. The work of West, who conducted a series of longitudinal studies of 'delinquency' between 1969 and 1982, provides a contemporary expression of this (masculinist and patriarchal) approach:

> The typical criminogenic family is beset by chronic problems ... parents who let their children spend most of the leisure time away from the family, fathers who never took part in their son's leisure activities and mothers whose expectations of their son's future career were low in comparison with his educational achievement, were all more likely than others to have sons becoming delinquent (West, cited in Cook, 1997, p. 13).

All the signs of a 'clamp down' on parents were in evidence before the publication of the Act. In Labour's pre-election publications the Home Secretary-in-waiting, Jack Straw, claimed that 'it is as children that people learn the difference between right and wrong and to behave in a socially acceptable way ... [but] too often parents are not made to face up to their responsibilities' (Straw and Michael, 1996). More recently Straw has expressed his dubious conceptualisations of parenting through the media: 'What I am trying to break is the excuse culture that has developed ... none of us should evade our responsibilities for our children. You have got to get parents to accept their responsibilities. The earlier you get to these parents and their children the better' (*The Guardian*, 26 September 1997). In September 1997, when the government published a series of 'consultation documents', it became clear that New Labour had plans to provide the courts with powers to deal with parents who are adjudged to 'wilfully neglect their parental responsibilities' (Home Office, 1997a, p. 5).

Sections 8–10 of the Crime and Disorder Act 1998:

> provide the courts with a new court disposal called a *parenting order*. The order is designed to *help* and *support* parents or guardians in addressing their child's anti-social or offending behaviour. It will be available in *criminal*, civil and family proceedings courts ... the parenting order can consist of two elements: a *requirement* on the parent or guardian to attend counselling or guidance sessions ... and *requirements* encouraging the parent or guardian to exercise a measure of *control* over the child ... If the parent *fails* without reasonable excuse *to comply* with any requirement of a parenting order he or she will be *guilty of an offence* and will be liable to summary *conviction* to a fine of up to £1,000 (Home Office, 1998, pp. 5–6, my emphasis).

The conceptual confusion intrinsic to the juxtaposition of 'help' and 'support' (albeit coercive and accessed through a court order) with a 'requirement' to 'control', and the visitation of substantial financial penalties for the 'offence' of 'failure to comply', is deeply problematic and insidiously authoritarian. The Order is predicated upon a pathologising and deeply offensive notion that parents of children in trouble 'wilfully refuse to accept their responsibilities' and negates the harsh material contexts invariably endured by such parents and their children. Two decades' worth of antagonistic social and economic policies have stripped resources and services from families with the greatest need for them, as public spending has been consistently pegged back. As I discussed earlier in this chapter, families have been increasingly cast to the vagaries of the free market as child poverty and all of its related problems has intensified and widened (Hewlett, 1993; Holterman, 1996; Goldson, 1997a). It is within this context that the Parenting Order is to impose – by way of criminal law – utterly unrealistic expectations on parents.

Criminalising and punishing parents is fundamentally at odds with established principles in child welfare including those provided by law, guidance and regulations: the Children Act 1989 'welfare checklist'; the 'non-adversarialist' approach and the 'no-order' principle of the same Act (Department of Health, 1991); working in partnership with families (Family Rights Group, 1991); and the more recent 're-focusing' initiatives in relation to 'family support' (Department of Health, 1995). The irrationality of the Parenting Order is self-evident, and, as Cavadino (1997, p. 5) notes 'punishing a parent because of a child's refusal to obey a control "requirement" could result in injustice, increase parents' resentment and put children more at risk than ever'.

Targeting Children (1): Distorting Protection – Imposing Confinement

The age of criminal responsibility in England and Wales is set at just 10 years and, as such, children may be formally criminalised earlier in their lives than in the overwhelming majority of countries in the European Union (Booth, 1991; McCarney, 1996; Ruxton, 1996), an important point to which I shall return shortly. The New Labour administration has stated that 'the government has no plans to change the age of criminal responsibility' (Home Office, 1997a: 6). However, the Crime and Disorder Act 1998, by providing for the Child Safety Order and local child curfews, has effectively widened the criminalising net by specifically targeting children below the age of criminal responsibility. These new powers re-focus the gaze from the 'problem' and 'criminogenic family' to the 'problem area' and 'crime-prone estate' and, not unlike the pathologising domain assumptions that underpin the Parenting Order, they have long-established antecedents. Indeed, the orders have their historical roots in the nineteenth century 'rookeries' of Dickensian England: 'deprived' and 'depraved' enclaves; 'fertile breeding grounds' for juvenile crime. Again, similar to the Parenting Order, there were early indications of these policy initiatives to specifically target the youngest children. The Conservative Party's 1997 Green Paper 'Preventing Children Offending' (Home Office, 1997b) proposed curfews for the under-10s, and earlier still Jack Straw had commented that 'there is very great concern about the number of younger children who are out on the streets late at night ... we are talking about the under 10s possibly being off the streets by 9.00 pm. ... I see them when I am driving back from the Commons and wonder where their parents are. Curfews seem to be a sensible way to deal with the issue' (*The Guardian*, 3 June 1996). However, it was not until the publication of the government's 'consultation paper' that the detail of its proposals emerged (Home Office, 1997a).

Indeed, the 'consultation paper' made proposals for:

> A child *safety* order to enable courts to impose conditions *protecting* children under ten who are *at risk* of *becoming involved* in crime; and new powers for local authorities to impose child *curfews* on children under ten in *public areas,* to deal with the real nuisance they *can* cause and to *deny* young children *temptation and the opportunity* to pick up anti-social *or* criminal habits (Home Office, 1997a, p. 3, my emphasis).

Sections 11–13 of the Crime and Disorder Act provide for the Child Safety Order, and sections 14–15 for the child curfew. Again, at first reading the benign language might conceal an authoritarian agenda. The 'safety' and 'protection' emphasis of the former order is interesting in its appeal to child-welfare discourse. The cold fact of the matter however, is that a child can be made the subject of a court order (with the looming threat of a full care order for 'failing to comply' (Home Office, 1998, p. 7)) for no more than a perceived 'risk of becoming involved in crime'. Equally, a child might be confined indoors and denied access to 'public areas' for no graver reason than their potential capacity to cause 'nuisance', and the proposed objective of the local child curfew to 'deny' 'temptation' is tantamount to the deification of the court: 'lead me not into temptation but deliver me from evil'! Indeed, the benign forms of expression anaesthetise overtly coercive practices. It is a language employed, in the words of Orwell (1954, p. 245), 'not so much to express meanings as to destroy them'. It is, as Garland and Young (1983, p. 18) once put it, a prime example of the political power of language to forge a distinction between the 'public realm of representations, significations and symbolic practices and the operational realm of sanctions, institutions and practices'. But there are other problems with these new powers quite apart from the way in which they are represented.

First, there is an uncritical assumption that the 'home' is a safe place for children. If a principal concern of these orders is really 'child safety' then serious recognition that the family can be a 'dangerous place' for some children is warranted (Parton, 1991). The complete absence of any such analysis with regard to either Child Safety Orders or Child Curfews might lead us to other conclusions. Donzelot (1980) is helpful here and we are reminded that the 'policing of families' has comprised a history of 'government through the family' as distinct from a record of humanity and welfare: the imperatives of surveillance and regulation overshadow any child-care priorities.

Second, relatively little is known in relation to the efficacy of child curfews. What we do know however leaves little room for optimistic prognoses.

Simpson from the Flinders University of South Australia, has possibly undertaken the widest research in this field. Simpson has studied child curfews in the USA and Australia where 270 cities have passed curfew laws. He has observed that the evidence in terms of the effectiveness of curfews regarding both child protection and crime prevention is very inconclusive; curfews represent a fundamental breach of human rights (both children's and parents'); and, in practice, curfews are implemented and applied in a targeted and discriminatory way with particular neighbourhoods and identifiable groups of children and young people more likely than others to be subject to the imposed forms of exclusion (particularly African-American children in the USA and Aboriginal children in Australia) (Simpson, 1997).

Third, and closer to home, child curfews have been applied in Scotland where the violation of the human rights of children and young people has been operationalised through a 'pilot' policing experiment. On 23 October 1997, Strathclyde Police and South Lanarkshire Council launched a 'Child Safety Initiative' in three areas of Hamilton. At the outset of the 'initiative' four key objectives were defined by the police: to protect the safety of children and young people; to address and cut down 'youth disorder'; to reduce crime concern; and to decrease the opportunities for children and young people to become involved in crime. The Chief Constable of Strathclyde Police, John Orr, stated that the 'principal aim' of the high profile after-dark police operation was 'to ensure that vulnerable youngsters ... are not exposed to dangers or tempted to become embroiled in crimes associated with being out too late in the dark and alone or with equally vulnerable company' (Scottish Human Rights Centre, 1998, p. 8). The Scottish Human Rights Centre (1998, pp. 8 and 11) note:

> ... even where no crime was being committed, the police considered they had a right to intervene if they thought that a crime *might* be. committed. Precisely how the police would make an assessment of that is unclear ... it is unprecedented for the police to take action where they thought there might be some possibility of a crime occurring at some point ... it is useful to see the wide powers that the police are giving to themselves ... what powers are they exercising to justify questioning children or even detaining them and removing them home or to a police station (original emphases)?

Clearly, there are fundamental human rights and civil liberties at stake. What if a child who the police think *might* commit a crime refuses to be taken home: are they to be detained? Article 8 of the European Convention on Human Rights provides for the respect for family life (Bell, 1998, p. 18). Is such police interference in the decisions that parents make about their children a violation of that article? Parents are not being left to make decisions about when their children can go out and where they may go. What about the right to free movement in a democracy? What about a breach of curfew? Is there to be such a thing? If so 'a breach of curfew would become dangerously close to a 'status offence' which would be in breach of articles 2 and 9 of the International Covenant on Civil and Political Rights which has been ratified by the UK' (Tanner, 1997, p. 7).

Fourth, and related to the human rights issue, is the question of legality. The Scottish Human Rights Centre (1998, p. 15) observe that:

> In America, curfews are enforced by way of laws, rather than police 'initiatives'. This has led to challenges to curfew laws which have resulted in some of them being overturned on the grounds that they interfered with children's fundamental freedoms of movement and expression. In one case, judges indicated that 'the number of juveniles engaged in safe and innocent activity almost certainly outnumbers those engaged in criminal activity, the courts have held that confining all of them to their homes ... without evidence that such draconian restrictions were necessary to address juvenile crime is not a response to the problem'.

The Child Safety Orders and the Child Curfews distort and corrupt the language of child protection to legitimise expanded forms of child confinement. Particular neighbourhoods and estates thought to be 'problem areas' will inevitably be targeted. Equally identifiable groups of children and young people will attract disproportionate levels of police attention and the black experience of 'stop and search' initiatives (see Goldson and Chigwada-Bailey, this volume) is ominous in this respect. The research findings that are available do little to validate the 'protectionist' or 'preventionist' claims that have been made in order to justify these new powers. In terms of child protection forcing children home may exacerbate the risks that some of them face from within the family. These new youth 'justice' initiatives undermine children's rights and parent's rights and represent an unwelcome encroachment upon fundamental civil liberties.

Targeting Children (2): Eroding Legal Safeguards – Institutionalising Injustice

I have noted already that the age of 'criminal responsibility' or 'criminal minority' in England and Wales is set at just 10 years. There is no international standard regarding the age at which criminal responsibility can be reasonably imputed on a child although Article 40 (3)(a) of the United Nations Convention on the Rights of the Child provides that States Parties should 'establish a minimum age below which children shall be presumed not to have the capacity to infringe the penal law' (United Nations, 1989). Furthermore, Article 4.1 of the 'Beijing Rules' states that 'in those legal systems recognising the concept of the age of criminal responsibility for juveniles, the beginning of that age shall not be fixed at too low an age level, bearing in mind the facts of emotional, mental and intellectual maturity' (United Nations, 1985). Although the UK is formally committed to these international instruments it nonetheless sets the age of criminal responsibility in England and Wales (and other UK jurisdictions: Scotland, eight years; Northern Ireland, 10 years) amongst the lowest level in Europe. This is clearly problematic from a children's rights perspective and is anomalous with other aspects of law including the age of consent for sexual relations, marital status and civil majority. Indeed, there have been campaigns to raise the age of criminal minority based, not least upon evidence that 'it can be shown that there are no negative consequences to be seen in terms of crime rates' (Dunkel, 1996, p. 38). However despite this, the government has recently stated that it 'has no plans to change the age of criminal responsibility' (Home Office, 1997a, p. 6).

Hitherto, the principle of *doli incapax* has provided some legal safeguards to the youngest children processed within the youth justice system. Under this principle children between the ages of 10 and 13 years are presumed to be incapable of criminal intent and this presumption must be rebutted by the prosecution before they can be convicted. In order to rebut the presumption, the prosecution must show beyond 'reasonable doubt' that the child appreciated that what they did was 'seriously wrong' as opposed to merely naughty or mischievous. Cavadino has observed that 'although in many cases the evidence needed to overturn the presumption is not great, the existence of the presumption currently makes lawyers, magistrates and judges stop and think about the degree of responsibility of each individual child' (Cavadino, 1997, p. 4). Thus the doctrine of *doli incapax* – a long established part of the law dating back to the time of Edward III – is an important legal safeguard for 10–13 year-old children: children, that is, who would be below the age of criminal responsibility in most other European countries. As the Penal Affairs Consortium (1995, p. 5) has noted:

> Far from being an outmoded survival from an earlier era, the doli incapax rule is fully consistent with our increasing knowledge of child development and learning, which tells us that children mature and learn over differing time spans.

A presumption of this kind acknowledges that there is variation in the speed of the maturation process.

Indeed, the importance of *doli incapax* was recognised by the Conservative government's White Paper in 1990:

> The age of criminal responsibility, below which no child may be prosecuted, is 10 years, and between the ages of 10 and 13 a child may only be convicted of a criminal offence if the prosecution can show that he knew what he did was seriously wrong. The Government does not intend to change these arrangements which make proper allowance for the fact that children's understanding, knowledge and ability to reason are still developing (Home Office, 1990, para. 8.4).

New Labour, however does not share this view and has referred to the need to 'reform' (Straw and Michael, 1996, p. 11; Home Office, 1997a, p. 5) and 'modernise' (Straw and Michael, 1996, p. 15; Home Office 1997a, p. 2) what it impatiently describes as an 'archaic rule' (Home Office, ibid.). Here we have further evidence of the New Labour 'iron fist' (authoritarianism and child criminalisation) crudely concealed within the 'velvet glove' (the benign language of reform and modernisation). Indeed, such 'soft tones' were little more than code for expunction. Section 34 of the Crime and Disorder Act 1998 provides for the abolition of the rebuttable presumption that a child is *doli incapax* and 'for the purposes of criminal law, this will mean that children who are over the age of criminal responsibility (10 to 13 year-olds) will be treated in the same way as other juveniles (14 to 17 year-olds) when deciding whether or not prosecution is appropriate' (Home Office, 1998, p. 9). Such an erosion of legal safeguards inevitably institutionalises fundamental injustice. But this is not all:

> Section 35 extends section 35 of the Criminal Justice and Public Order Act 1994 which allows a court to draw inferences from the failure of the accused to give evidence or answer questions at trial. This section now applies to all persons aged ten and over, ensuring that all juveniles (10 to 17 year olds) are treated in the same way (Home Office, 1998, p. 10).

The abolition of *doli incapax* now means that in England and Wales a 10 year-old child – still in junior school – is presumed to be as criminally responsible as an adult; an outrage only compounded by Section 35 of the Crime and Disorder Act, the practical implications of which will mean that any bewilderment that a child experiences when exposed to the formality of the police station and/or criminal courts (which may result in her/his incapacity to answer questions and/or give evidence) may also serve to criminalise them further. There is a grave risk here that the child will be punished not simply for their wrongdoing, but also for the very immaturity that inevitably, and naturally, besets the youngest and most vulnerable of children.

Targeting Children (3): Diversifying and Intensifying Incarceration

On 2 March 1993, Kenneth Clarke, the Home Secretary at the time, announced on behalf of the Conservative government new measures for the detention of 'that comparatively small group of very persistent juvenile offenders whose repeated offending makes them a menace to the community' (cited in Howard League, 1995b, p. 1). The Criminal Justice and Public Order Act received Royal Assent on 3 November 1994 and provided for the new child jails: secure training centres. Section 1 of the Act created a new sentence – a Secure Training Order – for children between the ages of 12 and 14 years. The criteria allow for an Order to be made in respect of a child convicted of three or more imprisonable offences (not necessarily on separate occasions and with no test relating to the seriousness of the offences) and who has been found to be in breach of a Supervision Order or to have committed an imprisonable offence whilst subject to such an Order. Technically, therefore, a 12 year-old child could be imprisoned for three offences of shoplifting.

The government's proposals were met with widespread opposition, not least because they were in breach of the principles contained within Article 37 of the United Nations Convention on the Rights of the Child to use imprisonment only 'as a measure of last resort and for the shortest appropriate period of time'; and in Article 40 to seek 'alternatives to institutional care ... to ensure that children are dealt with in a manner appropriate to their well-being' (United Nations, 1989). They were also in conflict with Article 17 (1)(c) of the 1985 United Nations Minimum Rules for the Administration of Juvenile Justice (the Beijing Rules) which states that 'deprivation of liberty shall not be imposed unless the juvenile is adjudicated of a serious act involving violence against another person or of persistence in committing other serious offences and unless there is no other appropriate response' (United Nations, 1985). The opposition to the new jails, however widespread and authoritative, went unheeded (Goldson, 1997b; 1997c). The Labour Party, whilst opposing various aspects of the Criminal Justice and Public Order Bill in its committee stages, abstained on the final vote (Howard League, 1997b, p. 3). It effectively colluded with the introduction of the new child jails which reversed a direction in youth justice policy dating back to the Children Act 1908. There are three principal grounds for opposing the secure training centres.

First, the issue of efficacy. Currie (1996, pp. 5–7) notes:

> The argument you are likely to hear nowadays, in brief, goes like this ... the strategy of radically increasing the incarceration rate as our main response to crime has 'worked', and would indeed work even better if we increased it a lot more ... all of these assertions are false ... within our poorest communities we're sending an unparalleled flood of young people into the jails and prisons ... the range of credible answers to the question of what we have gotten by way of crime reduction from our prison binge runs from 'not much' to 'virtually nothing'.

Indeed, as I discussed earlier, all of the available research confirms the miserable failure of child custody in terms of both deterrence and rehabilitation.

Second, the fiscal cost. £30 million was set aside for the start up costs of the secure training centres (Howard League, 1995b, p. 6), and the annual costs for each child is estimated at £120 thousand, well over £ 2,000 per week (Linehan, 1998, p. 6). The Penal Affairs Consortium (1994, p. 5) has observed that to 'devote such large sums of money to such a measure, at a time when resources for effective programmes of supervision in the community are being pegged back, is wholly unjustifiable.'

Third, and most important, the human cost. The very concept of incarcerating such children is grotesque. Many of the children will be held hundreds of miles from their home area. Removing children from their families, schools, friends and communities is deleterious to their welfare, maturational growth and development. Research and practice experience provides unequivocal evidence of this in relation to many children in the public care. Parker et al. (1991), Biehal et al. (1995), Sinclair et al. (1995) and Triseliotis et al. (1995) have each explored the health and health education deficits of children living away from home. Jackson (1989), Devlin (1995) and the Social Services Inspectorate and the Office for Standards in Education (1995) have focused on the difficulties that such children experience in relation to education and training opportunities. Similarly, there is no shortage of research evidence to confirm that the processes of acquiring life skills and preparing for 'adulthood' are severely hampered by institutional living (Stein and Carey, 1986; Garnett, 1992; Biehal et al., 1995). All of these problems are compounded for children who are incarcerated who also have to endure the brutalities endemic within the operational cultures of closed institutions

(Howard League, 1995a). The children who are sent to the secure training centres, by definition, will be children with behavioural and emotional problems. To develop trusting and meaningful relationships with such children takes time, but it also requires patience, developed skills and expertise. Despite whatever good intentions the staff in the secure training centres might have they will inevitably lack the necessary experience, training and qualifications (Goldson, 1995) and their priorities will have to be set on containment and institutional security (Howard League, 1995a). The secure training centres will be tinderboxes of human misery with anxious staff supervising deeply distressed and resentful children. The first of the new child jails, Medway in Kent, received its first 'trainee' in the middle of April 1998. Is it any surprise that the populist press were reporting a 'rampage' and 'a riot at children's prison' (*Daily Mail*, 27 June 1998), and the professional press were demanding an 'inquiry after child jail disturbance' (*Community Care*, 2–8 July 1998), no more than 10 weeks after it had opened its gates to that first child?

Despite such critique and concern, however, New Labour have not detracted from the legacy that they inherited from their Conservative predecessors and 'plans to open another four secure training centres seem to be moving apace' (Howard League, 1998, p. 4). The new child jails both intensify and diversify the penal estate for children. Not only do they represent material institutions they also symbolise the way that the state thinks about children. To borrow Mathieson's (1991, p. 183) words 'as a way of thinking [they] emphasise violence and degradation as a method of solving inter-human conflicts'. The building of new child jails implies in the wider society, that the incarcerative response is a necessary and effective response; for who would build such secure training centres without believing in them? In reality we can conclude that the (re)politicisation of youth crime is such that incarceration has a political life of its own irrespective of its effect or cost (fiscal or human). This is perhaps the most fundamental expression of the profound irrationality and cynicism that characterises contemporary youth (in)justice. Children, many of them amongst the most disadvantaged in modern Britain, are little more than defenceless pawns in a bigger political game. The social value of children in trouble is apparently worth nought, but the political price of expressing compassion and re-engaging a rational youth justice agenda is seemingly beyond the government's reach or ambition.

'Childhood' and 'Justice'

I have attempted here to analyse the politics of youth justice and to examine the contemporary developments in policy and practice that have stemmed from such politics. Rationality and political pragmatism has been eclipsed by the shrill punitive and retributive demands of a 'no excuses' agenda which has severed the policy-research linkage. Youth crime has been 'dematerialised' as the aetiological emphasis has crudely shifted to constructions of individual responsibility and morality. Brown (1998, p. 116) captures this phenomenon particularly well:

> 'youth' has been dragged along by adult institutions in their quest to secure a complex web of political interests. The young have been constructed through policy not as citizens, but as objects of increasingly repressive modes of governance. As adult anxiety and punitive desire escalate, the (metaphorical) body of the delinquent is carved up to serve political and popular appetites, and effectiveness and rationality are increasingly subsumed under ideological imperative.

All of this raises key issues in relation to our conceptualisations of 'childhood' and 'justice' (both social and criminal). Glendon (cited in Hewlett, 1993, p. 21) notes that the 'stories we tell', the 'symbols we deploy' and the 'visions we project' through state policy, forge the identity of the nation and help to construct public morality. What messages does the contemporary drift in youth justice policy convey in relation to 'childhood' and 'justice'? Increasing numbers of disadvantaged children are being condemned to systems of exile (the child safety order, the child curfew, the secure training centre, the young offender institution). What does this say regarding the identity of the nation, civil society and our public morality?

How are we to understand the place of children in contemporary Britain? How indeed has the broad public debate about youth crime (however ill-informed), the behaviour of some children and the very nature of 'childhood' – a debate too often fuelled by the irresponsible statements of politicians and the media – influenced conceptual constructions of 'children' and 'childhood'? Identifiable groups of children – the most disadvantaged and those in trouble – have seemingly been ascribed particularised identities which resonate with 'otherness', 'immorality' and 'failure'. In youth justice discourse the conflation of 'child' with 'offender' has apparently legitimised what Jenks (1996, p. 128) has called a 'conceptual eviction' whereby 'children who commit (offences) should be removed from the category of "child" altogether'. And so we have the 'adult-child', the 'child' whose recalcitrance betrays their very child-status and, as such, is no longer deserving of legal safeguards and compassion. These 'would-be children' have been relegated to another (anti)social order 'essentialised through images of evil and pathology' (Jenks, 1996, p. 129).

Politics is a question of deciding priorities and values. Youth justice policy is equally about deciding priorities and values. Is this the way that we want to treat our most disadvantaged and vulnerable children? Ultimately this is the question with which we are confronted. As Hewlett (1993,p. 2) observes, 'an anti-child spirit is loose in these lands'. It is a spirit that must be extinguished in any society that makes claims to human civility.

References

Bell, C. (1998), 'Clocking the Local Child Curfew', *Youth Justice Newsletter*, No. 9, pp. 18–19.

Biehal, N., Clayden, J., Stein, M. and Wade, J. (1995), *Moving On: Young People and Leaving Care Schemes*. London, HMSO.

Blackmore, J. (1984), 'Delinquency theory and practice: A link through IT', *Youth and Policy*, No. 9.

Booth, T. (ed.) (1991), *Juvenile Justice in the New Europe*, Sheffield, University of Sheffield Unit for Social Services Research.

Bottoms, A. (1995), *Intensive Community Supervision of Young Offenders: Outcomes, Process and Cost*, Cambridge, University of Cambridge Institute of Criminology.

Bottoms, A. and Stevenson, S. (1992), 'What Went Wrong? Criminal Justice Policy in England and Wales 1945–70' in Downes, D. (ed.), *Unravelling Criminal Justice*, London, Macmillan.

Brown, S. (1998), *Understanding youth and crime: Listening to youth?*, Buckingham, Open University Press.

Calouste Gulbenkian Foundation (1993), *One Scandal Too Many ... the case for comprehensive protection for children in all settings*, London, Calouste Gulbenkian Foundation.

Carlen, P. (1996), *Jigsaw – A Political Criminology of Youth Homelessness*, Buckingham, Open University Press.

Cavadino, P. (1997), 'Government Plans for Youth Justice', *Childright*, No. 141, pp. 4–5, Essex, Children's Legal Centre.

Children's Rights Development Unit (1994), *UK Agenda for Children*, London, CRDU.

Children's Society Advisory Committee on Juvenile Custody and its Alternatives (1993), *A False Sense of Security: The Case Against Locking Up More Children*, London, The Children's Society.

Commission on Social Justice (1994), *Social Justice: Strategies for National Renewal*, London, Vintage.

Cook, D. (1997), *Poverty, crime and punishment*, London, Child Poverty Action Group.

Crowley, A. (1998), *A Criminal Waste: A Study of Child Offenders Eligible for Secure Training Centres*, London, The Children's Society.

Currie, E. (1996), *Is America really winning the war on crime and should Britain follow its example?*, London, NACRO.

Department of Health (1991), *The Children Act 1989 Guidance and Regulations: Volume 1 Court Orders*, London, HMSO.

Department of Health (1995), *Child Protection: Messages from Research*, London, HMSO.

Department of Social Security (1993), *Households Below Average Income*, London, HMSO.

Devlin, A. (1995), *Criminal Classes*, Winchester, Waterside Books.

Donzelot, J. (1980), *The Policing of Families*, London, Hutchinson.

Dunkel, F. (1991), 'Legal Differences in Juvenile Criminology in Europe' in Booth, T. (ed.), *Juvenile Justice in the New Europe*, Sheffield, University of Sheffield Unit for Social Services Research.

Dunkel, F. (1996), 'Current Directions in Criminal Policy' in McCarney, W. (ed.), *Juvenile Delinquents and Young People in Danger in an Open Environment*, Winchester, Waterside Books.

Family Rights Group (1991), *The Children Act 1989: Working in Partnership with Families*, London, HMSO.

Garland, D. and Young, P. (eds.) (1983), *The Power to Punish*, London, Heinemann.

Garnett, L. (1992), *Leaving Care and After*, London, National Children's Bureau.

Gelsthorpe, L. and Morris, A. (1994), 'Juvenile Justice 1945–1992' in Maguire, M., Morgan, R. and Reiner, R. (eds.), *The Oxford Handbook of Criminology*, Oxford, Clarendon Press.

Goldson, B. (1994), 'The Changing Face of Youth Justice', *Childright*, No. 105, pp. 5–8.

Goldson, B. (1995), *A Sense of Security*, London, National Children's Bureau.

Goldson, B. (1997a), 'Locked Out and Locked Up: State Policy and The Systemic Exclusion of Children "In Need" in England and Wales', *Representing Children*, Vol. 10, No. 1, pp. 44–55.

Goldson, B. (1997b), 'Children in Trouble: State Responses to Juvenile Crime' in Scraton, P. (ed.), *'Childhood' in 'Crisis'?*, London, UCL Press.

Goldson, B. (1997c), 'Children, Crime, Policy and Practice: Neither Welfare nor Justice', *Children and Society*, Vol. 11, No. 2, pp. 77–88.

Goldson, B. (1998), *Children in Trouble: Backgrounds and Outcomes*, Liverpool, University of Liverpool Department of Sociology, Social Policy and Social Work Studies.

Hagell, A. and Newburn, T. (1994), *Persistent Young Offenders*, London, Policy Studies Institute.

Her Majesty's Inspectorate of Prisons for England and Wales (1997), *Young Prisoners: A Thematic Review by HM Chief Inspector of Prisons for England and Wales*, London, Home Office.

Hewlett, S.A. (1993), *Child neglect in rich nations*, New York, UNICEF.

Holterman, S. (1996), 'The Impact of Public Expenditure and Fiscal Policies on Britain's Children and Young People', *Children and Society*, Vol. 10, No. 1, pp. 3–13.

Home Office (1988,) *Punishment, Custody and the Community*, London, HMSO.

Home Office (1990), *Crime, Justice and Protecting the Public*, London, HMSO.

Home Office (1991), *Criminal Statistics in England and Wales*, London, HMSO.

Home Office (1997a), *Tackling Youth Crime: A Consultation Paper*, London, Home Office.

Home Office (1997b), *Preventing Children Offending*, London, Home Office.

Home Office (1998), *Crime and Disorder Act 1998: Introductory Guide*, London, Home Office.

Howard League (1995a), *Banged Up, Beaten Up and Cutting Up: Report of the Howard League Commission of Inquiry into Violence in Penal Institutions for Teenagers under 18*, London, The Howard League for Penal Reform.

Howard League (1995b), *Secure Training Centres: repeating past failures*, briefing paper, London, The Howard League for Penal Reform.

Howard League (1998), 'HLM: The Howard League Magazine', Vol. 16, No. 3, London, The Howard League for Penal Reform.

Hutton, W. (1996), *The State We're In*, London, Vintage.

Jackson, S. (1989), 'Residential care and education', *Children and Society*, No. 4, pp. 335–70.

Jenks, C. (1996), *Childhood*, London, Routledge.

Joseph Rowntree Foundation (1995), *Inquiry into Income and Wealth*, York, Joseph Rowntree Foundation.

Kumar, V. (1993), *Poverty and Inequality in the UK: the effects on children*, London, National Children's Bureau.

Kuper, J. and Williamson, J. (1993), *Treated with Humanity and Respect? Conditions for Young People in Custody*, London, Children's Legal Centre.

Lee, M. (1998), 'Young People in Prison', *Childright*, No. 143, pp. 12–13, Essex, Children's Legal Centre.

Linehan, T. (1998), 'Secure Training Centres: The Wrong Way to Deal with Young Offenders', *Childright*, No. 147, pp. 6–7, Essex, Children's Legal Centre.

Mathieson, T. (1991), 'The argument against building more prisons' in Muncie, J. and Sparks, R. (eds), *Imprisonment: European Perspectives*, London, Harvester Wheatsheaf.

McCarney, W. (ed.) (1996), *Juvenile Delinquents and Young People in Danger in an Open Environment*, Winchester, Waterside Books.

Miller, J.G. (1991), *Last One Over the Wall: The Massachusetts Experiment in Closing Reform Schools*, Ohio, Ohio State University Press.

Orwell, G. (1954), *Nineteen Eighty Four*, London, Penguin.

Parker, R., Ward, H., Jackson, S., Aldgate, J. and Wedge, P. (1991), *Looking After Children: Assessing Outcomes in Child Care*, London, HMSO.

Parton, N. (1991), *Governing the Family: Child Care, Child Protection and the State*, London, Macmillan.

Penal Affairs Consortium (1994), *The Case Against the Secure Training Order*, London, Penal Affairs Consortium.

Penal Affairs Consortium (1995,) *The Doctrine of 'Doli Incapax'*, London, Penal Affairs Consortium.

Pitts, J. (1988), *The Politics of Juvenile Crime*, London, Sage.

Pitts, J. (1990), *Working with Young Offenders*, London, Macmillan.

Pratt, J. (1987), 'A revisionist history of intermediate treatment', *British Journal of Social Work*, No. 15.

Rutherford, A. (1992), *Growing Out of Crime: The New Era*, Winchester, Waterside Books.

Rutherford, A. (1995), 'Signposting the future of juvenile justice policy in England and Wales' in Howard League for Penal Reform, *Child Offenders: UK and International Practice*, London, The Howard League for Penal Reform.

Rutherford, A. (1998), 'One year on', *HLM The Howard League Magazine*, Issue 1, London, The Howard League for Penal Reform.

Ruxton, S. (1996), *Children in Europe*, London, NCH Action for Children.

Scottish Human Rights Centre (1998), *Time to Go Home – Says Who: An analysis of the Hamilton curfew experience*, Glasgow, Scottish Human Rights Centre.

Simpson, B. (1997), 'Off the Street, Out of the Mall and Home to Your Parents: Curfews and the Social Exclusion of Children and Young People', unpublished paper presented at the *On the Margins: Social Exclusion and Social Work Conference*, University of Stirling 7–10 September, Stirling, Social Work Research Centre University of Stirling.

Sinclair, R., Garnett, L. and Berridge, D. (1995), *Social Work and Assessment with Adolescents*, London, National Children's Bureau.

Social Services Inspectorate and the Office for Standards in Education (1995), *The Education of Children who are Looked After by Local Authorities*, London, Department of Health and OFSTED.

Stein, M. and Carey, K. (1986), *Leaving Care*, Oxford, Blackwell.

Stern, V. (1998), *A Sin Against the Future: Imprisonment in the World*, London, Penguin.

Stewart, G. and Stewart, J. (1993), *Social Circumstances of Young Offenders Under Supervision*, London, Association of Chief Officers of Probation.

Straw, J. and Michael, A. (1996), *Tackling Youth Crime: Reforming Youth Justice. A consultation paper on an agenda for change*, London, Labour Party.

Tanner, P. (1997), 'A Child Safety Initiative or Simply a Curfew', *Childright*, No. 141, pp. 6–7.

Tonry, M. (1996), 'Racial Politics, Racial Disparities, and the War on Crime' in Hudson, B (ed.), *Race, Crime and Justice*, Aldershot, Dartmouth.

Triseliotis, J., Borland, M., Hill, M. and Lambert, L. (1995), *Teenagers and the Social Work Services*, London, HMSO.

United Nations (1985), *The United Nations Standard Minimum Rules for the Administration of Juvenile Justice*, New York, United Nations.

United Nations (1989), *The United Nations Convention on the Rights of the Child*, New York, United Nations.

United Nations (1990a), *The United Nations Guidelines for the Prevention of Juvenile Delinquency*, New York, United Nations.

United Nations (1990b), *The United Nations Rules for the Protection of Juveniles Deprived of their Liberty*, New York, United Nations.

Walker, A. and Walker, C. (1997), *Britain Divided: The growth of social exclusion in the 1980s and 1990s*, London, Child Poverty Action Group.

2 Troubled or Troublesome? Justice for Girls and Young Women[1]

ANNE WORRALL

> It is questionable whether it is necessary to keep the sentence of detention in a young offender institution for girls under 18 (Home Office, 1990, p. 45).

> Just what is going on? Does the new freedom that women have rightly gained include the freedom to act as foully as men? (Paul Barker, *Evening Standard*, 1 May 1996, on the kicking to death of 13 year old Louise Allen by other girls).

In September 1997 a pregnant 17 year-old girl from a 'criminal' family was imprisoned for persistent shoplifting (*The Independent*, 27 September 1997). She came to national attention because an appeal judge, Gabriel Hutton, refused to reduce her sentence by two weeks to avoid her being separated from her baby after its birth. His argument, that being separated from her baby was part of her punishment, appeared discriminatory (as well as inhumane), yet allowing the appeal would also have been seen by some as an example of chivalrous (and therefore discriminatory) leniency. As Judge Pickles remarked when sending Tracey Scott, another teenage mother, to prison:

> Would it be right to let young women know that one way of possibly or probably avoiding custody would be to deliberately become pregnant between the time they have been detected committing a crime and the time they were sentenced? One of the ways of discouraging them is to let them know that some others have been dealt with in an unpleasant way? (*The Independent*, 3 January 1990).

These incidents highlight the shortcomings of a criminal justice system which remains incapable of disentangling the criminal behaviour of a particular group of multiply-disadvantaged girls from their sexuality and which is prepared to lock them up in increasing numbers. Occupying the interface between youth justice and social work, 'troublesome' girls provoke anxiety in those professionals who work with them, and fear and suspicion in those who look on. This chapter will explore the range of legal, welfare and political discourses within which 'troublesome' girls are socially constructed, on the one hand, as deeply maladjusted misfits and, on the other, as dangerous folk devils, symbolic of post-modern adolescent femininity. It will conclude by highlighting some of the principles which already underpin the best of existing practice with girls and young women and which need to be more routinely addressed in the development of youth justice policy.

In the White Paper *Crime, Justice and Protecting the Public* (Home Office, 1990), which preceded the Criminal Justice Act 1991, the Conservative government suggested that the numbers of girls under the age of 18 years sentenced to custody by the courts were so small that the abolition of detention in a young offender institution for this group might be feasible in a civilised society. The 150 or so girls in custody (compared to over 7,000 boys) could be dealt with quite adequately by the 'good, demanding and constructive community programmes for juvenile offenders who need intensive supervision' (ibid., p. 45). Those few who committed very serious crimes could still be dealt with by means of Section 53 detention[2] in local authority secure accommodation. This liberal view of the way in which 'troublesome' girls should be treated by the criminal justice system reflected the long-standing belief that girls 'in trouble' require 'care' not punishment. In particular, difficult and deviant behaviour by adolescent girls has been interpreted for well over a century as a symptom of problematic sexuality requiring welfare regulation (Carlen and Wardaugh, 1991). As Annie Hudson (1989, p. 197) has argued:

> the majority of girls do not get drawn into the complex web of the personal social services because they have committed offences. It is more likely to be because of concerns about their perceived sexual behaviour and/or because they are seen to be 'at risk' of 'offending' against social codes of adolescent femininity.

Nearly a decade later, however, custody in young offender institutions remains for girls and the reason, we are led to believe, is that girls are committing more crime, especially violent crime. The ascendency of the 'just deserts' model of criminal justice, coupled with the inclusion of a supposedly anti-discriminatory clause[3] in the 1991 Criminal Justice Act, might have resulted in fewer girls being incarcerated. The principle of proportionality in sentencing should have led to the fairer sentencing of women (since their offending behaviour is generally less serious than that of men) and this trend should have been buttressed by greater access for women to community sentences.

But any such optimism was short-lived. As with the 1969 Children and Young Persons Act (see Pitts, 1988), the tide of political and public opinion had already begun to turn before the 1991 Act was ever implemented and by 1993 its more radical sections had been abolished, implicitly reversing most of its original principles. Although these changes affected adults and young offenders alike, the impact on girls and young women was particularly significant.

The 1990s have seen the emergence of several moral panics in relation to juvenile delinquency (Worrall, 1997). The first was 'rat boy', the elusive persistent offender who laughed at the system. The 'discovery' that a small number of children were committing a disproportionate amount of not-so-trivial crime, especially burglary and criminal damage, led to public outrage that, because of their age, these children could not be given custodial sentences (Morton, 1994; Hagell and Newburn, 1994). The government's response to this was to announce the introduction of secure training centres for 12 to 14 year-olds, the first of which opened in April 1998 . But this concern was to prove merely a precursor to the second moral panic, which followed the murder of Jamie Bulger in 1993. After this appalling event, it became increasingly difficult to argue that courts should retain any distinct system of justice for children based, as it is, on a belief in their still-developing understanding of right and wrong and their need for protection from the full weight of the criminal law. Increasingly, the media demanded that so-called 'adult' offences should be dealt with by 'adult' sentences, regardless of the age and maturity of the offender. The vexing issues of the age of criminal responsibility and *doli incapax* became matters of public and parliamentary debate.

This level of public anxiety was based on the scantiest of empirical evidence. Hagell and Newburn (1994), for example, found far fewer persistent young offenders (and virtually none of them girls) than Michael Howard (the Home Secretary at the time) had claimed existed. Nevertheless, it was against this backdrop that the third moral panic emerged. Newspapers and magazines claimed to have discovered 'all-girl gangs menacing the streets' (Brinkworth, 1994) and 'cocky, feminist, aggressive' superheroines targeting vulnerable women and other girls. Moreover, this 'new breed' of criminal girl apparently 'knows' that the criminal justice system is lenient on her. She 'knows' how to work the system, dressing smartly for court and playing up to the magistrates. The reasons for this supposed upsurge in young female crime are, however, confused. On the one hand, Brinkworth (1996) argues that women's liberation has raised women's expectations but has not delivered in terms of careers and wealth. Consequently, frustration and anger lead to street violence. On the other hand, women are supposedly sick of feeling unsafe in the home and are now fighting back. Either way, according to Brinkworth, the responsibility for all this lies with feminism. This is what happens when you loosen the controls on women. This is what happens when adolescent girls are allowed to think themselves equal or superior to boys. It is every mother and father's nightmare – their daughter's sexuality rampant and violent. But do the available statistics (despite their many flaws) support this fear?

'Invisible' Girls

Contrary to popular belief, the number of juveniles (male and female) found guilty or formally cautioned per 100,000 population has fallen steadily since 1986 (Home Office, 1997a, 1997b).[4, 5] The figures relating to girls, especially those aged 14–17, have fluctuated considerably from a low point of 1,300 per 100,000 in 1989 to a high point of 2,250 per 100,000 in 1993, but the corresponding figure declined to about 1,700 in 1996, compared with about 6,500 per 100,000 for boys in the same age range.

Cautioning rates for all juveniles reached a peak in 1992 and 1993 but have since fallen. The rates remain very high for 10–13 year olds (96 per cent for girls and about 85 per cent for boys) but rates for the 14–17 year range have fallen more markedly and in 1996 were 76 per cent for girls and 55 per cent for boys. The fall in cautioning rates has led to an increase in the numbers of juveniles appearing in court and being sentenced (42,200 in 1995 and 44,300 in 1996). Of these, 300 were girls aged 10–13 and 4,900 were girls aged 14–17. Although this latter figure represents an increase from 3,600 in 1993, a longer-term view shows a substantial decrease since 1986, when 6,900 girls in this age range were sentenced. In other words, there seems to be little evidence from official statistics to support the view that girls are committing more crime.

Over half of the girls sentenced in 1996 were given conditional discharges and a further 39 per cent were given community sentences (supervision orders, attendance centre orders, probation orders, community service orders and combination orders). During 1996, 214 were sentenced to young offender institutions. A similar number (193) of 17 year-olds were remanded in custody during the year. There may be some double counting between the two groups, since 140 of the sentenced girls served sentences of less than six months (and may, therefore, have been both remanded and sentenced in the same year). If one plays the percentage game, then one might argue that the number of girls sent to prison has increased by 175 per cent between 1992 and 1996 (Howard

League, 1997) – a far higher rate of increase than for boys. This is clearly a worrying trend, but since the absolute numbers are so small, there is a danger that such an argument could be misused by those who wish to demonstrate an increase in serious crimes by girls. The fact remains that very few girls indeed are considered by the courts to have committed crimes of such seriousness that custody is unavoidable. To pretend otherwise, even in a well-intentioned attempt to highlight judicial discrimination, is to risk a moral panic or backlash that serves only to demonise particular young women and lay ill-informed allegations of promoting female aggression at the door of 'women's liberation'. Researchers (see, for example, Campbell, 1995) have consistently found little evidence of 'girl gangs'[6] in Britain and the liïited available research on the influence of feminism on girls suggests that when girls raise their sights, broaden their horizons and increase their aspirations and self-esteem, they are less, not more, likely to behave deviantly (see, for example, James and Thornton, 1980). Young women, by and large, are not behaving badly and, given the parlous circumstances in which many of them exist, what should interest us is not that some girls and young women in these circumstances resort to crime (Carlen, 1988; Kempson et al., 1994) but that so many do not!

Part of the myth-creating problem is the difficulty in 'tracking down' the whereabouts of these 'welfare princesses' – the troubled and troublesome girls who are supposedly manipulating the criminal courts, social workers and the Social Security system. Apart from *Criminal Statistics* and *Prison Statistics,* published by The Stationery Office, information about girls in trouble can be found in the following publications: *Probation Statistics* (published annually by the Home Office); *Supervision Orders* (published by the Department of Health); *Children looked after by local authorities* (published by the Department of Health); *Children accommodated in Secure Units* (published by the Department of Health).

Although *Criminal Statistics* and *Probation Statistics* take their cut-off point for 'snapshot' figures as 31 December, *Prison Statistics* take theirs as 30 June and the Department of Health takes theirs as 31 March. So there is little compatibility between these publications, making comparison difficult. Setting aside such methodological problems, the following sections will attempt to identify the different institutional sites in which troubled girls are located, the policies governing their care or supervision and the existence or otherwise of evidence to suggest that girls are first, featuring increasingly in the statistics and, second, treated differently from boys and in a discriminatory fashion.

Girls Inside

The plight of girls in prison was highlighted in 1997 by three events: a thematic review of women in prison by HM Chief Inspector of Prisons (1997), a report by the Howard League on the imprisonment of teenage girls (Howard League, 1997) and a High Court ruling that a teenage girl should not be held in an adult female prison.[7] There are no institutions in the female prison estate designated solely as young offender institutions. There are two standard Prison Service justifications for mixing young and adult offenders in the female prison estate: first, there are too few young offenders to warrant separate institutions, which would, in any case, exacerbate the problem of women being imprisoned at unreasonable distances from their homes; second (and conveniently!), adult women are regarded as having a stabilising influence on young women (though, strangely, adult men are seen as having a corrupting influence on young men!) But such a role is not without its problems on both sides:

> Some older women prisoners show a willingness to parent and generally support younger women prisoners and have been observed to do this with care and sensitivity; in some cases this compensates women for being cut off from their own families. We heard from others that they resented the enforced parenting role. Living at close quarters with boisterous youngsters appeared to be particularly difficult for some long-term and lifer prisoners, who are keen to serve their time quietly (HM Chief Inspector of Prisons, 1997, p. 25).

Setting aside the complaints of adult women that young women have a disruptive influence on their lives, reports from the Chief Inspector and Howard League present a rather different picture of girls and young women being bullied, sexually assaulted and recruited as prostitutes and drugs couriers:

> There are serious child protection issues in mixing young prisoners with others who may include Schedule 1 offenders (women convicted of offences of violence against children under the 1933 Children and Young Person Act) which covers a multitude of behaviours .... We noted, for example, women convicted of procuring being held alongside 15 and 16 year olds (ibid., p. 26).

The exposure of girls to an environment that is seriously damaging is explored in detail by the Howard League (1997). In particular, the 'culture' of self-harm, or 'cutting up', which is endemic in most women's prisons, can socialise vulnerable girls into dangerous and disturbed ways of expressing their distress:

For the vast majority of the young girls we interviewed it was the first time they had come across self-mutilation and we were told by staff that it was rare a 15, 16 or 17 year old would come in self-harming. The danger is that they will copy this behaviour partly as a way of creating some control in their distressed and chaotic lives and partly because it is part of the culture of prison life to which they now belong (Howard League, 1997, p. 33).

The 'special needs' of adolescent women are not being addressed. Prison officers reported to the Howard League that girls in prison had disproportionate experience of sexual abuse, poor or broken relationships with parents, local authority care (between a third and a half of women in prison have been in care), drug or alcohol abuse, prostitution, school exclusion and truancy (see also Hudson, B., 1997). As with adult female prisons, black (African Caribbean) girls were over-represented,[8] though Asian girls were not. Both groups, however, reported feelings of marginalisation due to a lack of understanding of their backgrounds and cultural needs. In an attempt to address all these needs, and the more fundamental problem that prison officers receive no basic training to equip them to work with children, the Prison Service has worked with the Trust for the Study of Adolescence to produce a training pack, *Understanding and working with young women in custody* (Lyon and Coleman, 1996). Unfortunately, after initial interest, budgetary constraints now appear to have restricted the use of this pack in prison officer training (Howard League, 1997, p. 8).

If one has any lingering doubts about the 'special needs' of girls and young women in prison, one has only to consider the statistics of offences against prison discipline (Home Office, 1997c). The rate of disciplinary offending is considerably higher in all young offender institutions than in adult prisons, but the rate in female YOI establishments in 1996 was 624 offences per 100 prisoners, compared with 343 offences per 100 prisoners in male establishments. By far the most common offence was that of 'disobedience or disrespect'. However one chooses to explain this phenomenon (as being an indicator of either very badly behaved young women or of overly controlling female prison officers) it is clear that young women have great difficulty in 'settling' to prison life.

Although the holding of young women (from 18–21 years) in female prisons which are also designated as young offender istitutions looks set to continue, it has become clear that holding girls under the age of 18 alongside adult prisoners contravenes the UN Convention on the Rights of the Child and fails to protect them from harm under the provisions of the Children Act 1989. The Howard League has called for legislation prohibiting the use of prison custody for all girls aged under 18 years and the placing of 'those girls who genuinely require secure conditions in local authority secure accommodation units' (1997, p. 11). In the meantime, it calls for separate small units for juvenile girls and the promotion of noncustodial sentences in all but exceptional cases.

It is sometimes suggested that the apparent under-representation of girls in young offender institutions may be accounted for by their over-representation in local authority secure accommodation. In 1997 there were 348 places in 20 secure units for boys and girls (an increase of 20 per cent on 1996) (Department of Health, 1997a). On 31 March 1997 there were 290 children in secure units, of whom 241 were boys and 49 girls. There are two main routes into secure accommodation – the 'welfare route' and the 'justice route' (Goldson, 1995, p. 66) Children being looked after by a local authority may be placed in secure accommodation if they have a history of absconding from other accommodation *and* if they are likely to suffer 'significant harm' if they abscond, or are likely to injure themselves or others if not placed in secure accommodation. The 'justice route' has two distinct pathways – remands pending criminal trial (as a result of *either* a history of absconding from other accommodation *or* a likelihood of injury to self or others) and detention for 'grave offences' under Section 53 of the Children and Young Persons Act 1933. During the year ending 31 March 1997, there were 895 admissions – 648 boys and 247 girls (Department of Health, 1997a). Almost 200 of the girls were admitted through the 'welfare route', whereas over 400 of the boys were admitted through remand or Section 53 sentences. Where girls appear to have a history of absconding and are considered to be at risk of suffering 'significant harm', the latter is invariably interpreted as meaning prostitution, sexual abuse or pregnancy (Hodgkin, 1995). Only 18 girls were remanded and 15 were on Section 53 orders. It was also apparent that the average length of stay for girls was considerably shorter than for boys. Although there is no evidence to support the suggestion that girls who commit criminal offences are being processed disproportionately through secure accommodation, it is clear that considerable numbers of girls enter secure accommodation for short periods for 'welfare' reasons. This 'welfarisation' of certain troublesome girls is a distinctly gendered process which will be examined further later in this chapter.

The second place to search for troubled girls is in non-secure or 'open' local authority accommodation. In 1996 51,200 children were being looked after by local authorities – 16,000 fewer than in 1986 (Department of Health, 1997b). The proportions of boys and girls accommodated has changed little in the past 10 years and ranges from 54–56 per cent boys, 46–44 per cent girls.[9] Some two-thirds of these children were accommodated to provide relief to parents or because of parental abuse or neglect. Only 11 per cent were accommodated because of their own behaviour. Despite this, one study of girls leaving care found that:

> One in seven young women leaving care, and interviewed in a 1992 study, was pregnant or already had children (Triseliotis et al., 1995). This high number of pregnant young women may be influenced by their exposure/vulnerability to sexual exploitation, their acceptance of affection from inappropriate adults and the adoption of motherhood as a source of identity (Dennehy, Smith and Harker, 1997, p. 23).

The deleterious effects of leaving local authority care on some girls – notably homelessness and prostitution – and their over-determined path from care to custody have been well documented elsewhere (Carlen, 1988,1996; Carlen and Wardaugh, 1991). Although over 90 per cent of single homeless people sleeping rough are male, almost a quarter of single homeless people living in hostels or bed and breakfast accommodation are female and these are disproportionately girls and young women under the age of 25 years (Kemp, 1997). There appears to be a significantly vulnerable group of homeless girls, many of whom have been let down by Social Services departments who have failed to meet their obligations to support children leaving care (Carlen, 1996). Some of these will engage in prostitution (in its most dangerous form 'on the streets') in order to survive. Edwards (1997) explains that the numbers of girls being proceeded against for soliciting are declining but that this does not indicate any reduction in the numbers of girls soliciting. Rather, it is the result of new police initiatives in working with Social Services to deal with such girls as victims of sexual abuse and not as offenders. Such moves are clearly welcome and it would be simplistic to blame Social Services directly for their inability to prevent a proportion of the girls they are 'looking after' from engaging in prostitution. O'Neill (1997, p. 15) describes the problem comprehensively and succinctly:

> (T)he relationship between prostitution and residential care has to be explored within the context of the experiences and problems which bring young people into the care of the local authority; the residential care experience itself and the social stigma, marginalisation and 'otherness' related to being in care; financial resources allocated, training and education of social workers and carers; the overall management of care; the benefit system for young people; education, training and employment opportunities.

Supervising 'Criminal' Girls in the Community

Supervision orders come in several forms. They may or may not have additional requirements (such as residence, specified activities or night restriction) and they may be supervised either by local authority social workers or by probation officers. In the past, Intermediate Treatment (the pre-1991 Act generic term for the range of noncustodial Social Services provision for juveniles 'at risk') had an honourable tradition of work with girls, though girls tended to be involved at an earlier age than boys and were more likely to be involved in 'preventive' programmes than in 'alternative to custody or care' programmes (Bottoms and Pratt, 1989). Increasingly, youth justice teams are inter-agency based and the Crime and Disorder Bill proposes youth offending teams which are multi-agency in composition.

It is at this point that the available statistics become most confusing (Home Office, 1997d; Department of Health, 1997c). Despite the apparent disparities between the different statistics, it is clear that there has been a considerable increase in the numbers of girls being placed on criminal supervision orders by the courts since 1992, although this must be viewed in the context of a dramatic decline in such orders during the previous decade. The reason for this recent increase remains unclear, though one contributory factor may be the decline in the use of fines for girls (from 32 per cent of sentences in 1986 to 9 per cent in 1996). This argument seems to be supported by recent Home Office research on sentencing women (Hedderman and Gelsthorpe, 1997) which found that magistrates are increasingly reluctant to fine women and that this has resulted in an increase in the use of both conditional discharges and more restrictive supervisory sentences.

Troublesome girls also feature within the statistics for probation orders, community service orders and combination orders. Since the Criminal Justice Act 1991, courts have the so-called 'flexibility' to treat 16 and 17 year-old offenders as either 'juveniles' or 'adults' for sentencing purposes. Between 1992 (when the Act was implemented) and 1996 the number of boys placed on probation and community service orders declined, while those on combination orders increased. By comparison, while numbers of girls placed on probation declined, those on community service and combination orders increased. Although it might appear from this that girls are being placed on community service disproportionately, the longer-term picture again complicates that theory. The numbers of girls being supervised by the Probation Service now only appear high in relation to the dramatic reductions in supervision brought about by the implementation of the Criminal Justice Act

1991. To complete the picture, it should perhaps be noted that while some Attendance Centres cater for girls these are so few and far between as to be fairly irrelevant as female disposals (Gelsthorpe and Tutt, 1986).

It is well known that community service and probation (day) centre provision for women is inadequate (Worrall 1996). Probation officers complain that they receive very few referrals and that it is therefore difficult to make any special provision for women (such as all-female projects or groups). Courts tend to see community service and probation centres as unsuitable for women, both in principle and in practice. So a vicious circle exists whereby the male-orientation of both disposals is perpetuated. Despite (or perhaps because of) their small numbers, girls and young women who break the law encounter discrimination which is both subtle and indirect, based on a combination of inadequate provision and stereotyped assumptions about their 'needs' and the perceived changes in the nature of their offending behaviour.

Why Do(n't) Girls Commit Crime?

According to the most comprehensive recent self-report study of offending by young people (Graham and Bowling, 1995), young men are about two and a half times more likely than young women to admit having ever committed a crime and that ratio widens for more serious crime. For example, young men are about twice as likely as young women to have taken drugs but five times more likely to have taken heroin (ibid., p. 14). The most common offences admitted to by young women (and those where the gendered differences were narrowest) were handling stolen goods, fighting, shoplifting and vandalism. Traditional explanations of female offending have been widely rehearsed and challenged elsewhere (see, for example, Hudson, B., 1989; Heidensohn, 1996) but the most tenacious of those that purport to explain the criminality of some girls emphasise either their lack of femininity or their excess of (sexualised) femininity. Girls who commit crime – or rather, girls who have been criminalised – are thought to be either physically abnormal and masculine in appearance or emotionally maladjusted, attention seeking or promiscuous:

> There are few types that come before the juvenile courts that are more difficult to handle and more in need of expert diagnosis than some of these over-sexed adolescent girls (Elkin, 1938, cited in Harris and Webb, 1987, p. 131).

> Delinquent girls more often than boys have other forms of impaired physical health; they are noticed to be oversized, lumpish, uncouth and graceless, with a

varied incidence of minor physical defects (Cowie, Cowie and Slater, 1968, cited in Elliott, 1988, p. 7).

Girls in trouble are usually unhappy and disturbed, often sexually promiscuous and often rejected by their families (Home Office, 1968, cited in Gelsthorpe, 1989, p. 5).

By contrast, Graham and Bowling (1995) found that some offending is relatively 'normal', with approximately one in three girls having committed a crime at some time in their early teens. Their criminal activity correlates with the same combination of social circumstances that appear to apply to troublesome boys, including low parental supervision, poor relationships with at least one parent, poverty, truancy and delinquent associates. For girls, dislike of school and poor educational achievement appears to be particularly significant. Devlin's study (1995) of the school experiences of female (and male) prisoners confirms this view by providing numerous detailed case examples of 'girls with problems' being turned into 'problem girls' by failures of the education system.

The difference between the offending patterns of girls and boys, then, is not so much at the 'front end' or onset of offending (although the likelihood of greater parental supervision and the now widely acknowledged greater educational achievements of girls – see, for example, Ofsted, 1996; Bray et al., 1997 – may well contribute to their lower offending rates) but rather at the 'back end' of when and why young women desist from offending. According to Graham and Bowling (1995), young women 'grow out of crime' more successfully than young men do. Making a successful transition from adolescence to the responsibilities of adulthood is a much stronger and more clearly defined feature of the lives of young women than of young men. Completing schooling, gaining financial independence through employment, leaving home, living with a partner and motherhood all appear to have a strong influence on decisions by young women in their late teens and early twenties to stop committing offences. For young men, this social development is either less successful or appears to have less influence over their criminal activity. The suggestion that early motherhood might assist young women to desist from offending sits uncomfortably both with traditional concerns about 'moral danger' and with feminist concerns about the domestic oppression of women. Graham and Bowling do not pursue this point, except to suggest that motherhood needs to be accompanied by a stable relationship and economic independence if it is to be influential in preventing female offending. However, their broader argument about the significance of the gendered nature of 'growing out of crime' is forcefully made:

> (F)emales are less likely than males ever to start to offend and desist sooner than their male counterparts .... The data also suggest that the transition to adulthood and desistance from offending are closely associated for females: as girls become women, leave home and school, form partnerships and new families and become economically independent, so they desist from offending .... Males, however, are less likely than their female counterparts to achieve the independence, responsibility and maturity associated with adulthood by the age of 25 (Graham and Bowling, 1995, p. 64).

Government policy has persistently failed to acknowledge the significance of gender in youth offending. The Audit Commission Report (1996), *Misspent Youth*, makes fleeting reference to gender as a factor associated with high risk of offending, yet excludes it from its analytic 'cycle of antisocial behaviour' model. Similarly, The government White Paper *No More Excuses* (Home Office, 1997e) devotes two short and inconclusive paragraphs to selected statistics of female offending before resuming its gender-neutral analysis.

As many writers have observed, statistics on youth crime and punishment are more a reflection of the politics of juvenile justice than of the reality of offending by young people. As John Pitts (1988, p. 135) has remarked:

> The history of the theory and practice of juvenile justice in Britain from 1959 is ... a history of the perpetual and apparently random repudiation and replacement of one set of ideas by another.

Nowhere is this 'random repudiation and replacement' more clearly demonstrated than in the confusion and ambiguity of official statistics relating to the criminal activities and criminalisation of girls. Frankly, we don't know whether or not girls are committing more crime than they did a decade ago. If they are, then it is not, as the media suggests, the result of women's liberation. It has far more to do with certain impoverished young women seeing no future for themselves other than lone parenthood, state dependency and social stigma and saying 'anything must be better than that'. This is not an argument against agency in women's offending. Girls and young women choose to offend, but in conditions that are certainly not of their choosing. The narrowing of options and the absence of rewards for conformity result in what Carlen (1988, p. 126) graphically describes as the 'sod it syndrome' – the refusal of the gender deal:

For as the women talked, again and again they described situations in which, sometimes after months of going straight, of coping against all the odds, the four-hundredth blow had made them say 'Sod it', had occasioned an outburst of violence, a return to an addiction, the start of a new and flamboyant thieving spree.

We know that – partly thanks to feminist perspectives in criminology and partly to the unprecedented targeting of youth crime generally – the criminal justice system is more aware of criminal girls than it was a decade ago, and that is resulting in some rather strange fluctuations in the sentences they are receiving. But nothing, I would suggest, in the foregoing analysis supports the view that girls are becoming significantly more criminal or justifies the moral panic fuelled by media hyperbole. Barbara Wootton's cryptic comment remains relevant: 'If men behaved like women, the courts would be idle and the prisons empty' (quoted in Heidensohn, 1991, p. 9).

Controlling Girls

So if the lawbreaking behaviour of girls is as marginally problematic as the official statistics and research studies suggest, why is their social control considered such a moral and political imperative? The traditional answer to this question is that girls have problems with their sexuality, that they need protection from the 'moral danger' of pregnancy and/or prostitution. Preventing girls from becoming pregnant is one of the overriding concerns of all those parents, teachers, doctors and social workers who deal with 'vulnerable' or 'troublesome' girls and this concern is always justified as being in the girl's 'best interests'. Many health and educational projects are now funded as a result of the Health of the Nation agenda, which has as a target halving the number of teenage pregnancies by the year 2000 (Batsleer, 1996).[10] It is not disputed here that for girls to have babies before leaving school is likely to be 'a barrier to developing their "human capital"' (Burghes and Brown, 1995, p. 59) but the extent to which the agenda of adults in authority is this altruistic is questionable. The sexualising of girls' problematic behaviour is 'embedded at the heart of contemporary British welfare practice' (Hudson, A., 1989, p. 197) but girls are no longer (if they ever were) portrayed as hapless victims. Rather, their sexuality is constructed as being predatory and it is often boys, rather than girls, who are deemed to need the protection. Carrington (1993) goes further and argues that controlling the sexual activity of particular girls is the mechanism whereby society seeks to control the unacceptable sexual behaviour of men. Stricter controls on girls are seen to be the best way of preventing men from raping, sexually abusing and even killing them. And the 'clinching' argument for controlling girls comes from Charles Murray who views lone mothers as the root cause of juvenile male crime: 'The real problem with ... unmarried parenthood is that it offers no ethical alternative for socialising little boys' (Murray, 1994, p. 26).

So, as I have argued elsewhere, 'women may commit very little crime, but we can hold them responsible for a great deal of it' (Worrall, 1995, p. 141). In their roles as victims (of rape and domestic violence), bystanders (as partners of child sexual abusers) and as lone mothers (of young offenders), they are seen as provoking, colluding with or failing to socialise dangerous men. 'Henpecked' husbands who kill their wives are to be 'pitied' (Justice for Women, 1997) and sexual assault trials are notorious for their victim-blaming defence tactics (Chambers and Millar, 1987). After the murder of Jamie Bulger the *Daily Mirror* (25 November 1993) ran articles profiling the mothers of Robert Thompson and Jon Venables under the headline, 'Making of a monster'. Mrs Venables was described as 'very seriously depressive' following her divorce – she 'did not feel secure as a mother'. Robert Thompson's mother's 'upbringing was a classic case of deprivation'. Consequently, it should come as no surprise to us to learn that, when she arrived at her son's court appearance she:

> sat in the back of the car doing her make-up and hair. She is a short, stout woman with tight dark curls and a lost look about her. Her son was on trial for a week before she attended court.

Murray's solution is that unmarried mothers should either give up their baby for adoption or insist on marriage to the baby's father (which does not, as critics have pointed out, address the issue of divorced mothers). Those who refuse to do either and who do not work to support themselves should have all welfare benefits stopped (MacDonald, 1997). As Cook (1987) has argued, 'women on welfare' are all too easily perceived as 'scroungers', labelled by virtue of their life-style even when they have committed no 'crimes'. According to Murray (1994, p. 15), welfare queens and princesses need to be taught the New Victorianism of marriage and sexual restraint which he sees re-emerging among the affluent and well-educated middle classes (ibid.). If such policies are not pursued, he argues, then the 'New Rabble' of criminal, antisocial, feckless, single parent families will destroy British society (ibid., p. 18). If young men are not made to face up to their responsibilities – by women – then the cycle of 'feral'[11] masculinity will become inter-generational.

There are at least two responses to this argument. The first is to ask, with Sue Slipman (1994, p. 64), 'Would you take one home with you?' Why, she asks, should young women put up with this kind of behaviour from men if they can manage better without them? The second is to recognise, with greater empathy, that it is becoming harder and harder for young men to make the transition to responsible parenthood and that they experience a range of ambivalent feelings about commitment, which will not be resolved until they have realistic chances of working to support themselves and their families (Speak et al., 1997)

But Murray's views are only an extreme expression of a widespread assumption that 'girls learn to care' and have to be 'policed to care' (Reitsma-Street, 1991). As they grow up, girls learn three important lessons:

> (1) women, whether young or old, are the major providers of the love and labour that is caring; (2) young women are expected to restrict caring for themselves to personal appearance and demeanour; and (3) boyfriends become the special objects of caring (ibid., p. 119).

As Lees (1989) points out, the predominant feature of adolescent femininity is walking the tightrope of sexual reputation, avoiding being labelled as either a 'slag' or a 'drag'. Derisory appellations such as 'slag' (used initially by boys but internalised by girls) 'function as terms of abuse, to control single girls and steer them towards marriage as the only legitimate expression of sexuality' (ibid., p. 31). It is not that girls are unaware of the harsh realities of many marriages but, in learning to care, they use the language of romantic love to cushion their experiences and to rationalise their lack of choice. If you say you are 'in love' then that somehow justifies being taken over by a man, even if the resulting relationship is oppressive, abusive and patently unloving.

Name calling by peers and the management of sexual reputation is one of the most common ways in which girls are socially controlled. What is perhaps less often acknowledged is the extent to which unfamiliar adults use very similar crude methods to control the behaviour and self-image of girls. An Edinburgh study of young people's attitudes to crime and their own experiences of victimisation found that girls were particularly prone to harassment by adults in public places:

> (W)ithin the previous nine months, two-thirds of the girls interviewed had been harassed by adults following them on foot or by car, asking them things, shouting or calling after them or threatening them (Anderson et al., 1994, p. 1).

It is therefore not surprising that Loader found the use of public space to be 'a gendered process' (1996, p. 63). Girls have to negotiate their movements to take account of 'mundane, everyday forms of harassment' (ibid., p. 64) which are nevertheless set against a background fear of male sexual violence. Similarly, Pearce (1996), in her study of the gendered differences in the use of indoor and outdoor space by young people, found that girls made much more social use of their own and friends' homes and of enclosed supervised outdoor spaces such as shops, employing sophisticated harassment avoidance tactics to negotiate their way into male-dominated public space.

Working with Troubled Girls and Young Women

Working with girls causes anxiety (Hudson, A., 1989; Brown and Pearce, 1992; Aymer, 1992; Pearce, 1995; Spence, 1996) especially among female workers. Even Janet Batsleer's (1996) comprehensive and, at times, moving celebration of youth and community work with girls and young women starts with the following words: 'Somehow, youth work and informal education that focuses attention on girls has always been associated with threat' (p. 1).

Work with women and girls in trouble has always been seen as an optional extra by both Social Services and Probation Service management, requiring constant justification and being the first provision to be cut when time and funding is at a premium (Hudson, A., 1989). 'Separatist' work with women and girls in all-female groups is viewed with particular suspicion:

> Being keenly aware that their work is precarious at the best of times and that they are operating within agendas which have been set elsewhere by a masculine establishment, women workers are very self-conscious about the potential impact of acknowledging the influence of feminism in their work (Spence, 1996, p. 41).

They are concerned not to marginalise their work any further, nor to alarm or alienate the women and girls that they want to work with. Thus, feminism is muted in the discourse of work with girls and the focus is often on providing equal opportunities for girls to engage in the same activities as boys – to participate in a male-defined agenda.

But anxiety may be more personal than this. Women working with girls in trouble are often confronted with the challenge that 'You're not my mother, you can't tell me what to do' (Aymer, 1992). Working with angry young women provides women workers with an uncomfortable reminder of their own feelings of anger – feelings which they have learned to split off and repress in order to survive as adults in a male-dominated profession (Pearce, 1995). There is always the temptation to construct angry young women as 'other', as something different from us but successful work with girls starts by 'interrupting othering' (ibid., p. 32) and acknowledging the commonalities, as well as the differences, between the lived experiences of girls in trouble and the women who try to work with them.

One way of 'interrupting othering' in youth justice work with girls is to listen to women who have been 'through the system' talking about the factors that enabled them to turn their lives around (Eaton, 1993). Women offenders, Eaton found, will only change their lives if and when they have access to the structural preconditions of social justice – housing, employment and health facilities. Without these things, they have no chance of reconstituting their own lives and those of their 'families' – however they choose to define that term. But structural factors alone are insufficient. The women Eaton interviewed had all made a conscious decision to redirect their lives – they wanted things to be different. But such motivation was not something which just happened. In order to make that decision, they had to feel confident that change was possible. And to be confident, they had to achieve both self-recognition and recognition by others. They had to feel that they were people of worth who had something to contribute.

The key to this recognition was reciprocal relationships. For many women offenders, their only experience of relationships is subordination, exploitation and abuse. Whether in personal or official dealings, their expectations have been of hierarchical relationships in which they are told what they should do and how they should behave in order to please other people. Women offenders often demonstrate a healthy scepticism for, and resistance to, 'contracts' that appear to restrict their already limited choices and offer no obvious benefits (Worrall, 1990). Anything which contributes to the breaking down of those barriers and the development of mutuality in relationships will help to motivate women towards change.

Conclusions – the Dilemma of Visibility

This chapter has attempted to advance two main arguments. The first is that there is a need to distinguish between drawing attention to a neglected group of criminal justice and social service 'customers' or 'recipients' and the creation of a moral panic. By and large, girls still do not behave very badly. In their early teenage years they appear to experiment with petty crime, much as boys do (though less routinely, even then). As they get older they rapidly lose interest and very few become criminally 'embedded'. Those who do, however, have a predictable biography of sexual abuse, truancy, local authority care, drug misuse, homelessness, prostitution and pregnancy. They have not followed this over-determined path because they are born promiscuous, emotionally unstable, aggressive and maladjusted. To the extent that they are any of these things, it is the path of narrowing options that has made them so. The extent to which they can 'rehabilitate' themselves will depend on the means by which they are supported through the slow and painful process of reopening their options. There is no quick fix. However, there is one first step, without which there is no hope of avoiding criminal 'embeddedness' among troublesome girls. That step is the abolition of imprisonment for girls under the age of 18 – a step proposed nearly a decade ago by a Conservative government and shamefully resisted by the current Labour government (Howard League, 1998).

The second argument has been to demonstrate the impossibility of separating formal criminal justice for girls and young women from the social controls that routinely operate to constrain and circumscribe their behaviour. On a daily basis many girls and young women find their movements restricted and their moral reputations managed by real or threatened male intimidation and violence. The concept of 'moral danger' serves not only to restrict and 'protect' girls but also to blame them for their own plight and hold them responsible for the unacceptable behaviour of men and boys. The criminalisation of a small group of girls, the welfarisation of a larger group and the socialisation of all girls are processes which form a 'pyramid' of gendered social control. Youth justice for girls must take account of all levels of the pyramid.

This chapter opened with an account of a 17 year-old girl sent to prison during the last weeks of pregnancy in the autumn of 1997. As I conclude, another 17 year-old has given birth while on remand in Holloway Prison (*The Guardian*, 19 May 1998). She has been denied a place in a mother and baby unit, apparently because of her own bad behaviour in prison, and the baby is being cared for by relatives, although the young mother is still attempting to breast-feed the baby. She is facing a long prison sentence for arson and already has another child. There is no easy right answer but this 'solution' is surely the wrong one. A year after a change of government, the plight of girls and young women who offend seems to be worse than ever. At the end of the twentieth century, we really ought to have the will to look after our troubled and troublesome girls and young women with greater compassion and imagination – for the sake of future generations as well as the present one.

Notes

1   The term *girls* will be used in this chapter to refer to females under the age of 18 and the term *young women* will be used more loosely to include older teenagers and women in their early twenties.

2   Detention under Section 53 of the Children and Young Persons Act 1933 provides for the long-term detention of children and young persons under 18 for certain grave crimes such as murder, manslaughter and other serious crimes of violence.

3   Section 95 of the 1991 Criminal Justice Act required the Home Secretary to monitor the administration of criminal justice to ensure the absence of discrimination on grounds of race, sex or other 'improper' grounds.

4   Unless otherwise stated, all statistics are taken from *Criminal Statistics England and Wales 1996, Cm 3764* (Home Office, 1997a) and *Prison Statistics England and Wales 1996, Cm 3732* (Home Office, 1997b).

5   The Audit Commission Report (1996) questioned whether juvenile offending had actually fallen and purported to demonstrate its point by conflating *Criminal Statistics* with those from *The British Crime Survey* which were collected in different ways for different purposes.

6   The term *gang* is understood by researchers to refer to a highly structured group with clear identification and territorial location, which endures over time and outlives specific relationships (Campbell, 1995).

7   *R v Secretary of State for the Home Department and others, ex parte Flood.* Independent Law Reports, 2 October 1997, cited in Howard League (1997), *Lost Inside*.

8   Although Hood (1992) found no evidence of direct discrimination against black women by the courts, he did find that young black women with co-defendants of the same race, who were also of no fixed abode, were particularly vulnerable to imprisonment.

9   A study by Barn (1990) suggests that these proportions might be reversed for black children. She also suggests that black children are taken into care more quickly following referral than are white children.

10 The number of teenage pregnancies has steadily declined in the past decade but those under 16 appear to have increased again since 1993 and were about 8,000 in 1995. This is about 70 per cent higher than the Health of the Nation target for 2000 (Office for National Statistics 1997) On 13 March 1998, *The Guardian* reported that 'schoolgirl pregnancies' had reached 8,800 in 1996 – the highest figures since 1985.

11 I am grateful to Richard Sparks for using this graphic description on a recent Radio 4 programme about crime 'beyond the millennium'.

References

Anderson, S., Kinsey, R., Loader, I. and Smith, C. (1994), *Cautionary tales: young people, crime and policing in Edinburgh*, Aldershot, Avebury.

Audit Commission (1996), *Misspent Youth: young people and crime*, London, Audit Commission.

Aymer, C. (1992), 'Women in residential work' in M. Langan and L. Day (eds), *Women, oppression and social work*, London, Routledge.

Barn, R. (1990), 'Black children in local authority care: admission patterns', *New Community*, 16, 2, pp. 229–46.

Batsleer, J. (1996), *Working with girls and young women in community settings*, Aldershot, Arena.

Bottoms, A. and Pratt, J. (1989), 'Intermediate Treatment for Girls in England and Wales' in M. Cain (ed.), *Growing up good: policing the behaviour of girls in Europe*, London, Sage.

Bray, R., Gardner, C., Parsons, N., Downes, P. and Hannan, G. (1997), *Can boys do better?*, Leicester, Secondary Heads Association.

Brinkworth, L. (1994) 'Sugar and spice but not at all nice', *Sunday Times*, 27 November.

Brinkworth, L. (1996) 'Angry young women', *Cosmopolitan*, February.

Brown, H.C. and Pearce, J. (1992), 'Good practice in the face of anxiety: social work with girls and young women', *Journal of Social Work Practice*, 6, 2, pp. 159–65.

Burghes, L. and Brown, M. (1995), *Single lone mothers: problems, prospects and policies*, London, Family Policy Studies Centre.

Campbell, A. (1995), 'Creating a girl gang problem', *Criminal Justice Matters*, 19, pp. 8–9.

Carlen, P. (1988), *Women, crime and poverty*, Milton Keynes, Open University Press.

Carlen, P. (1996), *Jigsaw: a political criminology of youth homelessness*, Buckingham, Open University Press.

Carlen, P and Wardaugh, J. (1991), 'Locking up our daughters' in P. Carter, T. Jeffs and M.K. Smith (eds), *Social work and social welfare Year Book 3*, Milton Keynes, Open University Press.

Carrington, K. (1993), *Offending Girls*, Sydney, Allen and Unwin.

Chambers, G. and Millar, A. (1987), 'Proving sexual assault: prosecuting the offender or persecuting the victim?' in P. Carlen and A. Worrall (eds), *Gender, Crime and Justice*, Milton Keynes, Open University Press.

Cook, D. (1987), 'Women on Welfare: In Crime or Injustice?' in P. Carlen and A. Worrall (eds), *Gender, Crime and Justice*, Milton Keynes, Open University Press.

Dennehy, A., Smith, L. and Harker, P. (1997), *Not to be ignored: young people, poverty and health*, London, Child Poverty Action Group.

Department of Health (1997a), *Children accommodated in secure units year ending 31 March 1997, England and Wales*, London, Department of Health.

Department of Health (1997b), *Children looked after by local authorities year ending 31 March 1996, England*, London, Department of Health.

Department of Health (1997c), *Supervision Orders year ending 31 March 1996, England*, London, Department of Health.

Devlin, A. (1995), *Criminal classes*, Winchester, Waterside Press.

Eaton, M. (1993), *Women after Prison*, Milton Keynes, Open University Press.

Edwards, S. (1997), 'The legal regulation of prostitution: a human rights issue' in G. Scambler and A. Scambler (eds), *Rethinking prostitution: purchasing sex in the 1990s*, London, Routledge.

Elliott, D. (1988), *Gender, delinquency and society*, Aldershot, Avebury.

Gelsthorpe, L. (1989), *Sexism and the female offender*, Aldershot, Gower.

Gelsthorpe, L. and Tutt, N. (1986), 'The Attendance Centre Order', *Criminal Law Review*, pp. 146–53.

Goldson, B. (1995), *A sense of security*, London, National Children's Bureau.

Graham, J. and Bowling, B. (1995), *Young people and crime, Home Office Research Study 145*, London, Home Office.

Hagell, A. and Newburn, T. (1994), *Persistent Young Offenders*, London, Policy Studies Institute.

Harris, R. and Webb, D. (1987), *Welfare, power and juvenile justice*, London, Tavistock.

Hedderman, C. and Gelsthorpe, L. (1997), *Understanding the sentencing of women, Home Office Research Study 170*, London, Home Office.

Heidensohn, F. (1991), 'The crimes of women', *Criminal Justice Matters*, 5, p. 9.

Heidensohn, F. (1996), *Women and Crime*, 2nd edn, Basingstoke, Macmillan.

HM Chief Inspector of Prisons (1997), *Women in Prison: a thematic review*, London, HM Inspectorate of Prisons.

Hodgkin, R. (1995), *Safe to let out? The current and future use of secure accommodation for children and young people*, London, National Children's Bureau.

Home Office (1990), *Crime, Justice and Protecting the Public, Cm 965*, London, Home Office.

Home Office (1997a), *Criminal Statistics for England and Wales 1996, Cm 3764*, London, The Stationery Office.

Home Office (1997b), *Prison Statistics for England and Wales 1996, Cm 3732*, London, The Stationery Office.

Home Office (1997c), *Statistics of offences against prison discipline and punishment England and Wales 1996, Cm 3715*, London, The Stationery Office.

Home Office (1997d), *Probation Statistics for England and Wales 1996*, London, Home Office.

Home Office (1997e), *No more excuses: a new approach to tackling youth crime in England and Wales, Cm 3809*, London, The Stationery Office.

Hood, R. (1992), *Race and sentencing*, Oxford, Clarendon Press.

Howard League (1997), *Lost inside: the imprisonment of teenage girls*, London, The Howard League for Penal Reform.

Howard League (1998), ' Halt to detention of girls in prison blocked by government', *Howard League Magazine*, Spring, 4.

Hudson, A. (1989), 'Troublesome girls: towards alternative definitions and policies' in M. Cain (ed.), *Growing up good: policing the behaviour of girls in Europe*, London, Sage.

Hudson, B. (1989), 'Justice or welfare?' in M. Cain (ed.), *Growing up good: policing the behaviour of girls in Europe*, London, Sage.

Hudson, B. (1997), 'Lost inside', *Criminal Justice Matters*, No. 30, pp. 24–6.

James, J. and Thornton, W. (1980), 'Women's liberation and the female delinquent', *Journal of Research in Crime and Delinquency*, pp. 230–44.

Justice for Women (1997), *Information Pack*, 2nd edn, London, Justice for Women.

Kemp, P. (1997), 'The characteristics of single homeless people in England' in R. Burrows, N. Pleace and D. Quilgars (eds), *Homelessness and Social Policy*, London, Routledge.

Kempson, E., Bryson, A. and Rowlingson, K. (1994), *Hard times? How poor families make ends meet*, London, Policy Studies Institute.

Lees, S. (1993), *Sugar and spice: sexuality and adolescent girls*, London, Penguin.

Loader, I. (1996), *Youth, policing and democracy*, Basingstoke, Macmillan.

Lyon, J. and Coleman, J. (1996), *Understanding and working with young women in custody*, London, HM Prison Service and the Trust for the Study of Adolescence.

MacDonald, R. (1997), 'Dangerous youth and the dangerous class' in R. MacDonald (ed.) *Youth, the 'Underclass' and Social Exclusion*, London, Routledge.

Morton, J. (1994), *A Guide to the Criminal Justice and Public Order Act 1994*, London, Butterworth.

Murray, C. (1994), *Underclass: the crisis deepens*, London, IEA Health and Welfare Unit.

Office for National Statistics (1997), *Population and Health Monitor: Conceptions in England and Wales 1995*, FM1 97/2, Government Statistical Service.

OFSTED (1996), *The Gender Divide: Performance differences between boys and girls at school*, London, HMSO.

O'Neill, M. (1997), 'Prostitute women now' in G. Scambler and A. Scambler (eds), *Rethinking Prostitution: purchasing sex in the 1990s*, London, Routledge.

Pearce, J. (1995), 'The woman in the worker: youth social work with young women', *Youth and Policy*, No. 50, pp. 23–34.

Pearce, J. (1996), 'Urban youth cultures: gender and spatial forms', *Youth and Policy*, No. 52, pp. 1–11.

Pitts, J. (1988), *The politics of juvenile crime*, London, Sage.

Reitsma-Street, M. (1991), 'Girls learn to care; girls policed to care' in C. Baines, P. Evans and S. Neysmith (eds), *Women's caring*, Toronto, McClelland and Stewart.

Slipman, S. (1994), 'Would you take one home with you?' in C. Murray, *Underclass: the crisis deepens*, London, IEA health and Welfare Unit.

Speak, S., Cameron, S. and Gilroy, R. (1997), *Young single fathers: participation in fatherhood – barriers and bridges*, London, Family Policy Studies Centre.

Spence, J. (1996), 'Feminism in work with girls and women', *Youth and Policy*, 52, pp. 38–53.

Triseliotis, J., Borland, M., Hill, M. and Lambert, L. (1995), *Teenagers and the Social Work services*, HMSO.

Worrall, A. (1990), *Offending Women*, London, Routledge.

Worrall, A. (1995), 'Justice through inequality? The probation service and women offenders' in D. Ward and M. Lacey (eds), *Probation: working for justice*, London, Whiting and Birch.

Worrall, A. (1996), 'Gender, criminal justice and probation ' in G. McIvor (ed.), *Working with Offenders, Research Highlights in Social Work 26*, London, Jessica Kingsley.

Worrall, A. (1997), *Punishment in the community: the future of criminal justice*, Harlow, Addison Wesley Longman.

3 (What) Justice for Black Children and Young People?

BARRY GOLDSON AND RUTH CHIGWADA-BAILEY

Introduction

By way of introduction we begin this chapter by considering a range of perspectives relating to race and justice that have been expressed by others during the last 25 years or so:

> ... inequalities in the legal status of racial ... minorities, which were created by Parliament, have now been removed by Parliament, and, today everyone is equal before the law, whatever his (sic) race, colour or creed (Lester and Bindman, 1972, pp. 23–4).

> It is axiomatic that no court should treat a defendant differently from any other simply because of his (sic) race or ethnic origin. Any court that exhibited prejudice ... would be failing in its basic duty to treat all defendants before it equally (Judicial Studies Board Report 1987–91, cited in Hood, 1992, p. 192).

> The principle that everyone is equal under the law is fundamental to our system ... the legal system tries to deal with unique cases by applying universal rules and by making judgments anchored in general principles. In modern times, any rule or principle implying that members of one social group should be treated less favourably than members of another has been considered wrong and in conflict with the fundamental values of the system (Smith, 1994, p. 1042).

> I was a reluctant convert to the view that there appears to be an element of discrimination against ethnic minority offenders in our criminal processes ... those people will see the judicial system not as a means of maintaining law and order but as a means of keeping 'them' down and 'us' up (Lord Elton, a former Conservative Home Office Minister, cited in Penal Affairs Consortium, 1996, p. 2).

Goin' to court is frightenin' 'cos you know you're not goin' to get justice, no chance. We're black and that's enough to put you down (black young person, cited in Hil, 1980, p. 173).

In a land where fairness, justice and equality under the law are thought to be paramount ... equality under the law is not a right Black people in this country could automatically expect ... the important fact that emerges for us is that as a group Black People are victims of a systematic force of class and racial oppression carried out by a system through its institutions. The police, the courts of law, the prisons (Humphry, 1972, p. 233).

The confrontation between black children and young people and the apparatus of justice is the actual and symbolic moment at which the usually opaque institutionalised racist oppression which bears on all black people is made transparently clear in the official interventions and judicial disposals to which black young people are subjected (Pitts, 1988, p. 155).

The above statements extend across a conceptual continuum. They range from optimistic proclamations that parliament and the courts (the executive and judicial arms of the liberal democratic state) establish and maintain justice, through to more critical contentions that the 'apparatus of justice' not only fails to observe and preserve principles of 'fairness, justice and equality', but systematically subjects black people[1] to fundamental forms of injustice and oppression. Herein lies our primary question. At a time when youth justice policy and practice is witness to radical change, what 'justice' characterises the lived-experiences of black children and young people? By reviewing the principal findings from a wide range of research we intend to put the youth justice system, and, indeed, the very concept of 'justice' on trial.

Race, Crime and Justice

Gordon (1983) refers to 'white law', Gilroy (1987) observes that 'there ain't no black in the Union Jack' and Shallice and Gordon (1990) juxtapose the experiences of 'black people' with 'white justice'. Their argument is compelling. Those who define, administer and enforce criminal justice are overwhelmingly white, whilst the 'subjects' of their attention and endeavour, those upon whom the gaze of the justice and penal systems is most sharply focused, are disproportionately black. Let us consider these issues further.

In 1995 there were no High Court judges from minority ethnic groups, and only five of the 514 circuit judges, two of the 339 district judges, 13 of the 897 recorders and nine of the 341 assistant recorders were from minority ethnic groups. There are no current figures available relating to the ethnic composition of magistrates, although in 1989 the proportion from minority ethnic groups was less than 2 per cent. In 1995 there were no black justices clerks and only 1.6 per cent of the higher grade staff within the Crown Prosecution Service were from minority ethnic groups (a fall from 1.9 per cent in 1991). Four per cent of solicitors and 6 per cent of barristers were from minority ethnic groups but the corresponding figure for police officers was 1.75 per cent from a total of 127,222 (almost all of whom where occupying the lowest ranks – only eight had reached the rank of Chief Inspector and one had been appointed Superintendent). In the same year, 1995, 2.4 per cent of prison officers (again overwhelmingly employed at the lowest ranks) were from minority ethnic groups (National Association of Probation Officers and the Association of Black Probation Of ficers, 1995). Reardon (1993, p. 14) refers to the striking *whiteness* of the criminal justice system as 'grim ... a damning indictment of "equality of opportunity"'.

The contrast between the ethnic composition of the professional *'technicians'* of the criminal justice system with that of its *subjects* illuminates any analysis of race, crime and justice. Under Section 95 of the 1991 Criminal Justice Act the Home Secretary is required to 'publish such information as he (sic) considers expedient for the purpose of enabling persons engaged in the administration of criminal justice ... to avoid discriminating on the grounds of race or sex or any other improper ground'. The first report published under the auspices of this legal provision evidenced disproportionately high arrest rates for black people and variations in police charging practices which worked to their disadvantage (Home Office, 1992). Moreover, whilst people of African-Caribbean descent comprise approximately 1 per cent of the *general* population black males make up 11 per cent and black females 24 per cent of the *prison* population (Home Office, 1992; Penal Affairs Consortium, 1996, Chigwada-Bailey, 1997). Dholakia and Sumner (1993, p. 29) note that this 'disproportionate number of black, particularly Afro-Caribbean, people must be a matter of great concern for those involved with race issues and criminal justice policy and practice'. Put at its simplest the question is: does the disproportionate black presence within the regulatory and punitive dimensions of the criminal justice process stem from a high incidence of 'black crime' or a pervasive racism within 'white justice'?

Taking the crime question first, and for our purposes here we shall focus on youth crime, we immediately encounter knowledge deficit problems as there is a paucity of research into the offending profiles of black and white children and young people. However, Graham and Bowling (1995), in their oft-quoted and widely respected Home Office research, attempt to address this very issue. The researchers studied a random sample of 1,721 young people between the ages of 14 and 25, their 'core sample', together with a 'booster sample' of 808 young people of the same age from 'ethnic minorities'. Both the 'core sample' and the 'booster sample' were invited to self-report whether or not they had ever committed a range of specified offences. The data that was collated from this exercise 'allowed estimates to be made of how many people offend, when they start, how serious the offences are and how frequently they are committed. Comparisons are (then) made by sex, age, class and *ethnic origin*' (Graham and Bowling, 1995, p. 7 – our emphasis). The researchers conclude by noting:

> These data indicate that, taking all offences together, white and Afro-Caribbean respondents have very similar rates of participation in offending ... while each of the Asian groups have substantially lower rates of participation in offending ... This pattern of ethnic differences in participation in offending is broadly consistent for acquisitive and expressive property offences and for violence (ibid., pp. 14–15).

This evidence can offer little by way of explaining the startling under-representation of black people in positions of professional responsibility and power within the criminal justice system. What it does do, however, is indicate that the answer to the question as to why black (young) people are over-represented in the same system as 'subjects' is likely to lie somewhere other than with their rates of 'participation in offending' which, according to Graham and Bowling's study, are apparently no greater than those of white children and young people.

Such questions have also been addressed by way of theoretical contextualisation in which racism and criminalisation are understood as structural forms located within historical materialist processes, as opposed to expressions of individualised behaviours. Given the confines imposed here we can only offer a schematic review of such argument which is grounded in the economic history of postwar Britain. At this time an expanding economy demanded an influx of cheap labour and black people comprised what Sivanandan (1976) has called a 'bargain for capital' as immigration was actively encouraged in order to meet labour market requirements. However, 40 or so years later the combined effect of racism, recession and globalisation has served to 'residualise' many of today's young black people by consigning them to the ever-expanding pool of 'surplus labour'. Despite having been 'born and brought up in Britain', as Gordon (1983, p. 139) observes, 'they are unable even to find the "shit work" that had been forced on their parents (and grandparents)'. The black presence, far from being a 'bargain for capital' has been reconstructed, it is now commonly represented both as a 'drain on the economy' and a threat to public order and national equilibrium. Kushnik (1998, p. 176) notes:

> Margaret Thatcher first played the race card in 1978 during her infamous 'swamping' speech in which she declared that the British people had legitimate fear of being swamped by people of an 'alien culture' ... identity was being threatened by floods of violent, criminal and culturally inassimilable immigrants ...

In this way race has become the common denominator of the full range of social problems: too many 'blacks' means too few jobs; not enough houses; pressure on schools and public services; escalating welfare expenditure and ultimately too much crime. Shallice and Gordon (1990, p. 57) contend:

> the association of black people with crime so firmly made by the police and sections of the mass media, and the criminalisation of black people by the agencies of the criminal justice system have become central to racist ideology. Criminality and disorder ... have increasingly been identified as essential parts of black culture, emphasising the supposed 'otherness' of blacks in Britain, and serving as commonsense explanations for national crisis and decline.

Social and economic difficulties therefore, are conceptualised not in terms of antagonistic capitalist relations and underinvestment in public services but as inevitable consequences of the black presence; an 'alien' and 'lawless' culture. This 'way of seeing' both criminalises black people (and whole black communities) and legitimises their treatment within the criminal 'justice' process.

Although the case against the criminal justice process (in terms of its capacity to deliver 'racial justice') may seem watertight, however, the Home Office (1992) has claimed that 'at present there is only limited information available on any part of the subject (as) research findings to date have been patchy in their coverage'. Moreover, attempts to prove or disprove racism and discrimination in criminal justice processes – especially at the point of sentence – have been fraught with methodological problems. Shallice and Gordon (ibid., p. 31) are struck by the apparent contradiction that exists here:

In Britain, there seems to be an absolute discrepancy between the findings of researchers that there is no evidence of differential sentencing on racial grounds and the large numbers of people who readily assert the opposite, largely (though not unimportantly) on the basis of anecdotal, personal and collective experience. This discrepancy is further emphasised by the massive over-representation of black people in the prison population.

The methodological problematic essentially centres around how much weight can be attributed to 'race' without having the benefit of control over 'extra-racial' factors (for a recent discussion see Holdaway, 1997). Reiner for example, contends that no method 'can conclusively pin down the chimera of "pure" discrimination which is sought for' and proceeds:

> The main problem with any statistical or qualitative analysis of criminal justice practice is the inability to control all other relevant variables apart from 'race'. Statistical analyses in particular, invariably attempt to establish discrimination by seeking to show that there is a residual element of differentiation in the treatment of black people which is not explicable by 'legally relevant factors' … It is inconceivable that this approach could ever conclusively establish racial discrimination. The most obvious problem is the practical impossibility of holding constant more than a few 'legally relevant' variables. This means that it is always open to analysts of different persuasions to characterise any remaining differences in treatment as (so far) unexplained variation rather than discrimination (Reiner, cited by Smith, 1994, p. 1046).

It is not unimportant to take account of such methodological and scientific complexity, but, given what has gone before, we are less inclined to conceptualise the apparent 'racialised' injustices of the 'justice' process as 'unexplained variation' than we are to argue that systematic and endemic racist processes are evident. Moreover, we wish to contend that without *social justice* there can be no *criminal justice* for black children and young people and it is to a specific analysis of these phenomena that we now turn.

Social Injustice: Racism, Marginalisation and Exclusion

The institutions, structural arrangements and policies that influence – if not determine – the transitionary developments from childhood, through youth and into adulthood have been fundamentally reshaped and redefined over the last two decades or so. The cumulative impact of radical changes in relation to the distribution of income and wealth, patterns of schooling and education, employment and training opportunities and housing and household formations, have meant that the processes of 'growing up' have become more hazardous and insecure for identifiable groups of children and young people, many of whom experience hardening and intensifying forms of marginalisation and exclusion (Goldson, 1997a). Coles (1995) describes this process as the 're-structuration of youth' within which many young people endure what Westergaard (1992) has called 'outcast poverty'. Indeed, the postwar welfare state has not performed a redistributive function and the evidence generated from the Joseph Rowntree Foundation's (1995) comprehensive analysis of the national apportionment of income and wealth provides the rather stark conclusion that the rich are getting richer and the poor are getting poorer still.

Lister (1990, p. viii) argues that 'poverty does not make people a group apart from society so much as victims of the injustice and incivilities of the social order of which they are very much a part'. Such 'injustice and incivilities' have been visited upon children and young people in a particularly focused manner as child poverty has dramatically expanded and deepened. In 1993 there were 640,000 births in England (Central Statistical Office, 1996), 35 per cent of these babies were born into poverty (*Independent On Sunday*, 24 November 1996, p. 1). Indeed, there is no shortage of the most authoritative evidence that child poverty is widespread (The Commission on Social Justice, 1994; Joseph Rowntree Foundation, 1995; Hutton, 1996). Kumar demonstrates that 31 per cent of children in the UK (circa 4.2 million) live in poverty, with a further 10 per cent held at the 'margins of poverty' (Kumar, 1993), and Lansdown (1996, p. 63) adds that 'children have disproportionately borne the brunt of the increase of poverty in the UK'. In a nutshell, as Holterman's comprehensive analysis of public expenditure and fiscal policies illustrates, the state is 'underinvesting in its children' (Holterman, 1996, p. 3). The consequences of such underinvestment are applied (and thus experienced) unequally and the evidence is such to confirm that black children and young people are particularly disadvantaged (Oppenheim and Harker, 1996; Cook, 1997; Walker and Walker, 1997).

There can be little doubt that poverty is, in itself, a fundamental cause of marginalisation and exclusion. The 'racialisation' of poverty therefore, inevitably means that (working class) black children and young people are particularly prone to the consequences of this form of social injustice and the opportunity limitations that it imposes. Furthermore, poverty is interrelated with other dimensions of social and economic opportunity and here too black children and young people are disadvantaged. In order to develop this point further we will pay particular attention to education, employment and training, state benefits, and housing as these are both constituent imperatives of social justice and key elements which underpin the transitionary processes involved in 'growing up'.

Despite official guidance that 'unless other suitable arrangements are made, all children should be in school and learning (and) exclusion should be used sparingly in response to serious breaches of school policy and law' (Department for Education, 1994) the number of children and young people being permanently excluded from school has increased dramatically in recent years (National Union of Teachers, 1992; Stirling, 1992; Advisory Centre for Education, 1992; Garner, 1993; Bourne 1994; Parsons et al., 1995; Goldson, 1997b). The first national survey of school exclusions reported 4,000 permanent exclusions for the school year 1991–92, which represented a substantial increase from the previous year figure of 3,000; by 1994–95 the figure had risen sharply to 11,100; by 1995–96 it had increased further to 12,500; and the figure stood at a staggering 13,500 for the 1996–97 year (Social Exclusion Unit, 1998). Osler (1997, p. 22) observes:

> Although there is overwhelming agreement that there are significant differences between the rates of exclusion for different ethnic groups, the public debate about exclusion has paid little attention to concerns within ethnic minority, and particularly black, communities that their children are overrepresented in the exclusion statistics.

Similarly, Bourne et al. (1994) have noted that there has been 'absolute silence from the government on why black children are being disproportionately excluded'. Such silence is particularly conspicuous in view of the national evidence that black children are six times more likely to be excluded than their white counterparts (Social Exclusion Unit, 1998, p. 9) and a raft of local studies that provide similar findings (see for example, Gillborn, 1995; Klein, 1996). The implications of school exclusion for black children and young people are considerable and usually result in the complete termination of their state education. Although official guidance provides that children who are permanently excluded from secondary school should be reintegrated back into an alternative school as quickly as possible, this has been found to happen in only about 15 per cent of cases (Parsons, 1996). Being forced to exit the education system prematurely, with no qualifications and a blemished school record, clearly serves to disadvantage such children and young people in an increasingly competitive labour market.

Indeed, young people *per se* disproportionately face the worst of unemployment a consequence of the 1980s economic recession and demographic patterns which witnessed a sharp rise in the youth population. Currently the unemployment rate for young people is 18.6 per cent, almost one in five of all economically active 16 and 17 year-olds (Chatrik and Convery, cited in Walker and Walker, 1997, p. 180). However, the position of young black people is considerably worse and the labour market comprises a site of flagrant racism and institutionalised disadvantage. Among 16–24 year olds for example, the rate of unemployment for young black men stands at three times that of young white men: 51 per cent compared to 18 per cent (Sly, 1995), and Connolly and her colleagues in their study of black young people in Liverpool noted that 'racism was certainly a prominent if not the primary structuring force in our sample's lives ... our sample of young people had widespread experience of discriminatory treatment ... we visited far more firms where "equal opportunity" was little more than a public relations posture' (Connolly et al., 1992, pp. 85–6). Equally, research into youth training programmes has confirmed their particular failure in respect of black 'trainees' and despite the supposed universal availability of such schemes black school leavers are less likely to be provided with a place than are their white counterparts (Bhattacharyya and Gabriel, 1997). Indeed, the experiences of black young people within the labour market – experiences frequently underpinned by racism, marginalisation and exclusion – condemn disproportionate numbers of them to the miseries of claiming state benefits, where their difficulties are likely to be further compounded.

General entitlement to state benefits for 16 and 17 year-olds was withdrawn by the 1988 Social Security Act which consolidated the targeted diminution on the rights to claim welfare benefits for young people introduced by the 1985 Board and Lodgings Regulations and the 1986 Social Security Act. The legislation has institutionalised discretion, casualisation and short-termism with 'handouts' and 'bridging allowances' available only for those young people adjudged to be experiencing 'severe hardship'. The impact of such policy has been devastating, particularly for black young people who, as we have seen, are already those most likely to suffer the corrosive effects of poverty, school exclusion and unemployment. NCH Action for Children commissioned research which revealed that 35 per cent of the sample of young people who they interviewed had eaten either one meal or nothing over the period of the previous 24 hours; disproportionately high numbers had recently been ill; the overwhelming majority were depressed, worried or anxious; 66 per cent had gone into debt; and more than 80 per cent reported to being so desperate that they were compelled to consider illegal means of securing additional income in order to survive (NCH Action for Children, 1993).

Similarly, research undertaken by the Coalition on Young People and Social Security (COYPSS) concluded that many young people excluded from the benefits system are being forced to adopt 'survival strategies' which include loans, begging, theft and prostitution (cited in NCH Action for Children, 1996, p. 53). Indeed, it is such awful poverty that has been a key feature in the alarming rise of youth homelessness and/or the escalation of inadequate housing.

The importance of an adequate and secure home to the health and welfare of children and young people and to engender their sense of belonging and inclusion can hardly be overstated. However the National Housing Forum recently found that one in 12 homes in England is unfit for habitation, more than 600,000 are in a serious state of disrepair, and the money set aside by central government for housing renewal fell from £1.5 billion in 1983 to £500 million in 1993 (National Housing Forum, 1994). Furthermore, the London Research Centre has reported that 35 per cent of all children accommodated in local authority or housing association stock in London are living in overcrowded conditions. This amounts to 150,000 children, an increase of 30,000 since 1986/7, and black children are twice as likely to be living in such overcrowded conditions as are their white counterparts (London Research Centre, 1992). Many more children are condemned to the miseries of temporary accommodation and squalid bed and breakfast conditions (Clark, 1996) whilst others are literally denied homes as youth homelessness has emerged as one of the most vivid manifestations of systemic exclusion in the 1990s.

Indeed, the convergence of state policy in relation to youth employment, social security and housing has produced crisis conditions for many young people in need of accommodation. The National Inquiry into Preventing Youth Homelessness was established in 1995 by 10 leading housing and children's organisations and it calculated that up to 300,000 young people had experienced homelessness in Britain in 1995; that youth homelessness besets every part of Britain; that particularly disadvantaged teenagers aged under 17 years are especially vulnerable; and that by ignoring the plight of homeless children and young people 'we undermine the principles and values of a caring society' (Inquiry into Preventing Youth Homelessness, 1996). Moreover, with depressing predictability, recent research has indicated that black young people are particularly disadvantaged (Rooney and Brown, 1996; Davies et al., 1996) and Julienne (1998, p. 33) observes:

> Homelessness among young black single people can be seen as part of a problem of housing shortages and short-sighted dis-integrated social policies. It can also

be analysed and identified as part of the more fundamental issue of entrenched racism which is buried deep in the British psyche.

Shelter (1996, p. 7) add that 'the consequences ... will be to further alienate them from a society they see as offering them little and valuing them less.

This last point is of critical importance. A polarised society within which the stark 'haves' and 'have nots' dichotomy serves as a constant reminder of social injustice, and yet which continues to vaunt the merits of 'enterprise culture' and condemn the 'scourge' of 'welfare dependency', is a society which can not claim to be at ease with itself. It is a society which offers little in terms of material opportunity and human respect for its most disadvantaged citizens. It is a society which is predicated upon forms of 'racialised' injustice, marginalisation and exclusion. It is a society within which many young black people endure a penetrating sense of alienation as their experience of poverty, school exclusion, labour-market exclusion, inadequate benefits, poor housing and homelessness interrelate and combine to produce complex and layered institutionalised forms of social injustice.

It is in some senses such a socioeconomic context that occupied the minds of criminologists such as Merton (1938) in his development of 'anomie' theory and Cloward and Ohlin (1960) in their conceptualisation of 'opportunity' theory. Here the theoretical arguments appear to make perfect sense: if material goals are emphasised in a society but access to achieve them legitimately is denied for identifiable groups, then individuals within such groups will seek illegitimate or illegal means to reach the prized goals. Pitts (1993, p. 115) notes:

> If a century of sociological studies of crime in cities has any validity, it would be astonishing if we did not find that the crime rate among the young who inhabit the poorest sections of our inner cities was not disproportionately high. We would expect this to be the case ... The fact that a disproportionately large number of young black Britons are located in such areas would suggest that their crime rate would, in consequence, be higher than average.

This is not an unreasonable hypothesis. However there are problems with such hypothesising (as Pitts himself acknowledges), not least because it is largely untested due to the shortage of available evidence. Moreover, the evidence that is available, such as that provided by Graham and Bowling's 1995 study which we discussed earlier, indicates that the offending rates between black and white children and young people are not as dissimilar as such theorising would lead us to suspect. Indeed, the Home Office study found

– notwithstanding some methodological limitations – that the comparative rates of 'participation in offending' between black and white young people were remarkably similar. Despite the pervasive social injustice, racism, marginalisation and exclusion that black children and young people endure, it does not in itself appear to result in any greater proclivity to 'offend'. Thus explanations for their over-representation in the criminal justice system must be sought elsewhere and Mathieson (1974, p. 77) offers an alternative theoretical proposition:

> In our society 'productivity' is to a considerable and increasing degree geared to activity in the labour market. At the same time, our social structure ... increasingly creates groups which are 'unproductive' according to this criterion ... the 'unproductive' brutally remind us of the fact that our productive system is not so successful after all. A society may get rid of its 'unproductive' elements in many ways. One way is to criminalise their activities and punish them ... this may be done towards a sub-category of the 'unproductive'.

Criminal Injustice: Racism, Criminalisation and Punishment

We referred earlier to Section 95 of the 1991 Criminal Justice Act. The central provision of this section – 'to avoid discriminating against any person on the grounds of race or sex or any other improper ground' – not only represents an explicit duty in criminal law to 'avoid discrimination' (the first of its kind in England and Wales, albeit at Section 95 rather than Section 1!) but, by definition, it also acknowledges the existence of discrimination and injustice. We have also noted the over-representation of black young people within the criminal justice process as 'subjects', and this observation is comprehensively established and grounded in a wealth of evidence that has accumulated over some time. In 1991 for example, the Runnymede Trust in its submission to the Royal Commission on Criminal Justice claimed that unequal treatment occurred at all stages of the system, from initial contact with the police to imprisonment (Runnymede Trust, 1992, p. 11) and more recently, the Audit Commission (1996, p. 45) has expressed concern that 'African Caribbean's are over-represented throughout the system'. In the same way that the processes of social injustice and exclusion take multiple and interrelated forms, so the processes of criminal injustice, criminalisation and punishment are multidimensional and cannot be reduced to any one part of the criminal 'justice' system. Rather, racism is endemic and operates – at times overtly and at others more insidiously – at each discrete point of the process, producing a cumulative and compounding configuration of injustice. Lord Justice Taylor observed how different points of the criminal justice process might connect in this way: 'a multiplier effect could operate, amplifying discrimination at several points ... (and) the effect could produce startling discrepancies' (Taylor, cited in Cook, 1997, p. 78). It is our intention here to examine briefly the impact of the 'multiplier effect' on black children and young people as it gathers momentum from the point of operational policing, through the process of caution, prosecution, bail and remand decisions, to sentencing and punishment by incarceration.

To begin with street-level policing, there is substantial evidence that black people, and particularly black young people, are much more likely than white people to be stopped and searched under police powers provided by the 1984 Police and Criminal Evidence Act (Smith, 1983; Institute of Race Relations, 1987; Skogan, 1990; Hood, 1992). Indeed, Pitts (1988, p. 127) argues that 'black young people are subject to more intensive policing than any other section of the population'. Up until recently however, there was little by way of systematically collated evidence of such surveillance, regulation and harassment because police forces were not required to use ethnic monitoring systems in relation to operational practices. Further to the 1991 Criminal Justice Act and the provisions of Section 95, though, the police are now legally obliged to undertake such monitoring. In March 1995, following discussions within the Home Office, Her Majesty's Inspector of Constabularies and the police, a system of ethnic monitoring was agreed and subsequently introduced in 1996. In December 1997 – six years after the formulation of the Section 95 provisions – the Home Secretary published the first set of figures (Home Office, 1997) despite the fact that 'some police forces are still not in a position to supply all the data required ... an extraordinary situation given the length of time the police have had to introduce monitoring systems' (Statewatch, 1998, p. 16). The monitoring exercise reveals widespread differentials in the proportions of minority ethnic people subject to police powers of stop and search and arrest, with 'those recorded as being of black appearance' four or five times more likely than white people to be targeted. Moreover, by analysing the Home Office data and applying it across England and Wales Statewatch concludes that:

> The variation in the use of these powers between white people and ethnic minorities ... is extremely wide ... The rate for white people is 14 per 1000, for black people 108 per 1000 ... In other words black people are nearly 8 times ... as likely to be subject to stop and search by the police than white people in

England and Wales ... The arrest rate for white people is 34 per 1000, for black people 155 per 1000... nearly 5 times as great (Statewatch, 1998, p. 18).

The Commission for Racial Equality described the stop and search and arrest rates for black children and young people as 'ludicrously high' and postulated that they help to explain the 'deep alienation' that many of them experience regarding the police (*The Guardian*, 27 July 1998, p. 1). Indeed, even the Metropolitan Police Commissioner Sir Paul Condon, has recently acknowledged that 'too many young black men are stopped and searched without good cause (and) the challenge is not to pretend it doesn't happen, the challenge is to understand that it does happen and how we can work together to combat it' (*The Guardian*, 3 April 1996, p. 9). Despite such apparent determination, however, racism within the police cuts deep and exists at all levels. Reiner's research among chief constables found that they tended to conceptualise black people as a source of crime and disorder (Reiner, 1991, p. 206), and Smith and Gray, following extensive observational research noted (1983, p. 335):

> Although there were variations in the extent of racial prejudice and racialist talk between different groups of officers ... these things are pervasive: they are, on the whole, expected, accepted and even fashionable. Senior officers seldom try to set a different tone ... and there were some cases where they initiated racialist talk and kept it going.

Nor is police racism confined to what Smith and Gray refer to as acts of individual 'racial prejudice', but it is entrenched and institutionalised within the organisation and operation of *policing* as Scraton has argued (1982, p. 21):

> ... the black population 'as a whole' has been targeted as 'the problem'. Saturation policing, using special task force units, has encouraged an aggressive, siege-like attitude within the police. The emergence of offensive methods as force policy, as opposed to the use of individual officers' discretion, has elevated racism from the personal to an institutional level.

Black children and young people are further criminalised at the point of the criminal 'justice' process where decisions are taken whether to caution and *divert from*, or prosecute and formally *commit to*, the court system. The widely referenced study by Landau and Nathan (1983) found that black children and young people were more likely to be prosecuted than white children and young people, and the National Intermediate Treatment Federation have reported that 'the chances of apprehended Black juveniles obtaining a caution are considerably smaller than those of their white counterparts' (NITFED, 1986, p. 2). More recently, the Commission for Racial Equality has concluded that:

> In the majority of forces, proportionately more ethnic minority young people – and particularly Afro-Caribbean's – were referred for prosecution than white young people: in inner city areas the difference was very substantial indeed. The widespread police view that such differentials would indicate that, on average, ethnic minority young people were committing more serious offences was not borne out (cited in Chigwada-Bailey, 1997, p. 30).

Similar forms of racism are evident at the court stage where bail and remand decisions are taken. The legal presumption in favour of bail does not appear to apply to black children and young people who are 'more likely to be remanded in custody' (Hood, 1992, p. 181). Despite there being widespread concerns in relation to the welfare of children remanded into prison custody (Howard League, 1995) the Howard League found that an astonishing 45 per cent of the 15 and 16 year-old remanded prisoners that they met were black or Asian (Howard League, 1997, p. 3).

The methodological complexities and confusions that we discussed earlier are most evident in relation to research into sentencing patterns, and it is this stage of the process that has paradoxically been the source of both greatest anxiety and least agreement. Some researchers have concluded that differences in the use of custodial sentences between ethnic groups can be accounted for by referring to differences in their offending and criminal histories (Moxon, 1988), whilst others contend that 'there is sufficient evidence to support the case that unequal and unfavourable treatment of black defendants exists' (Shallice and Gordon, 1990, p. 36). Kirk (1996) found that black children and young people received significantly more 'high tariff' sentences than white defendants in his study, and Hudson's (1989) research produced similar results with a higher proportion of black people receiving custodial sentences than white people irrespective of the comparability of their offences. However, perhaps the most detailed and comprehensive study (which is also widely regarded as having overcome many of the methodological limitations that are thought to have beset earlier sentencing research) is Hood's (1992) analysis of sentencing in the West Midlands region of England. Hood adopted sophisticated analytic methods to examine sentencing outcomes in respect of 2,884 men and 433 women in five Crown Courts and filtered his findings meticulously, using a range of variables. He concluded that, all else being equal, black people had an overall 5 per cent greater probability of being sentenced to custody than white people, and that there were worrying inconsistencies between some of the courts in his study:

> Given the number of cases which appeared before these courts in the course of a year, these differences were sufficiently large to be to the disadvantage of a considerable number of black defendants ... there was strong evidence to suggest that factors which would have been regarded as mitigating the seriousness of the case if the defendant was white were not given the same weight if the defendant was black ... there were substantial racial differences in the sentencing patterns and it seems inconceivable that similar variations would not be found in other regions of the country ... to have a considerable impact on the proportion of black offenders in the prison system ... when one contrasts the overall treatment meted out to black Afro-Caribbean males one is left wondering whether it is not a result of different racial stereotypes operating on the perceptions of some judges (Hood, 1992, pp. 184–8).

Whilst methodological precision and the nuances of interpretation have comprised the source of academic debate in relation to 'race and sentencing' research, however, the prisons and other custodial institutions have steadily been filling with black people. The trends are staggering and what Hood (ibid., p. 193) refers to as 'the very substantial over-representation of males and females of Afro-Caribbean origin in the prisons and young offenders institutions of England and Wales' is a grotesque and unmistakable manifestation of racist criminalisation and punishment. Indeed, black people now account for 18 per cent of the prison population in England and Wales: 17 per cent of male prisoners and 24 per cent of female prisoners (Penal Affairs Consortium, 1996, p. 3). The number of female prisoners from minority ethnic groups doubled from 12 per cent in 1986 to 24 per cent in 1990 (Chigwada, 1991; Carlen, 1992; Home Office, 1992) and 26 per cent of the children serving custodial sentences who were referred to the Howard League were black (Howard League, 1997). Moreover, the skewed ethnic profile of custodial institutions only tells part of the story in relation to racism and punishment by incarceration. Black young people are likely to be serving longer sentences than their white counterparts (Howard League, 1997) and the operational practices of custodial institutions are also tarnished by racism. Genders and Player (1989, p. 131) conclude their study of 'race relations in prisons' with the observation that 'racial discrimination is intrinsic to the social organisation of prisons'. If we are to recall the words of the Chief Inspector of

Prisons following his most recent thematic review that 'there is no such thing as a neutral experience for children in custody (as) they are either helped or damaged' (HM Inspectorate of Prisons, 1997, p. 69), and overlay the permanent omnipresence of racism within custodial institutions, the implications for black children and young people are of utmost concern.

What is commonly referred to as the criminal justice or youth justice system is not really a *system* at all. A system is underpinned by scientific regularity and predictability which serves to produce methodical and reliable outcomes. This is not always the case, as we have seen. Similarly, we may wish to take a step further and challenge the semantic legitimacy of the very term 'justice'. Indeed, the means by which black children and young people are *processed* through the administrative and institutional arrangements that are charged with the responsibility for dispensing youth 'justice' raise profoundly discomforting questions. The interrelated and interdependent stages of the *process* are each predicated upon human discretion and judgment as opposed to scientific laws. Our analysis and review of the research evidence reveals that racism operates within this discretionary milieu and its interactive form produces a 'multiplier effect' connecting street-level harassment with systematic criminalisation and ultimately disproportionate levels of punishment by incarceration. There is little getting away from the reality that criminal 'injustice' compounds social 'injustice' and consolidates the individualised and institutionalised forms of racism that black children and young people are compelled to endure.

Towards Justice for Black Children and Young People?

There is no shortage of policy and practice initiatives that have been established to address the racialised injustices of the 'justice' process. We have referred already to monitoring initiatives that have been instituted to record aspects of police operations. The Lord Chancellor's Department and the Home Office have issued guidance to courts in relation to equality of treatment. The Judicial Studies Board created an Ethnic Minorities Advisory Committee in 1991 and training on race issues has been provided for the full range of sentencers. The Law Society and the Bar have established race relations committees. The Probation Service has produced policy statements and practice guidance and introduced monitoring and quality assurance mechanisms to cover all aspects of race equality. In 1993 the Association of Chief Police Officers and the Commission for Racial Equality issued equality guidance to all police forces and HM Inspectorate of Constabulary produced thematic reports on equal opportunities in 1992 and 1996. The Crown Prosecution Service has adopted a policy statement on race relations and the Prison Service has done likewise. Finally, in 1994 the Criminal Justice Consultative Council published a report in which it made 50 recommendations for criminal justice agencies and government departments in relation to race equality (Penal Affairs Consortium, 1996, pp. 7–8). These initiatives are to be welcomed, but it would be foolhardy to assume that in themselves they can eradicate the forms of injustice that we have considered here, and they are not beyond critique, as Shallice and Gordon (1990, p. 56) have argued:

> This is an approach which is best described as 'multicultural' in which the 'answer' is seen to lie in greater 'sensitivity' towards black people, greater understanding of their cultures and lifestyles, and so on – usually to be achieved through multifarious forms of 'training' – combined with 'equal opportunity' policies and the recruitment of more black personnel, whether as lawyers, probation officers, magistrates or whatever. Such an approach ignores the central question of racism, the institutionalised practices of a society based on unequal social, economic and power relations.

It is a society in which black children and young people, all black people, are routinely, systematically and institutionally disadvantaged. This is not simply the product of technical accident, and has to be understood and conceptualised in conjunction with the political economy of contemporary British society. It is not a society which can guarantee either justice or safety to black people and it is not a society in which injustices can readily be 'trained' away.

Indeed, turning briefly to the issue of welfare and safety, Britain is a disproportionately dangerous place for all black people and the growing incidence of racial harassment and violence is such that even the right to walk the streets freely and without fear or trepidation is compromised. The European Parliament's Committee of Inquiry into Racism and Xenophobia indicted Britain for its 'intolerably high level of racial harassment and violence' (Kushnik, 1998, p. 179) and the British Crime Survey 1996 estimated that approximately 200,000 black or Asian people experienced some form of racially-motivated victimisation or harassment in 1995 (Home Office, 1998). Racism here has a double edge. Not only are black people subject to harassment, intimidation and violence but 'despite the wealth of information available to the police, there (is) a conspicuous absence of action against perpetrators ... the police appear to put little effort into identifying suspects' (Sibbitt, 1997, p. 95). In other words, forms of racism and *criminalisation* are so deeply embedded and institutionalised that there is substantial resistance to conceptualising black people as *victims* and responding accordingly. This presents fundamental challenges to the 'equality' initiatives that we have just reviewed and serves to remind us of the context within which they are located. Indeed, an uncomfortable contradiction emerges here which is graphically illustrated in recent pronouncements by the Metropolitan Police Commissioner.

In March 1993 Paul Condon, the newly-appointed Commissioner of the Metropolitan Police, made opposing racism within the police force the subject of his first major speech (Smith, 1994, p. 1095). In July 1995 Condon – seemingly oblivious to the penetrating analysis provided by Hall and his colleagues almost 20 years earlier (Hall et al., 1978) – wrote a letter to prominent black organisations and individuals inviting them to a briefing to launch 'an important police operation to combat street robbery' (Operation Eagle Eye). Condon's letter was based on the 'fact' that 'very many of the perpetrators of muggings are very young black people' (cited in Holdaway, 1997, p. 383). The Commissioner's 'evidence' was drawn from an internally conducted, unpublished study of victims' descriptions of their attackers in areas of London heavily populated by black people. Inevitably, newspaper headlines about 'black muggers' followed. In June 1998 the Metropolitan Police Commissioner again made a high profile statement in which he made an unprecedented apology to the parents of Stephen Lawrence for failing to bring their son's murderers to justice. Condon's message of contrition was delivered by his Assistant Commissioner Ian Johnston at the public inquiry into Stephen's murder (*The Guardian*, 18 June 1998, p. 1). The apology followed a catalogue of utter incompetence and 'serious shortcomings' in which at least 11 potential leads went unchecked by the police and those responsible for the racist slaughter of a young black person on the streets of London were not brought to justice. The Commissioner's bold statement of anti-racist intent in 1993, which was followed in 1995 by his spectacular criminalisation of black people, concluded in 1998 with a meek and inadequate apology for the most flagrant form of police negligence (at best). This is not intended as a slight towards London's most senior police officer but rather as a powerful and evocative symbol of the depth and complexity of the 'race-crime' issue and the profound injustice to which black people are subjected.

So, at a time of radical change, is the youth justice system moving towards a point where it might provide justice for black children and young people? Can black children expect justice from (white) adult deliberations with regard to child curfews? Will the courts ensure that black children are not over-represented in secure training centres? Will the new 'corporatism' of youth offender teams facilitate the effacement of the social and criminal injustices that confront black children? Will New Labour's apparent assault on 'social exclusion' target the particular and institutionalised forms of disadvantage and poverty that impact upon black children? As we approach the new millennium, will the British state seriously address the institutionalised injustices that systematically undermine the rights and potential of black children, or are we to follow the pernicious example of the USA, where some states have become 'minimum security penal colonies' where 60 per cent of young black men are 'under the control of the criminal justice system'? These same states are 'being turned literally into hollow shells – places without stores or jobs, without health care or mental health care, with crumbling schools and nonexistent recreation programmes – with virtually no legitimate things for young people to do' (Currie, 1996, p. 6). If the latter is to be the case, what are we to do when the secure training centres, young offender institutions and prisons are full? Will we follow the USA here too, where 160 children have been sentenced to death since 1973, where the number of children executed has doubled during the last decade, and where 75 per cent of all the juveniles executed this century were black (Block, 1998, p. 2)? Is this what we want? Could we call this 'justice' too?

Note

1   The very term 'black' is conceptually problematic. Although 'black' has a particular political significance and value it is certainly not the intention here to posit crude notions of homogeneity in the experiences of black people. For example, the Asian and the African-Caribbean experience of criminal 'justice' is dissimilar in important respects. Pitts (1993, p. 111), observes that the 'tendency to treat as homogeneous groups of people whose only characteristic is that they are not caucasian … is to lead to the denial of complexity which, Richard Titmuss warned us, is the essence of tyranny'. For our purposes here, 'black' will primarily refer to children and young people of African-Caribbean descent, which in itself does not take account of issues of class and gender. Where particular forms of structural analysis are examined we will attempt to draw out the specifics within the space that we have.

References

Advisory Centre for Education (1992), 'Exclusions', *ACE Bulletin*, 45, pp 9–10
Audit Commission (1996), *Misspent Youth*, London, Audit Commission.

Bhattacharyya, G. and Gabriel, J. (1997), 'Racial Formations of Youth in Late Twentieth Century England' in J. Roche and S. Tucker (eds), *Youth in Society*, Buckingham, Open University Press.

Block, B. (1998), 'Killing Children: Past and Present', *Youth Justice Newsletter*, 9, June, pp. 1–3.

Bourne, J. (1994), 'Stories of Exclusion' in J. Bourne, L. Bridges and C. Searle (eds), *Outcast England: how schools exclude black children*, London, Institute of Race Relations.

Bourne, J., Bridges, L. and Searle, C. (eds) (1994), *Outcast England: how schools exclude black children*, London, Institute of Race Relations.

Carlen, P. (1992), 'Criminal women and criminal justice: the limits to, and potential of, feminist and left realist perspectives' in R. Matthews and J. Young (eds), *Issues in Realist Criminology*, London, Sage.

Central Statistical Office (1996), *Social Trends*, London, HMSO.

Chigwada, R. (1991), 'The policing of black women' in E. Cashmore and E. McLaughlin (eds), *Out of Order? Policing Black People*, London, Routledge.

Chigwada-Bailey, R. (1997), *Black Women and Criminal Justice*, Winchester, Waterside Press.

Clark, A. (1996), 'Policy and Provision for the Schooling of Children Living in Temporary Accommodation: Exploring the Difficulties', *Children and Society*, Vol. 10, No. 4, pp. 293–304.

Cloward, R. and Ohlin, L. (1960), *Delinquency and Opportunity*, New York, Free Press.

Coles, B. (1995), *Youth and Social Policy*, London, UCL Press.

Commission on Social Justice (1994), *Social Justice: Strategies for National Renewal*, London, Vintage.

Connolly, M., Roberts, K., Ben-Tovim, G. and Torkington, P. (1992), *Black Youth in Liverpool*, Netherlands, Giordano Bruno Culemborg.

Cook, D. (1997), *Poverty, crime and punishment*, London, Child Poverty Action Group.

Currie, E. (1996), *Is America really winning the war on crime and should Britain follow its example?*, London, NACRO.

Davies, J. and Lyle, S. with Deacon, A., Law, I., Julienne, L. and Kay, H. (1996), *Discounted Voices: homeless young black people and minority ethnic people in England*, London, Federation of Black Housing Organisations and CHAR.

Department for Education (1994), *Excluded Pupils. DfE Circular 10/94*, London, DfE.

Dholakia, N. and Sumner, M. (1993), 'Research, Policy and Racial Justice' in D. Cook and B. Hudson (eds), *Racism and Criminology*, London, Sage.

Garner, P. (1993), 'Exclusions: the challenge to schools', *Support for Learning*, 8, 3, pp. 99–103.

Genders, E. and Player, E. (1989), *Race Relations in Prisons*, Oxford, Clarendon Press.

Gillborn, D. (1995), *Racism and Antiracism in Real Schools*, Buckingham, Open University Press.

Gilroy, P. (1987), *'There Ain't No Black in the Union Jack': the cultural politics of race and nation*, London, Hutchinson.

Goldson, B. (1997a), 'Locked Out and Locked Up: State Policy and the Systemic Exclusion of Children "In Need" in England and Wales', *Representing Children*, Vol. 10, No, 1, pp. 44–55.

Goldson, B. (1997b), 'From Exclusion to Inclusion: Educationally Disadvantaged Children and Young People – A Child Centred Approach to Practice', *Journal of Child Centred Practice*, Vol. 4, No. 2, pp. 47–68.

72   Youth Justice: Contemporary Policy and Practice

Gordon, P. (1983), *White Law: racism in the police, courts and prisons*, London, Pluto Press.
Graham, J. and Bowling, B. (1995), *Young people and crime*, Research Study 145, London, Home Office.
Hall, S., Critcher, C., Clarke, J., Jefferson, T. and Roberts, B. (1978), *Policing the Crisis: Mugging, the State and Law and Order*, London, Macmillan.
Hil, R. (1980), 'Black kids, white justice', *New Society*, 24 January.
HM Inspectorate of Prisons (1997), *Young Prisoners: A Thematic Review by HM Chief Inspector of Prisons for England and Wales*, London, Home Office.
Holdaway, S. (1997), 'Some Recent Approaches to the Study of Race in Criminological Research', *British Journal of Criminology*, Vol. 37, No. 3, pp. 383–400.
Holterman, S. (1996), 'The Impact of Public Expenditure and Fiscal Policies on Britain's Children and Young People', *Children and Society*, Vol. 10, No. 1, pp. 3–13.
Home Office (1992), *Race and the Criminal Justice System*, London, HMSO.
Home Office (1997), *Race and the Criminal Justice System*, London, HMSO.
Home Office (1998), *Ethnicity and Victimisation: Findings from the 1996 British Crime Survey*, Home Office Statistical Bulletin 6/98, London, Home Office.
Hood, R. (1992), *Race and Sentencing*, Oxford, Clarendon Press.
Howard League (1995), *Banged Up, Beaten Up and Cutting Up: Report of the Howard League Commission of Inquiry into Violence in Penal Institutions for Teenagers under 18*, London, The Howard League for Penal Reform.
Howard League (1997), *The Howard League Troubleshooter Project: Lessons for Policy and Practice On 15 Year Olds in Prison*, London, The Howard League for Penal Reform.
Hudson, B. (1989), 'Discrimination and Disparity: The Influence of Race on Sentencing', *New Community*, Vol. 16, No. 1, pp. 23–34.
Humphry, D. (1972), *Police, Power and Black People*, London, Panther Books Ltd.
Hutton, W. (1996), *The State We're In*, London, Vintage.
Inquiry into Preventing Youth Homelessness (1996), *We Don't Choose to be Homeless*, London, CHAR.
Institute of Race Relations (1987), *Policing Against Black People*, London, Institute of Race Relations.
Joseph Rowntree Foundation (1995), *Inquiry into Income and Wealth*, York, Joseph Rowntree Foundation.
Julienne, L. (1998), 'Homelessness and Young Single People from Black and Minority Ethnic Communities', *Youth and Policy*, 59, pp. 23–37.
Kirk, B. (1996), *Negative Images*, Aldershot, Avebury.
Klein, R. (1996), 'A steering hand away from trouble', *Times Educational Supplement*, 12 January.
Kumar, V. (1993), *Poverty and Inequality in the UK: the effects on children*, London, National Children's Bureau.
Kushnik, L. (1998), *Race, Class and Struggle*, London, Rivers Oram Press.
Landau, S.F. and Nathan, G. (1983), 'Selecting Delinquents for Cautioning in the London Metropolitan Area', *British Journal of Criminology*, 23/2, pp. 128–49.
Lansdown, G. (1996), 'Implementation of the UN Convention on the Rights of the Child in the UK' in M. John (ed.), *Children in Our Charge: The Child's Right to Resources*, London, Jessica Kingsley.
Lester, A. and Bindman, G. (1972), *Race and Law*, Harmondsworth, Penguin.
Lister, R. (1990), *The Exclusive Society: Citizenship and the Poor*, London, Child Poverty Action Group.

London Research Centre (1992), *London Housing Survey*, London, London Research Centre.

Mathieson, T. (1974), *The Politics of Abolition*, Oxford, Martin Robertson.

Merton, R.K. (1938), 'Social Structure and Anomie', *American Sociological Review*, Vol. 3, pp. 672–82.

Moxon, D. (1988), *Sentencing Practice in the Crown Court*, Home Office Research Study No. 103, London, HMSO.

National Association of Probation Officers and the Association of Black Probation Officers (1995), *Race Discrimination and the Criminal Justice System*, London, NAPO and ABPO.

National Housing Forum (1994), *Papering Over the Cracks*, London, National Housing Forum.

National Intermediate Treatment Federation (1986), *Anti-Racist Practice for Intermediate Treatment*, London, NITFED.

National Union of Teachers (1992), *Survey on Pupils' Exclusions: information from LEAs*, London, NUT.

NCH Action for Children (1993), *A Lost Generation*, London, NCH Action for Children.

NCH Action for Children (1996), *Factfile 96/97*, London, NCH Action for Children.

Oppenheim, S. and Harker, L. (1996), *Poverty the Facts*, London, Child Poverty Action Group.

Osler, A. (1997), *Exclusion from School and Racial Equality*, London, Commission for Racial Equality.

Parsons, C., Hailes, J., Howlett, K., Driscoll, P. and Ross, L. (1995), *National survey of local education authorities' policies and procedures for the identification of, and provision for, children who are out of school by reason of exclusion or otherwise*, London, Department for Education.

Parsons, C. (1996), *Exclusions from School: the public cost*, London, Commission for Racial Equality.

Penal Affairs Consortium (1996), *Race and Criminal Justice*, London, Penal Affairs Consortium.

Pitts, J. (1988), *The Politics of Juvenile Crime*, London, Sage.

Pitts, J. (1993), 'Thereotyping: Anti-racism, Criminology and Black Young People' in D. Cook and B. Hudson (eds), *Racism and Criminology*, London, Sage.

Reardon, D. (1993), 'The Reality of Life for Black Professionals in the Criminal Justice System' in D. Woodhill and P. Senior (eds) (1993), *Justice for Black Young People*, Sheffield, Pavic Publications.

Reiner, R. (1991), *Chief Constables*, Oxford, Oxford University Press.

Rooney, B. and Brown, M. (1996), *Locked Out: Housing and Young Black People on Merseyside*, Liverpool, Shelter and the Federation of Black Housing Organisations.

Runnymede Trust (1992) *The Runnymede Bulletin*, October. London, The Runnymede Trust

Scraton, P. (1982), 'Policing and Institutionalised Racism on Merseyside' in D. Cowell (ed.), *Policing the Riots*, London, Junction Books.

Shallice, A. and Gordon, P. (1990), *Black People, White Justice? Race and the Criminal Justice System*, London, Runnymede Trust.

Shelter (1996), *Compound Homelessness: Young People, Housing Benefit and Homelessness*, Gloucestershire, Shelter.

Sibbitt, R. (1997), *The perpetrators of racial harassment and racial violence*, Home Office Research Study 176, London, Home Office.

Sivanandan, A. (1976), 'Race, Class and the State: The Black Experience in Britain', *Race and Class*, No. 4.

Skogan, W. (1990), *The Police and Public in England and Wales*, Home Office Research Study No. 117, London, HMSO.

74   *Youth Justice: Contemporary Policy and Practice*

Sly, F. (1995), 'Ethnic groups and the labour market: analyses from the Spring 1994 Labour Force Survey', *Employment Gazette*, June, pp. 251–62, London, HMSO.

Smith, D.J. (1983), *Police and People in London 1: A Survey of Londoners*, London, Policy Studies Institute.

Smith, D.J. and Gray, J. (1983), *Police and People in London 1V: The Police in Action*, London, Policy Studies Institute.

Smith, D.J. (1994), 'Race, Crime and Criminal Justice' in M. Maguire, R. Morgan and R. Reiner (eds), *The Oxford Handbook of Criminology*, Oxford, Clarendon Press.

Social Exclusion Unit (1998), *Truancy and School Exclusion: Report by the Social Exclusion Unit*, London, HMSO.

Statewatch (1998), 'UK: Stop and search and arrest and racism', *Statewatch*, Vol. 8, Nos 3 and 4, May–August, pp. 16–19.

Stirling, M. (1992), 'How many pupils are being excluded?', *British Journal of Special Education*, 19, 4, pp. 128–30.

Walker, A. and Walker, C. (eds) (1997), *Britain Divided; The growth of social exclusion in the 1980s and 1990s*, London, Child Poverty Action Group.

Westergaard, J. (1992), 'About and beyond the underclass: some notes on influences of social climate on British Sociology', *Sociology*, 26, pp. 575–87.

4 Youth Crime and the Politics of Prevention

BARRY ANDERSON

Introduction

Few would deny that the best approach to crime is to prevent it from happening. Even a modest reduction in crime offers potentially significant gains: fewer victims suffering injury or loss; fewer lives blighted by the fear of crime; reduced public expenditure on the criminal justice system and an end to overcrowding in the prisons. Additionally the prevention of youth crime offers the prospect of fewer 'child offenders' leading adult lives damaged by their early involvement in crime and the criminal justice system. In short, the potential human, social and economic benefits of prevention are considerable. Only comparatively recently however, (mainly during the 1980s and 1990s) have policy-makers paid serious attention to the question of crime prevention (other than by conventional policing) and there remains little consensus as to how it can be best achieved. Indeed, to many observers the current crime prevention scene is confused and fragmented with little clarity about goals or methods, direction or leadership, and with structures which in some cases are arguably counterproductive.

If anything, the youth crime situation is even more complicated and the outlook still less optimistic. To understand the current state of *youth crime prevention*, one has to understand both the 'rise of prevention' over the past 20 years together with the contemporary youth justice debates. Indeed, the highly emotive public debate about 'child offenders' which has taken place during the 1990s has radically altered the terms in which crime by young people is both understood and managed. A series of changes to youth justice legislation by successive governments has produced a criminal justice system which arguably deals with children more harshly than with adult offenders. Moreover, such developments have meant that youth justice policy has been rendered inconsistent both with current policy on crime prevention (insofar as that can be discerned), and with the more recent policy emphasis on tackling social exclusion. It remains to be seen whether the events of the past five years or so will eventually be seen as an unfortunate 'blip' in the evolution of a rational and coherent social policy framework, or will continue to exert their discordant influence on the development of future crime prevention initiatives. Much will depend on the ability of today's policy-makers to resolve the inherent contradictions between current responses to crime and the more general social policy thrust. The challenge will be to establish a more inclusive and coordinated approach – a genuine 'third way'- in order to tackle the issue of youth crime alongside the (often formidable) problems confronting 'young offenders'.

The Rise of Prevention

Historically, those people most concerned with crime – professionally, politically or through personal experience – have been preoccupied with the criminal justice system and the way it deals with offending *after the event*. Even the most recent crime measures from successive governments seem wedded to a belief in the preventive and deterrent value of the punishments handed down by the courts, despite all the evidence to the contrary. The modern crime prevention landscape is dominated by the Crime and Disorder Bill 1998, the provisions of which (in relation to whose provisions for joint police and local authority 'Community Safety Plans') provide a framework for future developments. However, the 'rise of prevention' commenced some two decades earlier.

In the late 1970s concern about rising crime rates and the seeming inability of conventional policing, and the criminal justice system to check the upward trend, prompted a number of local authorities and police forces to examine new ways of reducing crime in 'high-crime areas'. The programmes varied; some concentrated on new policing methods and others focused on improved security, environmental change or upgraded community facilities. Often they had 'outside' help, notably from the voluntary sector. NACRO (National Association for the Care and Resettlement of Offenders), for example, traces its first involvement in crime prevention to a project in Widnes, in the northwest of England, in 1976 (NACRO, 1988). At central government level a lead was given by the Department of the Environment, which made funding available for projects similar to the Widnes project as long ago as 1979. It was the Home Office, however, which continued to drive crime prevention policy, establishing the 'Crime Prevention Unit' in 1983. Again, the trend was collaborative, with the development of partnerships at a local level paralleled by interdepartmental activity centrally.

The 1980s were a busy time for central government departments concerned with crime prevention. The 'Inter-Departmental Group on Crime' reported in January 1984 (Home Office, 1984a), the report forming the basis for a joint Circular (Home Office, 1984b) which was issued that same month. In 1985 the Home Office 'Standing Conference on Crime Prevention' was established and in October that year, the 'Crime Prevention and Community Programme' was launched, foreshadowing the introduction, early in 1986, of the 'Five Towns Initiative', subsequently described as 'an experiment which sought to foster community support to reduce opportunities for crime' (Morgan Committee, 1991, p. 38). The 'Ministerial Group on Crime Prevention' also met for the first time in the spring of 1986, bringing together ministers from no fewer than 13 government departments. Despite this activity, however, it would be misleading to imply any significant degree of similarity or coherence between the various early programmes. Nonetheless, some common themes did emerge which informed subsequent policy developments. In particular there was a concern with the disadvantaged urban neighbourhoods where crime rates are highest, the impact of crime greatest, and repeat victimisation most likely. However, the aim was generally to reduce crime not by tackling the social and economic problems of such areas, but by concentrating on '*target-hardening*' and other '*situational*' approaches, which were designed to make offending more difficult through security and environmental measures. Such an emphasis probably reflected the principal concerns and activities of the main agencies involved at a local level: the police and Housing and Chief Executives departments of local authorities. Early Home Office activity also concentrated on situational measures but its focus was more concerned with specific offences than with particular kinds of neighbourhood (Home Office, 1984c, 1985a, 1986a, 1986b, 1986c, 1986d, 1986e).

Even at the outset, however, there were a number of initiatives which addressed what became known as '*social crime prevention*'. This somewhat vague term covered a wide range of measures, variously intended to prevent crime by reducing unemployment, tackling poverty, improving housing conditions and filling gaps in community facilities. The approach (with its focus on specific neighbourhoods) probably owed something to the community development initiatives of the 1970s The emphasis on the engagement of local communities clearly informed the development of the 'Five Towns Initiative', although in other respects this retained situational priorities and was concerned with reducing *opportunities* for crime (NACRO, 1988). Clearly social crime prevention initiatives lent themselves much more readily to a youth focus than most situational measures, and there were early attempts specifically to address the problem of youth crime by tackling youth unemployment and improving services and facilities specifically for young people.

Ultimately the distinction between *social* and *situational* approaches to crime prevention is neither clear nor absolute. A programme to improve household security across a 'high crime estate' for example, might be seen as 'target-hardening' *and* as a 'situational' measure *and* as a 'social' initiative leading to improved public safety and a reduction in the fear of crime among local residents. Nonetheless, the distinction is important, since it is rooted within a different view of causation. Social crime prevention measures are frequently criticised, especially by commentators on the political right, who are keen to dispute the implied relationship between social disadvantage and crime which is at odds with notions of individual responsibility. Situational measures, on the other hand, are often criticised for *displacing* crime (transferring the problem elsewhere) rather than *preventing* it. Probably the most cited example in this respect is closed circuit television, the deployment of which in busy commercial areas is thought to relocate crime into nearby residential neighbourhoods. However, the same point is made about other forms of target-hardening, from perimeter fences to security patrols: all – at least potentially – displace crime to areas which are less well-'defended'.

Perhaps the strongest crime prevention theme to emerge during the late 1980s, however, involved *multi-agency cooperation* and the development of *local partnerships*. In 1988, the Home Office established 'Crime Concern' – an independent national organisation, with a brief to promote and develop local crime prevention strategies – and launched the 'Safer Cities' programme. The first two rounds of this Home Office programme established three-year projects (directly managed by the Home Office) in 20 English towns and cities. Subsequently a further 29 projects in England and three in Wales were set up by Crime Concern (14), NACRO (15) and SoVA (3), working under contracts awarded by the Home Office. Essentially the role of the project teams was to act as catalysts in the development of multi-agency crime prevention partnerships and strategies and to stimulate new prevention initiatives. 'Safer Cities' projects were intended to act as models for partnerships elsewhere. By the end of the 1980s some form of crime prevention partnership was to be found in most major urban areas, and in May 1990 the government reiterated its support for this approach with the publication of a report (Home Office, 1990a) and the dissemination of an interdepartmental

Circular somewhat prematurely entitled 'Crime Prevention: The Success of the Partnership Approach'.

Local authorities and police forces were still the key players at a local level, with the wider range of local government functions and concerns (notably for housing, education and social services) reflected in the development of *community safety* policies and structures as distinct from the narrower *crime prevention* focus. The Morgan Committee (1991) commented:

> The term 'crime prevention' is often narrowly interpreted and this re-inforces the view that it is solely the responsibility of the police. On the other hand, the term 'community safety' is open to wider interpretation and could encourage greater participation from all sections of the community in the fight against crime.

The Morgan Committee's recommendations sought both to promote the concept of community safety and to create the conditions – nationally and locally – within which community safety partnerships might operate effectively. In particular they proposed that the police and local authorities should be given statutory responsibility for community safety, including the establishment and support of broader community safety partnerships. Morgan's recommendations were not endorsed by the government and the Home Office felt it necessary, when publishing the committee's report, to print a caveat on the title page to the effect that the report was 'the work of an independent working group' and that 'the views expressed in it are not necessarily those of the Home Office' (Morgan Committee, 1991).

What went wrong? The Morgan Committee appeared to have endorsed and developed an approach to crime prevention which the government itself had supported enthusiastically. However, proposing new powers for local councils was perhaps taking a 'step too far' for a government with an ambivalent approach to local authorities and keen, if anything, to curb their existing powers. Or perhaps this was an early indication of the government's apparent change of heart on crime, which was to be marked by a radical shift to the right in law and order policy, commencing with the departure of Douglas Hurd as Home Secretary and subsequently pursued with ever-increasing vigour by his successors (David Waddington, Kenneth Clark and Michael Howard). Whatever the explanation for the government's apparent rejection of the Morgan Committee recommendations, the report nonetheless had a significant effect on the subsequent development of local policy and practice. Indeed, a number of areas went some way towards implementing the report's recommendations on joint policy and planning, with many more local authorities developing community safety structures. However, the absence of legislation and official guidance has inevitably meant that the pattern of development has been decidedly 'patchy'; not every area has established a partnership and the size, composition and focus of those which do exist varies enormously.

To sum up, the past 20 years have seen some encouraging developments and some worrying trends. On the positive side, there has been a greater willingness on the part of policy-makers to take prevention seriously: a growing commitment to partnership at both a national and a local level; a range of promising projects and practical initiatives; and a general consensus on the relative merits of a broad approach to community safety, rather than a narrow concentration on crime prevention. However, the current situation is still far from satisfactory. Bright summarises the key concerns expressed by Professor David Smith about the current state of crime prevention in describing a period

> characterised by experimentation; few resources; little evaluation; a 'shotgun' approach to problem solving; a reliance on voluntary partnerships; and no training or professional standards (and observing that) at a national level, government has found it difficult to articulate a national strategy and co-ordinate the work of its own departments (while) at a local level, ... there is a confusing range of active groups and the respective roles of these ... are unclear (Bright, 1997, p. 17).

There is a concern too at the tendency for this area of work to have become both over specialised and professionalised in recent years. Community safety is a broad concept bringing together a wide range of interests and activities in an essentially local strategy. More than almost any other sphere of activity it calls for 'joined-up thinking': cooperation and collaboration between agencies, and inclusive partnerships between those agencies and the communities they serve. In reality, however, some local authority crime prevention/community safety structures appear to have defined and bureaucratised their 'professional' territory in a way which is essentially exclusive; marginalising 'non-crime' agencies, stifling attempts at genuine partnership and precluding meaningful community involvement. Almost inevitably, such units have a tendency to channel 'their' limited resources into special (usually short-term, 'bolt-on') projects, whose impact on mainstream services (housing, education, health, social services) is transient and/or negligible. The recent Crime and Disorder Bill only partially addresses these concerns in providing a broad statement of national policy and placing the police and local authorities under a statutory duty to produce *community safety plans*. This is an improvement on the purely voluntary commitments required under existing partnerships, but the Bill leaves many important questions unanswered, preferring instead to leave the key issues to be determined locally. There are perhaps more hopeful signs in the government's broader social policy agenda. If the stated commitments to tackle social exclusion and youth unemployment and raise educational standards inform local community safety strategies (and the partnership arrangements required to deliver them) they should result in a greater emphasis on 'social' crime prevention measures and encourage agencies to look beyond 'special projects' and focus on the preventive potential of effective mainstream and universal services.

The Fall of Youth Justice

If crime prevention had developed and consolidated since the late 1970s, the history of contemporary 'youth justice' arguably commences a decade earlier with the passage of the Children and Young Persons Act in 1969. This Act sought to: *divert young people from prosecution* (by requiring the police to consult with other agencies prior to a decision to prosecute); *expand the range of community penalties available to juvenile courts* (by introducing the Intermediate Treatment Order) and *limit the use of custodial sentences for 'children in trouble'* (by abolishing the 'short, sharp shock' Detention Centres). The 1969 Act was one of the last major pieces of legislation passed by the Wilson government prior to its defeat in the 1970 general election. The incoming Heath administration was no more inclined to implement some of the key new provisions in government than it had been to support them in opposition. Large sections of the Act, including the abolition of Detention Centres, were never implemented: nevertheless, it was to have a lasting impact on the (then) 'juvenile justice' system. Initially the Act's influence was practice-led. In a number of areas local agencies (notably Social Services departments) worked to establish the kind of consultative arrangements and develop the sort of community-based programmes for children and young people in trouble which the Act had envisaged. It was not until the 1980s, however, that policy 'caught up' with practice. This is not the place for a detailed review of the welter of youth justice legislation, guidance and policy development which the decade brought forth, but mention of the key milestones is itself instructive: the Criminal Justice Act 1982; the DHSS Intermediate Treatment Initiative (DHSS, 1983); the Police and Criminal Evidence Act 1984; the Home Office

Circular on the Cautioning of Offenders (Home Office 1985b); the establishment of the Crown Prosecution Service and the publication of its guidelines on prosecuting juveniles (Crown Prosecution Service, 1987); the Criminal Justice Act 1988; the Children Act 1989; a further Home Office Circular on Cautioning (Home Office, 1990b); and the Criminal Justice Act 1991.

Juvenile justice policy and practice during the 1980s was underpinned by three primary principles – diversion, decriminalisation and decarceration – the combination of which had significant impact (Goldson, 1997). By 1990, 70 per cent of boys and 86 per cent of girls who offended between the ages of 14 and 16 years were cautioned by the police and the use of custodial sentences for juveniles fell from 7,900 in 1981 to 1,700 in 1990 (Home Office, 1991). Indeed, despite the rapid pace at which criminal justice legislation and guidance was developed during the 1980s, the direction of juvenile/youth justice policy remained not only fairly constant but also entirely compatible with the developments that were taking place in crime prevention. Indeed, the 'juvenile justice revolution', as it was sometimes described during the 1980s, could probably be said to have created the conditions for the growth of interest in prevention, especially from within the Home Office. However, criminal justice policy (and especially youth justice policy) was about to undergo a radical change of direction with the inevitable consequence that the political consensus on youth crime and the synergy between crime prevention and criminal justice policy were lost.

How and why 'young offenders' suddenly came to occupy such a prominent (and negative) place in the national consciousness during the 1990s is open to question. There can be little doubt, however, that the death of James Bulger in 1993 and the subsequent conviction of two 10 year-olds for his murder, was a catalyst for what Scraton (1997, p. vii) has described as 'this outpouring of adult condemnation, directed remorselessly against contemporary childhood'. Though the nation was periodically given to what Cohen (1973) famously termed 'moral panics', youth crime had never previously been a major political issue, yet the general election campaign of 1997 saw law and order ranked alongside the economy, health and education in electoral importance (largely as a result of public anxiety and anger about youth crime). Whatever prompted the youth crime debate of the 1990s, it is likely that the tough measures contained in the 1994 Criminal Justice and Public Order Act and the 1998 Crime and Disorder Bill reflect growing public concern about rising levels of crime and the perceived inability of the criminal justice system to stem the tide of lawlessness among the young. The popular view, echoed (and frequently amplified) in the newspapers, is that society has 'gone soft' on young 'criminals' and that harsher sentencing is needed to re-establish the rule of law. Though a succession of high-profile miscarriages of justice may have dented public confidence in the criminal justice system, it is apparently still widely seen as our only means of tackling the (juvenile) crime problem.

There are, of course, those who point to the apparent success of a very different approach during the 1980s, and others who argue that crime statistics are misleading and that all the evidence suggests our fear of crime is greatly exaggerated. Such arguments have apparently had little or no impact on the public mood, however, and if they have had more influence among Labour's policy-makers it is well disguised. Labour fought the election on their leader's slogan 'tough on crime, tough on the causes of crime' and have produced a Crime and Disorder Bill which has sought to 'balance' tough new sentencing options with wider reform of the youth justice system and measures to promote community safety. The difficulty for those charged with implementing these 'schizophrenic' new arrangements is that they appear to be driven by conflicting policy objectives. To put it more bluntly, current youth crime policy appears equally committed to preventing the social exclusion of children and young people considered to be 'at risk' and increasing the exclusion of those who go on to offend.

A Third Way?

One reason for this muddled thinking is an apparent failure to distinguish between 'crime' and 'the criminal'. When politicians talk about being tough on crime for instance, they tend to mean getting tough with 'offenders', which may or may not be appropriate, but is undeniably a different proposition. In the field of prevention (as noted above) there has been rather more progress, with commentators making a conscious distinction between 'crime prevention' and 'preventing criminality' and a greater willingness to look at crime and criminality as part of the wider social fabric. Inevitably, but nonetheless ironically, some of the most important contributions to this area of work were being prepared or published just as the 'great youth justice debate' was getting up steam.

Reporting on their longitudinal 'Cambridge Study in Delinquent Development', Farrington and West suggested that the three most important predictors of offending were poor parental child-rearing behaviour, school failure and economic deprivation (Farrington and West, 1990). A strategy for tackling these often interrelated social problems, therefore, offers the greatest prospect of preventing young people from turning to crime. Just what such a strategy might look like (and what its policy implications might be) was the subject of a report by Utting and his colleagues, who also emphasised the wider benefits of this approach to crime prevention in noting that

> [a] number of the most promising ingredients for inclusion in a campaign to prevent delinquency ... belong equally in strategies to combat other social ills. If the increasing human and financial costs of crime can convince society that preventing criminality is a desirable goal, then it is encouraging to know that action addressing the main risk factors will yield potential benefits in other spheres. If, on the other hand, the survival of valuable ... work is threatened by restricted funding for education or social services, then it is in the public interest that its crime prevention potential should be better-known and understood (Utting, Henricson and Bright, 1993, p. 73).

Support for this view has come from the influential and much-quoted Home Office research study of 'Young People and Crime' which was concerned not only with the factors affecting *resistance* (i.e. why some young people become involved in offending and others do not) but also with those influencing *persistence* and *desistance*:

> Criminality prevention entails preventing individuals from ever starting to offend and, in the event that they do start to commit crimes, to stop them from offending as soon as possible thereafter. The former can be achieved by developing a range of policies which impact upon the factors which predispose young people towards committing offences. The latter can also be achieved this way, but more often the prevention of reoffending is considered to be the responsibility of the criminal justice system. However, ... this is a comparatively expensive way to reduce crime. An alternative ... might be to identify the strongest influences on offending and reoffending during the transition to adulthood in the context of an individual's personal and social development and develop policies which encourage natural processes of desistance and discourage criminogenic influences (Graham and Bowling, 1995, p. 83).

In their conclusions the authors discuss the potential benefits of measures aimed at 'strengthening families' and 'improving parental supervision'; 'strengthening schools'; 'reducing truancy' and 'reducing school exclusions'; 'promoting family : school partnerships'; 'preparing young people for leaving home'; 'supporting the forming of new families'; 'reducing risks during adolescence'; and 'harnessing informal to formal sources of social control' (ibid., pp. 85–103). These have much in common with the recommendations for 'preventing youth crime' made by the Audit Commission (1996). Here, the measures include: 'helping with parenting'; 'structured nursery schooling'; 'school support'; 'positive leisure opportunities'; 'housing needs and leaving care'; 'employment and training opportunities'; 'drugs and alcohol services'; and 'reinforcing community institutions' (Audit Commission, 1996, pp. 91–4). In short, even while proposals for harsher new regimes for 'young offenders' have been working their way through the parliamentary process, a new consensus has been emerging on how to tackle crime; a consensus which appears to be consistent with both the 'established' values of crime prevention and more recent political developments. The new consensus is focused on children, young people and families and may help to narrow the antagonistic divide between the positive direction of crime prevention policy and the continued negativism of the youth crime debate. Moreover, in its rejection of the sterile debate about 'tough' and 'lenient' approaches and its support for a more constructive and practical approach, such developments can justifiably be said to offer a 'third way'. Equally a broadly-based preventive strategy embracing a wide range of social measures is clearly consistent with both the principles of 'partnership' and broadened notions of 'community safety' and with the government's pledge to tackle social exclusion. But what would a 'third way' programme based on such an approach actually look like?

Communities that Care

In Britain, the principal initiative concerned with what is sometimes referred to as 'positive' or 'holistic' prevention is the 'Communities that Care' programme, an approach which was originally developed in the USA by Professors J. David Hawkins and Richard Catalano of the University of Washington in Seattle (Communities that Care, 1997). Their starting point is a powerful *meta-analysis* of international research into youth crime, drug abuse, school failure and school-age pregnancy, and the identification of the *risk and protective factors* which make children and young people's involvement more or less likely. Of particular importance is their ability to demonstrate and explain the interrelated nature of these problems which confirms the need to address youth crime (and work with 'young offenders') within the context of a much broader 'holistic' strategy or, as Hawkins and Catalano (1993) put it, 'multiple problems require multiple solutions'. Based on this knowledge Hawkins and Catalano have developed an evidence-based, community-led, long-term programme for building safer neighbourhoods where children and young people are valued, respected and encouraged to achieve their potential. This programme is now operational in over 500 American communities and the approach was introduced to the UK on the initiative of, and with funding from, the Joseph Rowntree Foundation. In 1997, following some 18 months research and development and pilot work, the Joseph Rowntree Foundation established 'Communities that Care UK'; an independent charitable organisation which would support the development of CtC programmes in the UK. Three 'demonstration programmes' – in Barnsley, Coventry and Swansea – commenced in 1998, to be followed by three Scottish 'demonstrations' as the next stage of a number of further programmes planned for throughout the UK.

CtC's work is *evidence-based* and *community-led.* Having secured the commitment of '*key leaders*', programmes are managed by local '*community boards*' comprising local residents and 'front-line' professionals: teachers, police officers, social workers, GPs, health visitors, youth workers and many others. The job of 'key leaders' and CtC (UK) is to support and assist 'community boards' in their work. Great emphasis is placed on the provision of resources, information and training in a bid to ensure that the '*empowerment*' of the local community goes beyond fashionable rhetoric. Equally, the 'community board' is not necessarily seen as a proxy for the community as a whole and it is constantly encouraged constantly to engage and involve all local people, and in particular to make every effort to secure the active participation of young people. This conscientious approach to the '*community development*' aspect of the CtC programme is seen as essential if the initiative is to take root and produce lasting change. Moreover, CtC's unique feature is its distinctive analysis of *risk* and *protective factors,* which informs the development of 'action plans' based on an audit of such factors within specific local communities. Unlike most conventional audits (including crime audits) a CtC audit provides not only a '*snapshot*' of the circumstances and concerns of a community (levels of crime and poverty, for example) but also a '*map*' of the known risk and protective factors which are 'driving' that situation. The 'action plans' are designed to tackle the main risk factors, and promote the known protective factors, in order to reduce the *future likelihood* of children and young people becoming involved in crime or drug abuse, or experiencing school failure or school-age pregnancy. By definition these 'action plans' are long-term and mainstream; they typically contain recommendations both for new provision to 'fill gaps' and for action to improve and/or refocus existing community services, they are designed to: support and strengthen families; promote school commitment and success; encourage responsible sexual behaviour; and achieve a safer, more cohesive community

Clearly, it is not possible to generalise about the content of CtC 'action plans', as each is determined by the local evidence. However, where family risk factors predominate, there may be an emphasis on pre- and postnatal care and support services, parental support and/or parenting education. Where there are particular problems concerning education (and depending on which of the school-related risk factors are to be addressed) options may include preschool education, organisational change in schools, special teaching programmes and 'whole school' programmes to tackle bullying, truancy and exclusion. What matters most in designing action plans is that decisions are based on the evidence and informed by an understanding of *what works*. This effectiveness issue is extremely important and whether advocating changes in current arrangements or the provision of new services, 'community boards' have access to what CtC calls *'promising approaches'*: a constantly updated database of evaluated best practice designed to ensure that existing knowledge about what works is put to good use.

CtC can perhaps best be described as an *holistic prevention* initiative. The approach is *evidence-based, community-led* and *positive* in that it does not employ what is frequently referred to as a *deficit model* but seeks to harness and build on a community's *strengths*. Furthermore, the approach is *long-term,* aiming to produce *sustainable* benefits in the form of both reducing 'problem behaviours' and improving community life especially for children and young people. Perhaps most importantly, CtC is essentially concerned with *changing the mainstream* and in this respect it is distinctive. As Bright (1991) observes:

> there have been few attempts to apply the knowledge drawn from special projects to mainstream practice. The substantial amount of energy and commitment devoted to prevention over the past ten years does not amount to a national strategy. Indeed, it sometimes seems that the whole is rather less than the sum of its parts. What is needed is a more coherent attempt to agree priorities, mobilise resources and apply what we know works.

Conclusion: Respecting Children – Preventing Crime

CtC is probably the best example presently available of what is generally described as a 'criminality prevention strategy'. Holistic or criminality prevention is broadly consistent both with the general direction of current UK social policy and with the 'prevailing wisdom' on crime prevention and community safety. It would be wrong, however, to see it either as problem-free or uncontentious. At a local level, for example, existing community safety mechanisms often do not embrace the full range of agencies whose involvement is required for a successful criminality prevention initiative and resistance to expanding the partnership may be a two-way problem. Not only are the agencies traditionally in the forefront of crime prevention sometimes reluctant to share 'their' professional territory with new players, but those 'new' players can also be reluctant to become involved, perhaps feeling that their work is being redefined in terms of its preventive effect rather than for its intrinsic value. Equally, professionals may have problems about engaging in a community-led process as may their (elected) leaders. Can these potential difficulties be resolved?

The creation of broadly-based multi-functional partnerships at a community level with a vision of, and responsibility for, the well-being of a local community rather than a purely preventive brief or a particular remit to deliver specific services is of crucial importance. This may seem naive or idealistic, but there are a number of innovative CtC pilots currently taking place (in Coventry and Salford for example) which give some grounds for optimism. At the same time, however, recent policy and legislative development seems to point in the opposite direction. It is unlikely, for instance, that the exclusively professional youth offending teams to be established under the Crime and Disorder Act (with responsibilities for both youth justice and youth crime prevention) will be *either* sufficiently broadly-based to encompass 'criminality prevention' *or* willing and able to engage creatively with local communities around a preventive agenda. There must also be a danger that they will be hampered by the conflicting demands of youth crime prevention and youth justice policy that were discussed earlier. Nor is it clear how either set of responsibilities will interface with broader criminal justice and community safety arrangements and we should perhaps remind ourselves that – contrary to the impression sometimes given by press and politicians – some offences are still committed by adults!

Notwithstanding such tensions and difficulties, the *children and youth-focused* 'criminality prevention' approach is an extremely important development which offers a more rational and intellectually coherent response to youth crime *and* youth justice. It is a response which is consistent with, and an essential part of, a wider strategy to tackle the problems of socially excluded children, young people, families and communities. This is not to say that other measures can or should be jettisoned in favour of 'criminality prevention'. If we have learned anything about crime prevention in the past 20 years it must surely be that the temptation simply to follow the diktats of fashion or funding has to be rejected in favour of a more broadly-based incremental approach. In short, we need both national and local strategies which embrace both crime prevention and criminal justice. We need strategies which might adopt a 'mixed economy' approach to crime prevention, including community policing, target-hardening, situational and social measures and which conceive of crime not as an isolated and individualised phenomenon, but as part of a wider social picture. We need a strategy which recognises that 'multiple problems require multiple solutions'. Above all, we need a strategy which is informed by a consistent set of values and principles in which 'children and young people are valued, respected & encouraged to achieve their potential' (Communities that Care, 1997). The analysis of risk factors influencing young people's involvement in crime, school failure, drug abuse and school-age pregnancy leave little doubt that the current 'youth crime problem' is largely due to our failure as a society adequately to value, respect and encourage our children. The ultimate goal of a preventive strategy must be to change that.

References

Audit Commission (1996), *Misspent Youth*, London, Audit Commission.

Bright, J. (1991), *Turning the Tide: Crime, Community and Prevention*, London, Demos.

Crown Prosecution Service (1987), *Code for Crown Prosecutors*, London, HMSO.

Cohen, S. (1973), *Folk Devils and Moral Panics: The Creation of the Mods and Rockers*, London, Paladin.

Communities that Care (1997), *Communities that Care UK: A New Kind of Prevention Programme*, London, CtC.

DHSS (1983), *Intermediate Treatment Initiative*, Local Authority Circular 83(3), London, DHSS.

Farrington, D.P. and West, D.J. (1990), 'The Cambridge Study in Delinquent Development: A Long-Term Follow-Up of 411 London Males' in G. Kaiser and H.J. Kerner (eds), *Criminality: Personality, Behaviour and Life History*, Berlin, Springer-Verlag.

Goldson, B. (1997), 'Children in Trouble: State Responses to Juvenile Crime' in P. Scraton (ed.), *'Childhood' in 'Crisis'?*, London, UCL Press.

Graham, J. and Bowling, B. (1995), *Young People & Crime*, Research Study 145, London, Home Office, 1995.

Hawkins, J.D. and Catalano, R.F. (1993), *The Social Development Model: A Theory of Anti-Social Behaviour*, Cambridge, Cambridge University Press.

Home Office (1984a), *Report of an Inter-Departmental Group on Crime*, London, HMSO.

Home Office (1984b), *Joint Inter-Departmental Circular on Crime Prevention*, London, Home Office.

Home Office (1984c), *Reducing Burglary*, London, Home Office.

Home Office (1985a), *Car Security*, London, Home Office.
Home Office (1985b), *The Cautioning of Offenders*, Circular No. 14/85, London, Home Office.
Home Office (1986a), *Situational Prevention: From Theory into Practice*, London, Home Office.
Home Office (1986b), *Commercial Robbery*, London, Home Office.
Home Office (1986c), *Violence Associated with Licensed Premises*, London, Home Office.
Home Office (1986d), *Residential Burglary*, London, Home Office.
Home Office (1986e), *Car Security*, London, Home Office.
Home Office (1990a), *Partnership in Crime Prevention*, London, Home Office.
Home Office (1990b), *The Cautioning of Offenders*, Circular No. 59/90, London, Home Office.
Home Office (1991), *Criminal Statistics in England and Wales*, London, Home Office.
Morgan Committee (1991), *Safer Communities: The Local Delivery of Crime Prevention through the Partnership Approach*, London, Home Office.
NACRO (1988), *National Safe Neighbourhoods Programme*, London, NACRO.
Scraton, P. (ed.) (1997), *'Childhood' in 'Crisis'?*, London, UCL Press.
Utting, D., Bright, J. and Henricson, C. (1993), *Crime and the Family: Improving Child Rearing and Preventing Delinquency*, Occasional Paper 16, London, Family Policy Studies Centre.

5 Diverting Children and Young People from Crime and the Criminal Justice System

ADRIAN BELL, MIKE HODGSON AND SANDY PRAGNELL

Introduction

The description and analytical account of diversionary policy and practice contained within this chapter stems from experience in Northamptonshire, but the lessons learned from this experience have broader resonance and can, and perhaps should, be applied elsewhere. The principal aim of the chapter is to examine the various 'strands' which, taken together, comprise the 'cloth' of diversionary policy and practice, and to analyse both the strength of each strand and its fitness for purpose, in order to explain and understand the practice which has evolved to divert children and young people from crime and the criminal justice system.

Diversion: A Brief Historical and Theoretical Background

The 1969 Children and Young Persons Act represented the legislative expression of a *'welfare model'* in relation to children and young people in trouble (Blagg and Smith, 1989). The Act was intended to reduce the criminalisation of young people, and to increase the support and care available to them. As Nellis (1991) observed courts were to lose their power to sentence to Attendance Centres and Detention Centres when adequate schemes of Intermediate Treatment (IT) became available, and to Borstal when adequate secure accommodation had been provided. However significant sections of the Act were never implemented and paradoxically, during the period when IT was gaining ground as a new 'wonder treatment', the use of custody for juveniles increased. In 1969 about 2,600 young people were locked up in prison service establishments and by 1979 this figure had increased to 7,100

(Home Office, 1989). Similarly, whilst the 1969 Act abolished approved schools it also introduced the use of 'criminal care orders', which were to number 9,000 by the end of the 1970s. There was a real contradiction between the apparent success of programmes of IT *for the individual* and the very real increases in incarceration and punishment experienced by young people *as a whole* (Thorpe et al., 1980).

Labelling theorists supplied an explanation for this conundrum. They suggested that by being exposed to formal and interventionist systems of justice (including visits from the police, social workers, appearances at court, *and/or packages of preventative Intermediate Treatment*) young people become labelled as young 'criminals' (Schur, 1973; Blackmore, 1984). This process results in the young people 'internalising' the criminal 'label', eventually believing it themselves, and continuing to behave as a delinquent. The theory demanded an approach which diverted young people away from forms of intervention which might cause this 'labelling' process, and adopted strategies grounded in *minimum intervention*. This position became one of the foundation blocks of the '*justice model*' in relation to children and young people in trouble. Labelling theory and 'justice approaches' speedily gathered momentum, not least because they offered practical ways of reducing the numbers of children and young people having to be dealt with by the courts and care systems. This created a strong alliance between the liberal intentions of social work practitioners and the demand for efficiency, effectiveness, but above all economy, from the new Conservative governments in the 1980s. Within this context *systems intervention approaches* developed, based on an acknowledgment that overzealous intervention in individual cases may cause more problems than it solves. The original thinking was not to avoid all intervention but to apply only minimum appropriate interventions at the level of casework.

From here the focus turned towards strategic and diversionary interventions within the criminal justice process itself. In Northamptonshire dramatic changes occurred, which had significant national impact following an influential conference organised in the County in 1986. There was little theorising at the conference and the emphasis was very definitely on the effectiveness of the approach. Stevens and Crook (1986) reported that:

> between 1980 and 1985 the number of juveniles prosecuted decreased by 80%; the number of custodial sentences decreased by 65%; the number of care orders decreased by 82%; the number of remands to care decreased by 81%; the number of remands in custody decreased by 64%; the commission of detected juvenile crime (as a % of all detected crime) decreased by 11% (from 33.3% to 22.3%)

and the actual commission of detected juvenile crime (since 1983) decreased by 3.2%.

During this same period there was an increase in the cautioning of juveniles in Northamptonshire from 49 per cent in 1981 to 84 per cent in 1985. The Northamptonshire strategy was based upon a considered approach to diversionary activity with an emphasis on *informal community responses* and *minimum appropriate intervention*. Moreover, the diversionary practice demonstrated that the careful balance between reducing unnecessary, ineffective and sometimes damaging forms of intervention and ensuring informal responses to juvenile crime was actually very effective.

However, in other areas of the country the message which was taken back from the 1986 conference was, at least in some cases, crude. Nationally, in the realisation that they may have been part of the problem of increased social policing and custodial responses, IT workers enthusiastically embraced systems theory, and the pendulum swing led to *non-* or *minimal* intervention schemes developing. This became part of the 'justice' movement during the 1980s. Moreover, the 1982 Criminal Justice Act, and Home Office circular 14/85 (Home Office, 1985), which introduced guidance on the cautioning of 'young offenders', facilitated these justice-based developments with young people who offended. The justice model dominated the last half of the 1980s and it led to enthusiastic endorsements by the then Home Secretary, who also stated that 'locking people up is now generally accepted as being an expensive way of making bad people worse' (Waddington, 1991). Indeed, Jones (1989) summarised the optimism which prevailed among juvenile justice workers towards the end of the 1980s:

> The 1980s have seen a revolution in the way the juvenile justice system operates in England and Wales. ... While there is no room for complacency, there is a core of good practice and inter-agency co-operation which can be built on in the 1990s. Many notions, which once seemed totally unrealistic, such as the abolition of juvenile imprisonment, are now viewed as achievable.

This positive sense was based upon dramatic changes in custodial sentencing. In 1981, for example, 7,900 juveniles received custodial sentences and by 1990 that figure had fallen to 1,700 (Home Office, 1991; NACRO, 1993).

A further swing of the policy pendulum was about to occur, however, and the optimistic mood of the late 1980s has since been severely undermined. As soon as the political capital of being tough on crime (with or without its causes) outweighed the fiscal imperative of reducing the numbers of children and young people in public care and prison custody, the Conservative government and youth justice professionals, who had previously appeared united, started to diverge dramatically. The speed with which this divergence and change of government policy occurred was arguably accelerated because some areas had adopted *the systems approach* as a complete alternative to providing services.

Indeed, some commentators, including John Pitts, described minimum intervention as 'benign neglect' or in the worst of cases 'culpable negligence'. The tensions between the two extremes of 'welfare' and 'justice' were clear to see. Bell (1992) questioned whether 'we can in all conscience leave communities *(both offenders and offended against)* to fend for themselves' given the close link between deprivation and crime and Raynor (1993) argued that there was danger in 'the uncritical over-generalisation or over-extension of a good idea until it becomes, at least in some of its applications, a rather bad idea'.

The Northamptonshire Diversion Unit is one example of an attempt at a mediated solution to the polarised 'welfare'–'justice' debate. It involves targeting resources in the context of what we know about the potentially 'damaging effects of over- *and* under-reaction' to criminal behaviour (Thorpe, 1998). It also balances forms of intervention and support which are needed by victims with those which will be effective with offenders. It seeks to have an impact on people as well as on systems, and is integrative rather than divisive.

The Development of the Northamptonshire Juvenile Liaison Bureau

In 1980 in Northampton, as elsewhere, court sentencing trends in relation to children and young people indicated that an enormous number of cases were being processed through the court (532 young people were sentenced in the Northampton Borough Juvenile Court in 1980) resulting in large numbers of adjournments and lengthy delays in sentencing. The Court Users' Committee (a committee comprising all those agencies involved within the Juvenile Court, including Probation and Social Services, magistrates and court clerks) recommended that the consultation process regarding the decision to prosecute should be improved between the agencies. The result was the formation of the Juvenile Consultation Meeting; a weekly meeting attended by senior representatives of Probation and Social Services and police, when files from arrests made on juveniles during the previous week were considered and decisions made immediately as to whether to caution or prosecute. This resulted in the rate of cautioning increasing from 45 per cent to 70 per cent of cases and, due to the subsequent decrease in numbers appearing before the courts, a marked reduction in the number of adjournments and delays (Cooper, 1990). The agencies began to recognise the value of diversion and, following pilot projects in the north of the county in 1984, the Northampton Juvenile Consultation Meeting was discontinued to be replaced by the *Northampton Juvenile Liaison Bureau.*

The philosophy and practice of the Northamptonshire Juvenile Liaison Bureau (henceforth JLB) was based on the increasing weight of practice experience and research evidence that indicated the dangers of premature prosecution and consequent escalation into offending (Farrington and Bennett, 1981; and Rutherford, 1986) and by the mid-1980s there were three JLBx covering the whole county. These teams comprised full-time, seconded representatives from the police, the Education Department, the Youth Service, the Probation Service, and the Social Services Department. The JLBx worked with young people aged between 10 (the age of criminal responsibility within England and Wales) to 16 inclusive[1] who had been arrested for an offence and where there was a clear admission of guilt. The sole source of referrals to the JLB was the police. They agreed to consult with the JLB in all cases involving juvenile offenders except those who had committed grave offences (murder, rape and endangering life). The policy was that no juvenile should be prosecuted until every consideration had been given to the alternatives. Although the police retained the ultimate right to make the decision regarding the formal outcome of the case, it was the decision of the multi-agency practitioners within the Bureau as to who they intervened with and what and how much work was undertaken. The police, particularly in the latter half of the scheme, agreed with some 97 per cent of JLB recommendations. Blagg following research into the Bureaux, noted that the JLBx were the 'first examples of such inter-agency co-operation where the police agreed to be directly influenced in their decision making by other professionals' (Blagg, 1986, p. 24).

The JLB was predominantly an offender-based scheme operating on a 'systems' approach to juvenile justice. This was based on evidence that the court and formal criminal justice processes, rather than having beneficial effects, often served to exacerbate the very problems they sought to reduce. The axiom of the JLB was that for most children and young people offending is a one-off, relatively minor and transient occurrence, and the research evidence confirmed this (Rutherford, 1986). The *aims* of the JLB were:

• to divert young people wherever possible from penal and welfare

intervention systems into informal networks of control, support and care;
- to avoid the imposition of those forms of penalties and welfare intervention which tend to aggravate the very problem they seek to reduce;
- to enable agencies to respond to delinquent behaviour in ways which may reduce offending and enable young people to become more responsible adults;
- to encourage the normal institutions of society to respond constructively to adolescent behaviour.

In addition to clearly defined aims, the Juvenile Liaison Bureau had an equally sharp focus in relation to the principles and rationale of formal interventions. The *principles* of intervention comprised:

- the reason for intervention must be clear, explicit and have positive consequences for the offender or injured party;
- intervention should be directed towards resolving offences informally and treating the offender as a 'normal' adolescent;
- minimum appropriate intervention should be used;
- intervention should aim to increase the amount of community involvement and create a greater tolerance and understanding of the problem of juvenile crime;
- concern should be shown for the injured party as well as the offender.

The *reasons* for intervention included:

- a claim for financial compensation resulting from an offence needed resolving;
- relatively serious or persistent offences had been committed;
- problems were being experienced within the family, school or community relevant to the offence or offending behaviour;
- concern in the community about particular or recurrent types of offence;
- failure of the community or a parent agency to respond to the problem of juvenile crime in a positive and constructive manner.

The Juvenile Liaison Bureau interrogated the whole process of diversion. Cautions were seen as viable alternatives to prosecutions, but this raised the issue of diversionary alternatives to cautions themselves. It was here that the use of 'no further action' and 'informal action' played their part and became a crucial element in the evolution of the Bureau system. The JLB encouraged the police to recognise the use of 'no further action' as a valuable disposal in its own right. This enabled the offence to be recorded as having been detected but a record was not kept on the child or young person, and this was a major move towards decriminalisation. The development of using 'informal action' was supported by the local management group and, by 1985, nearly a quarter of all cases were dealt with informally, leading to a significant fall in the number of prosecutions and formal cautions. The argument and justification for this strategy was clear:

> If we aim to make a positive response to offending behaviour then informal networks of control, support and care become crucial. The ability of the community to resolve an offence and show tolerance is a more important feature of diversion than the record of a formal caution (Pragnell, 1991).

'Informal action' was a non-citeable disposal, that is the 'record' was not registered with the Central Criminal Records Office and thus could not be cited should the young person subsequently appear in court for a further offence. Equally, the 'record' could not be declared to an employer. Individual and parental responsibility were seen as an important part of this process. An 'informal action' was considered a positive step to take as distinct from 'benign neglect' and the use of 'informal actions' did not preclude intervention with a child or young person although any involvement was on a voluntary basis. Flexibility of response allowed for the resolution to suit the needs of the offender and offence within an individually shaped and tailor-made process. It was this 'elasticity' and flexibility of 'informal action' that in practice appeared to be its principal strength. Although it aimed to avoid drawing young people into the vortex of formal welfare provision it did not prevent children and young people with 'needs' benefiting from short-term intensive intervention. The immediacy of the disposal coincided with the young person's sense of justice which was so often eroded by the alienating procrastinations of perpetual adjournments in the Juvenile Courts. Statistics in 1990 showed that of those young people detected for committing an offence 70 per cent offended only once, 20 per cent two or three times, with only 10 per cent being detected four or more times. This encouraged the police to deal with many children and young people at source, particularly first time offenders, by way of 'no further action' or 'informal action', without the need to refer to the JLB for additional intervention.

In 1992 (the final full year of operation) the JLB dealt with 2,399 referrals representing 1,389 individuals (some young people were referred more than once). For the same year only 9 per cent of young people were prosecuted, with over 80 per cent receiving a non-citeable disposal of 'no further action' or 'informal action'. The fall in the number of prosecutions allowed the Social Services to develop a specific youth justice team to service the courts and deal with all statutory court duties. The Probation Service, other than the representation within the JLBx, was able to withdraw its services from all young people under 17 within the county. The youth justice team was able to concentrate on the small number of young people appearing before the court and offer substantial packages of support as a direct alternative to custody. The result was a decrease in the number of young people being sentenced to a custodial institutions by the Northampton court from 37 in 1980 to four in 1991.

The Review of Diversion and Government Policy Revisions

From 1986 a parallel model of diversionary practice had developed in Northamptonshire which involved working with adults outside the court system. This model of diversion contrasted with that of the JLB in that it had the specific aim of intervening not only with the 'offenders' referred, but also with their victims. The work concentrated on reparation and mediation between both parties to the offence. Whereas the JLB maintained an emphasis on changing the means by which agencies responded to children and young people, the concentration of the Adult Reparation Bureau (ARB) was on changing people's behaviour.

After six years of parallel development the Chief Officers who were responsible for the inter-agency management of both models of diversion undertook to review the overall practice in the county. The *Review of Diversion in Northamptonshire* took place in 1992, which led, amongst other things, to the creation of the Diversion Unit to consolidate all diversionary strategy underpinned by four primary principles:

- there would continue to be a central role for noninterventionist diversion for nonpersistent and non-serious, usually first time, offenders;
- that action is needed when it becomes obvious that offenders are becoming more persistent or have admitted more serious offences, and that inter-agency partnership is seen as an essential basis for Diversion Unit activity;
- that work across all ages would take place (from 10 years upwards);
- that the inclusion of work with victims was crucial to the development of

good/best practice.

This approach built upon the strengths and foundations that had been established within both the JLB and the ARB, and developed them further to work in ways which included both victims and offenders, and combined both systems management and reparation strategies and practices.

Perhaps one of the greatest challenges to the Northamptonshire diversionary strategy, immediately following the Review and the establishment of the Diversion Unit, was Home Office Circular 18/94 a key part of the government's burgeoning policy revisions (Home Office, 1994). Although previous Home Office circulars on cautioning (Home Office, 1985 and 1990) had positively encouraged the police to consult with multi-agency partners and develop panels and units to assist in the decision making process regarding young offenders, this circular went a long way in retracting this policy commitment. Circular 18/94 stated that although the police could seek advice from multi-agency panels, this should not be done as a matter of course. It also determined that the police should not be involved in negotiating reparation or mediation between victim and offender. The circular called for more consistency between police forces and discouraged local discretion and regional initiatives. The Review of Diversion had, however, already dealt with some of the issues raised in the circular, and the commitment of the local Chief Officer group to the Diversion Unit in the face of this threat to balanced practice, along with a staff and management commitment to explaining the practice to various government inspectors, ensured the Unit's survival and continued development.

The Northamptonshire Diversion Unit and the Principles of Restorative Justice

The review of diversion placed a restorative approach at the heart of the practice of the newly-formed Diversion Unit. The two chief objectives of the Unit became:

- to resolve or put right the harm created by individual offences;
- to reduce the likelihood of re-offending.

Diversion Unit practice involves staff from the Unit visiting each 'offender' and victim and, on the basis of a thorough assessment, constructing a plan of action designed to meet the Unit's two core objectives. These individual action plans are prepared and worked through for each referred 'offender' and their victim(s) within the context of their local communities. Any involvement with the Unit is on a voluntary basis. Regular action planning meetings are held so that staff from each of the six seconding agencies can contribute to its design. Typically, action plans address offending behaviour, the possibilities of mediation and the potential for reparation, and, importantly, link 'offenders' and victims with resources and organisations in their own community in order to achieve these aims. The Unit also ensures that the wider social issues that affect and are affected by offending can be addressed through the active involvement of county agencies, other bodies and local communities.

The Diversion Unit is primarily committed to being effective and, in this pursuit, new and innovative (as well as tried and tested) methods of working with people are used. The work of the Diversion Unit is carefully monitored and evaluated and action plans benefit from information about the success of previous interventions, and their impact on offending and its consequences. A database has been developed which monitors the effectiveness of the Diversion Unit's work in terms of reducing re-offending and offence resolution, and to assist in developing best practice methods.

Some of the aims of a restorative justice approach include the victim's (and the community's) need for healing, together with the need to reintegrate offenders back into the community. Accordingly, young people should be actively responsible for putting things right without the escalation of legal processes being necessary (Braithwaite, 1989). On this basis the Diversion Unit has operated since its inception within a restorative framework. Defining restorative justice, Marshall (1998) has observed:

> Restorative Justice is a problem solving approach to crime which involves the parties themselves and the community generally in an active relationship with statutory agencies *(including Local Authority Departments).*

The Diversion Unit's approach to working with victims and offenders has developed in accordance with restorative principles (Zehr, 1991) in the following ways:

- personal involvement (of victims and offenders) is central;
- crime is seen in its social context which is where work is undertaken to attempt resolution;
- a problem solving (and solution finding) approach is adopted, which looks

forward to find ways to put things right, as well as back in order to acknowledge and 'heal' hurt or harm done;
* every case is different, because of its social context, and sufficient room for manoeuvre and flexibility must be present for creative solutions to be found.

Overall, the inter-agency partnership approach adopted and developed by the Diversion Unit has been based on, and has provided considerable supporting evidence for, the idea of synergy – the whole is greater than the sum of the parts – and the concept of partnership is of critical importance.

Inter-Agency Strategy and Working in Partnership

Inter-agency strategy and working in partnership involve complex and dynamic processes which require intellectual, emotional and practical commitments. In Northamptonshire the success of such arrangements has been underpinned by a number of primary principles.

Interdependency and the Importance of Secondment

The Diversion Unit gains a great deal from being a dynamic organisation which draws the majority of its front-line staff from full-time secondments. This is not to undermine the contribution of the Unit's permanent administrative staff, its managers, or its 'practitioners', each of whom have valuable roles to play (particularly by way of stability and continuity). But it is to recognise that it is the secondment process which ensures continuous attention is paid both to the dynamic nature and to the 'interdependency' of the agencies. Seconded staff also have responsibility to keep alive networks of communication and access resources within their seconding agencies. This helps immeasurably with a whole range of important work; from marshalling the best and most appropriate skills and experiences in order to meet the needs of individual victims and offenders, to gaining assistance in securing training for the staff team or help with working with the media. It is important to the Diversion Unit that its seconded staff maintain their 'parent' agency identity and represent the strengths of their organisation. The live representation of the contributing agency's views helps the Unit to have a dynamic understanding of the 'community of agency' perspectives. This in turn can help the Unit better to represent the people it serves.

Inter-agency partnership is particularly appropriate for a Unit which works with both offenders and their victims and recognises the importance of their social context. An 'offender's' perspective of their crime is necessarily limited, as is the victim's. A police officer's or a social worker's perspective, by way of examples, are equally likely to be limited. However, a combination of these perspectives from both a personal and professional perspective is likely to be much more accurate, and therefore productive as a basis for appropriate action.

The inter-agency partnerships represented by full-time seconded commitments have had the following practical benefits:

- an ability better to represent 'the community' from a number of perspectives, including the victim's and the offender's;
- a subsequent ability to recognise and then respond positively to differing perspectives and complex problems;
- a coordinated and substantial staff resource which can benefit from true teamwork;
- a substantial and dynamic network of agency resources which can be accessed through seconded staff members who keep live channels of communication and have relatively recent local experience in the 'parent' agency setting;
- an integrated structure which avoids duplication of effort and coordinates resource inputs, information monitoring and analysis, and management;
- an integrative practice which adds inter-agency value to individual workers' abilities, skills and experiences.

Quality Tensions and Constructive Conflict

In drawing 'client' and 'professional' perspectives together it is important to note that there are likely to be initial tensions between victims and 'offenders' and between different agency perspectives. Indeed, given the nature of crime and the fact that different agencies have different focuses, philosophies and 'core objectives', it would be strange if there were not tensions. It has been our experience that these tensions can be resolved, and that, through their resolution, high quality solutions can be found. For this reason we sometimes refer to them as 'quality tensions' or 'constructive conflict'.

Simple solutions can be effective, but often the lives of 'offenders' and victims are complex, and certainly their relationship is likely to contain ambivalent elements. We have found that processes of resolution which recognise complexities and different perspectives and work towards dealing with ambivalence and likely tensions provide more effective solutions than more obvious uni-dimensional 'quick fixes' that are easier to organise. Inter-agency seconded structures help us to recognise the complexities which exist, to marshall the community resources which can assist, and to recognise and deal with the ambivalent nature of our work and the tensions between 'offenders' and victim's perspectives. The dynamic nature of the inter-agency partnership is analogous to the nature of the relationships between victims and offenders, and makes us more effective in their resolution.

Form and Function

When the overall framework is one which encourages 'social inclusion' partnership function arguably becomes more important. Diversion leads naturally to a partnership approach which deals with crime from both the victim and the 'offender' perspectives, makes an impact on the community, and recognises the correlation between crime and other difficulties, including school exclusion and other educational difficulties; health pressures, including mental health problems and drug and alcohol misuse; lack of or disrupted employment; family breakdown, violence or disruption; and financial difficulties and poverty (Audit Commission, 1996). Partnership forms follow both diversionary purposes and the purpose of 'working together to prevent offending' outlined by the government (Home Office, 1997).

The Focus on Purpose and Vision

There is a particular need to be absolutely clear about purpose and vision within an inter-agency approach. There is also a need to allow for distinct styles, experiences and skills, and even for different agencies having differing organisational values. At first this can cause difficulties as different agency perspectives surface in terms of language, culture and methods. However, working with such variation of perspectives, and debating and experimenting with different methods in an inter-agency team often leads in time to more effective practice. It is the 'testing' of these differing perspectives in the inter-agency 'fire' which can be so productive. Continuous review and improvement focused on practice in the context of complex problems and solutions needs a clarity of purpose and vision. Without it a downward spiral of wasted energy and fruitless debate can result.

The Challenges Ahead: Diversion and the New Youth Justice System

Current proposals for reforming and restructuring the youth justice system contain a number of positive aims which *in principle* appear to be consistent with diversionary values and practice. There is a commitment to 'processing' young people less and providing effective diversionary services more. There is a formula which provides for two possible diversionary episodes before prosecution – the reprimand delivered by the police, and the final warning which will normally be expected to be accompanied by inter-agency activity. There is a commitment to including victims in the process and there is a clear intention to marshall partnership resources to address the causes of crime as well as confront behaviour. However criminal justice legislation has often produced unintended consequences and some of the detail of the new proposals are potentially problematic. Much will depend on how the new arrangements are implemented, but there are also aspects within the government's proposals which appear to work against the overall perceived intended direction.

Room for Manoeuvre

The use of repeated diversionary decisions needs to be carefully targeted and based on clear evidence of their effectiveness. It is also very important that if diversionary decisions are repeated appropriate action is taken. Young people need to be given real opportunities to change and to take responsibility for their actions. This often complex task will sometimes take more than one intervention (possibly in addition to previous noninterventionist warnings) but can nevertheless be productive.

Young people may need intensive support and guidance if their behaviour is to be constructively challenged. This is a necessary element in helping them to take responsibility for their actions and to mature into positive adults. Any successful system of pre-court intervention must provide *room for change* and credibility of multiple interventions can be maintained. In Northamptonshire, for example, this is possible because of its extensive experience: a highly-developed intervention process; strong multi-agency commitments; and a sophisticated and objective targeting procedure.

The proposed single reprimand and final warning limitations within the Crime and Disorder Bill 1997 are too inflexible a response to the variety of 'offending career paths' which can be positively influenced by diversionary processes. In Northamptonshire a small minority of young people, carefully targeted by an objective decision-making process, are successfully diverted from the court process by providing up to four consecutive pre-court options. Without this room for manoeuvre – certainly in areas where sophisticated diversionary services have proven to be effective – the unintended consequence will be to channel more young people unnecessarily *into* the court system. This is likely to be more costly, take more time, but most importantly will, based on the evidence, be less effective in meeting the new overall purpose of the criminal justice system to 'prevent offending' (Home Office, 1997). In other words this potential unintended consequence could lead to a large increase in court activity resulting in overloaded court processes and subsequent slow and inappropriate decision making: the very reverse of what is intended.

Control Versus Assessment to Change Behaviour

Throughout the government's new proposals there is a tension between the principles of controlling youth justice systems and changing young people's behaviour. This is a difficult balance and there have been times when youth justice practice itself has either over- or under-reacted to young people's offending behaviour. Both appropriate and high quality intervention and knowing when it is most effective *not to* intervene are important elements of a sophisticated diversionary response. The emphasis on controlling the system has led to the reprimand and final warning, which do not give sufficient discretion for workers to make judgments based on effectiveness rather than simple predetermined mechanics. This problem is also present at the interface between pre-court diversion and court decisions. The government is intent on legislating to remove the use of the conditional discharge as a decision of the court after a final warning with intervention has been applied within the previous two years. This removes the discretion of the magistrates to use a disposal which has shown itself to be useful in terms of reducing further offending. The rationale appears to be that once intervention has been tried (and failed) only more intensive intervention is legitimate. There is a clear danger that in emphasising control using a linear process of increasing intervention, good assessment and decision-making will be stifled and opportunities to respond with constructive and timely interventions will be restricted within the straitjacket of proscribed practice. Good practice is most effective after careful assessment when it is delivered to the right people in the right environment at the right time.

Working in Partnership

The strengths of inter-agency partnership in diversionary practice have already been outlined, and this is an area where the government has proposed, we believe, some very sensible arrangements. The full-time secondment of education, health, police, probation, and social services workers to youth offending teams who will have responsibility for delivering final warning packages is welcome. The inter-agency arrangements and responsibilities for this work is also welcome. Working in partnership is not always easy but it is, in our experience, often very productive and can provide effective quality services (Northamptonshire Diversion Unit/NACRO, 1998).

When organising partnership areas should not restrict themselves to stereotypes of what individual workers and individual agencies can bring to both policy and practice. To assume that any particular worker or agency can only perform certain restricted tasks is to under-use and underestimate the full potential of the partnership. Obviously this does not preclude using the particular strengths and specialist expertise of individual staff and their agencies, but the point is also to maximise the potential of corporate strategy.

Working with Victims

The government's proposals encourage work with victims, and the White Paper points towards adopting restorative principles (Home Office, 1997). This fits well with the inclusion of victims in diversionary practice which has been a developing feature of the Northamptonshire strategy (Northamptonshire Diversion Unit/NACRO, 1998). There are, however, some difficulties which will need to be considered in widening the scope of work with and for victims. In the pre-court setting voluntarism is possible and this allows young people the opportunity to *make the decision to take responsibility* for their actions. This is most often something which they and the victim of their crime find useful and is an important element in the effectiveness of plans of action. As soon as the voluntary participation of either the 'offender' or the victim is compromised, however, the dynamic of the process and the relationship is negatively affected. Taking personal responsibility for the harm done and wanting to put it right by reparative actions is very different from taking reparative actions as part of enforced punishment.

At the pre-court stage within the new youth justice system the decision to issue a final warning will have been taken prior to an assessment involving the 'offender' or victim. Currently, whilst the victim does not determine the decision to caution or not (and neither should they), it is important that they are offered an opportunity to contribute their views fully in the assessments made regarding decisions and plans of action. Removing this opportunity for them to participate will undermine their ability to engage in a process of restorative justice. This process of engaging people in activities of resolution before informed decisions are made also affects the 'offender'. At the court level the problem will be exacerbated further. It will often be difficult for victims to see an enforceable reparation order as a genuine and willing response to the suffering to which they have been subject. The formality and statutory nature of court proceedings will have to be changed to make this a possible restorative venue.

Conclusion

At the beginning of this chapter, we undertook to examine and evaluate the various strands which comprise diversionary policy and practice. The analysis has established that diverting young people from crime and the criminal justice system has developed in many ways during the last 20 years. Concepts of working in partnership have been developed and have proved to be very productive. Victim work has grown and improved, and has become more than just a way of diverting young people from the criminal justice system. Considerable room for manoeuvre has been effectively employed to facilitate targeted forms of intervention without the need for court process. There has been real progress and strong elements of positive and progressive practice have developed in Northamptonshire and elsewhere. The present government has, we believe, recognised some of these positive aspects, and has attempted to integrate them within its current legislation. This is intended to consolidate a consistency of best practice in England and Wales and has the potential to be successful. However, without careful implementation a number of unintended, if not unforeseen, consequences could result. To avoid the quality of the cloth becoming obscured in the potential unintended muddle of all the emperor's new clothes, careful attention will have to paid to the detail of *how* he is to be dressed, as well as being clear as to what overall impact is required.

Note

1   The work of the JLB extended to include 17 year-olds in 1992, in line with the implementation of the Criminal Justice Act 1991 when it was renamed the Youth Liaison Bureau accordingly.

References

Audit Commission (1996), *Misspent Youth*, London, Audit Commission.

Bell, A. (1992), *Two Urban Programme applications concerning Social Crime Prevention in Dudley*, unpublished, Birmingham, Aston University.

Blackmore, J. (1984), 'Delinquency Theory and Practice: A Link Through IT', *Youth and Policy*, No. 9.

Blagg, H. (1986), *The Final Report on the Juvenile Liaison Bureau, Corby*, Lancaster, University of Lancaster.

Blagg, H. and Smith, D. (1989), *Crime, Penal Policy and Social Work*, Harlow, Longman.

Braithwaite, J. (1989), *Crime, Shame and Re-integration*, Cambridge, Cambridge University Press.

Cooper, K. (1990), 'Northamptonshire – Ten Years On' in C. Wilkinson (ed.), *Police Cautioning*, Department of Social Policy and Social Work Conference Series No. 1, papers presented to a one day conference May 1989, Birmingham, University of Birmingham.

Farrington, D. and Bennett, T. (1981), 'Police Cautioning of Juveniles in London', *British Journal of Criminology*, 21 (2).

Home Office (1985), *The Cautioning of Offenders*, Circular No. 14/85, London, Home Office.

Home Office (1989), *Demographic changes and the criminal justice system*, Circular No. 41/89, Surrey, Government Statistical Service.

Home Office (1990), *The Cautioning of Offenders*, Circular No. 59/90, London, Home Office.

Home Office (1991), *Cautions, court proceedings, and sentencing in 1990*, Circular No. 31/91, Surrey, Government Statistical Service.

Home Office (1994), *The Cautioning of Offenders*, Circular No. 18/94, London, Home Office.

Home Office (1997), *No More Excuses – A New Approach to Tackling Youth Crime in England and Wales*, London, The Stationery Office.

Jones, D. (1989), 'The successful revolution', *Community Care* (inside supplement), 30 March 1989.

Marshall, T. (1998), 'Values of Restorative Justice', unpublished paper, Social Concern seminar, April.

NACRO (1993), *Juvenile Crime: Some Current Issues*, London, NACRO.

Nellis, M. (1991), 'The last days of "juvenile justice"' in *The Yearbook of Social Work and Social Welfare*, Buckingham, Open University Press.

Northamptonshire Diversion Unit and NACRO (1998), *Diverting People from Crime*, London, NACRO.

Pragnell, S. (1991), 'Pre-Caution Decisions: the use of Informal Warnings and No Further Action Decisions', unpublished paper presented at Nottingham Polytechnic conference on police cautioning, January.

Raynor, P. (1993), 'Systems Purists, Client Refusal and Gatekeeping: is help necessarily harmful?', *Journal for the Centre for Social Action*, No. 2, London, Whiting and Birch.

Rutherford, A. (1986), *Growing Out of Crime: Society and Young People in Trouble*, London, Penguin.

Schur, E. (1973), *Radical Non-Intervention: Rethinking the Delinquency Problem*, Englewood Cliffs, New Jersey, Prentice Hall.

Stevens, M. and Crook, J. (1986), 'What the devil is I.T.?', *Social Work Today*, 8 September.

Thorpe, D., Smith, D., Green, C. and Paley, J. (1980), *Out of Care*, London, Allen and Unwin.

Thorpe, D. (1998), *Y.O.T. Steering Group Review Papers*, unpublished, Northamptonshire, Northamptonshire County Council.

Waddington, D. (1991), *Today*, London, BBC Radio Four.

Zehr, H. (1991), *Changing Lenses: A New Focus for Crime and Justice*, P. Herald.

6 Managing Juvenile Remands and Developing Community-based Alternatives to Secure Accommodation in Wales: Towards a Strategic Approach

HELEN DAVIES

Introduction

In 1991 the Welsh Office published an influential report in which it stated that there was not only a need to develop a secure unit for children and young people in Wales, but there was an equally pressing need to develop a range of services to offset the use of secure accommodation in all but the most serious cases (Welsh Office, 1991). Following the publication of this report the Welsh Office commissioned the National Association for the Care and Resettlement of Offenders (NACRO) to undertake a survey of policy and practice relating specifically to pre-court and pre-sentence services for children and young people in trouble in a sample of local authorities. NACRO subsequently reported that although there was evidence of positive practice and effective services for children and young people on remand, there were also marked gaps in services and inconsistencies within and between the authorities that were surveyed (NACRO, 1993). These two reports have been of critical importance in focusing attention on juvenile remands in Wales (particularly custodial remands) and in generating policy and practice development at this particular stage of the youth justice process.

This chapter will consider the development of the Community Alternatives to Secure Accommodation (CASA) project in Wales: a strategically targeted policy and practice initiative to address juvenile remands in general, and juvenile custodial remands in particular. Some emphasis will be placed on the central importance of monitoring (the systematic collection and analysis of quantitative data) in the development and delivery of effective youth justice practice. The chapter will examine the background to CASA by reviewing the principal findings from the two reports referred to above before outlining some of the key issues to have emerged from the *'All Wales Monitoring of Remands'* initiative. Finally the chapter will highlight some of the policy and practice issues that will comprise future developments in effectively managing juvenile remands.

Welsh Office Report: 'Review Of Secure Care in Wales'

The purpose of the Welsh Office review of secure care in Wales (Welsh Office, 1991) was essentially twofold. First was the imperative of legislative change. The Children Act 1989 was in the process of implementation and placed a new duty on local authorities 'to take reasonable steps designed to avoid the need for children within their area to be placed in secure accommodation'. Furthermore, proposals to end the remanding of juveniles in prison accommodation provided by Section 60 of the Criminal Justice Act 1991 meant that a review of existing secure provision was timely. Second, in the course of undertaking the review of secure accommodation there appeared to be a groundswell of opinion that existing provision was inadequate and needed to be addressed. These two primary issues were galvanised and consolidated by the death of a 15 year-old boy, Philip Knight, while on remand in Swansea prison.

The Welsh Office report proposed to address the situation through a number of recommendations, aimed at strengthening both policy and practice. The recommendations essentially fell into two categories. The first related to what might be done in terms of providing alternatives to secure accommodation, and the second related to the perceived necessity of providing a secure facility in Wales to contain a limited number of young people described as being 'the most troubled or troublesome' (Welsh Office, 1991, p. 13).

For the purposes here I will focus on those recommendations concerned with reducing the need to remand young people into secure accommodation or prison custody. There are five key issues: policy statements; reviews; new initiatives; inter-agency cooperation; and information and monitoring.

Policy Statements

The report recommended that policy statements should be drafted by both the

Welsh Office, and the local authority Social Services departments. The statements, should establish clear practice principles to inform the development and monitoring of services:

> All Welsh Social Services Authorities should establish and endorse a policy for the care of the most troubled and troublesome young people for whom they have responsibility ... They should form an integral part of the authority's overall child care policy but nevertheless be distinct and explicit. The Welsh Office should have sight of these policies with a view to ensuring that they conform to best practice and are compatible with the departments own policies (Welsh Office, 1991, p. 24).

Reviews

The report recommended that a series of reviews should be implemented to comprehensively assess the current situation. This primarily related to the need to review existing secure facilities, and to draw up plans for the development of alternatives to secure accommodation.

Local authorities were expected to assess the place that secure accommodation had within the context of their overall child care responsibilities. Running alongside the local authority-led reviews, the Welsh Office sought to gain an understanding of the overall picture by reviewing the use of the existing secure units in Wales. These recommendations were based on evidence that authorities which managed secure facilities also used them most: supply seemingly determining demand!

New Initiatives

The report explicitly recommended that alternatives to secure accommodation should be rigorously explored:

> An initiative should be set up to identify best practice in the provision of community based and open residential alternatives to secure accommodation concentrating on measures of effectiveness. The resulting information should be made available to the local authorities and to the Welsh Office (ibid.).

The Welsh Office wanted an independent assessment of the current situation with particular emphasis being placed on what local authorities said they did (policy statements) and what they could demonstrate they did (service provision). The report recognised that there would be resource implications in terms of monitoring and developing services in line with best practice and community-based provision.

Inter-Agency Cooperation

The report urged local authorities and other agencies to develop collaborative policy and practice strategies. Much had been achieved elsewhere in the juvenile justice process and the report recommended that this should be applied to the pre-trial arena:

> We feel that there is also scope for reducing the need for secure accommodation through improvements in inter-agency consultation and collaboration (Welsh Office, 1991, p. 25).

In particular, delay in the system had been identified as having detrimental consequences in terms of the length of time children and young people spent on remand and this should be addressed within inter-agency contexts:

> the police, crown prosecution service, courts, probation service and voluntary organisations should seek to maintain close links for consultation and collaboration ... they should concentrate on avoiding the need for young people to be placed in secure accommodation and on reducing remand periods to the minimum demanded by due process (ibid.).

Information and Monitoring

In reviewing the use of secure accommodation in Wales, it transpired that there were significant information and monitoring deficits within some local authorities. Given that effective and comprehensive monitoring had been associated with best juvenile justice practice for some time, it was surprising that inadequate information appeared to be at the root of the remand problem. In order to tackle this issue the report recommended that 'local authorities should be asked to keep a wider range of information on their use of secure accommodation and its alternatives' (ibid., p. 26). More specifically, local authorities were being instructed to collect information at specified points of the system: overnight holds under Section 38(6) of the Police and Criminal Evidence Act 1994 (PACE); remands on bail which involved the use of local authority resources; details of remands to local authority accommodation; details of remands to prison custody; and details of placements in secure accommodation whether in, or outside of, Wales.

The *Review of Secure Care* paved the way for an independent review to take place which would be charged with responsibility for highlighting good practice where it existed, but would also report on failure to develop successful strategies for managing remands.

The NACRO Survey: Juvenile Remands in Wales

In September 1993 the report of the NACRO Youth Crime Section survey of remand practices in Welsh Social Services departments was published (NACRO, 1993). The survey had two primary objectives. First, to examine the policy and provision each local authority had established in relation to juveniles alleged to have committed an offence at the pre-court and pre-sentence stages of the juvenile justice system. Second, to examine the monitoring systems and the statistical information held by local authority Social Services departments on juvenile remands. The findings of the survey were presented in two categories: *policy statements* and *strategies and services*.

Broadly speaking, the survey concluded that whilst the majority of local authorities had developed youth justice policy statements which incorporated the management of juvenile remands there was some evidence of a gap between rhetoric and reality. This gap was most evident in relation to monitoring:

> One of the key tasks of this review, was to establish the extent to which the remands process is being monitored by local authorities. 5 of the 6 authorities who have produced statements acknowledge the importance of monitoring as a key to achieving policy objectives ... However, with notable exceptions, the practice which preceded the development of those policy statements ... fell way short of what was required (NACRO, 1993, p. 19).

Furthermore, there was a similar problem evident in relation to inter-agency collaboration:

> even when formal agreements had been reached, elements of dissent frequently affected actual practice. There remain quite different attitudes amongst individuals and amongst agencies relating to the nature and levels of juvenile crime and the appropriate response. The differences continue in the absence of reliable data and jointly agreed monitoring procedures at a local level (ibid., p. 21).

Further gaps between policy statements and practice reality, especially in relation to monitoring, were highlighted in the survey. None of the local authorities was able to demonstrate any monitoring regarding the numbers of young people detained in police stations for example, and more startling was the apparent lack of information in relation to remands to local authority accommodation. The report observes:

> The apparent lack of availability of data on young people remanded to local authority accommodation was remarkable ... The actual monitoring of remands ... stood in stark contrast to the requirements for monitoring espoused in policy statements and demonstrates the change required if policy objectives are to be met (NACRO, 1993, p. 29).

Taken together, the Welsh Office report and the NACRO survey provided clear evidence that although some progress had been made in relation to diverting children and young people from the formal justice process and reducing the numbers being sentenced to custody, far less had been achieved regarding the effective management of juvenile remands. A glaring deficit concerning the latter issue related to the shortcomings and inconsistences in remand monitoring and information systems: quite simply there was a disjuncture between policy claims and practice realities.

Community Alternatives to Secure Accommodation (CASA)

In 1996 the Child and Family Services Division of the Welsh Office supported an application from the Youth Crime Section of NACRO and allocated funding to develop a Community Alternatives to Secure Accommodation (CASA) project in Wales. Funding was allocated for a three year period to work at a strategic level with the 22 newly-established local authorities in Wales (following local government reorganisation and unitarisation: see later) together with other agencies involved in the youth justice process. The function of the project is to develop and coordinate policies and practices consistent with the aim of reducing the need for secure accommodation, and providing alternatives to custodial remands and remands to local authority accommodation. In pursuing these objectives CASA offers a range of services including: casework consultancy; service development; a best practice initiative which includes the promotion of examples of good practice in all areas of the youth justice pre-trial process; national monitoring to specifically identify trends in the use of remands in local authority accommodation, secure accommodation and prison service custody by courts in Wales, and an information request (advice) service.

Particular emphasis has been placed on the issues of monitoring and information systems which is consistent both with the reports outlined above and with other relevant research. Hill (1992, p. 18) for example, notes:

> Monitoring has been one of the most important aspects of juvenile justice practice for the last 10 years. The monitoring of court disposals and of diversion from court has, in many areas, been the most significant factor in the dramatic reduction in numbers receiving custodial sentences and of those appearing before the court. Remands in general, have not benefited from the same level of monitoring as other aspects of the juvenile justice system. The reason for this is not hard to find: decisions about remands get taken at unpredictable times and in a number of different places. For these reasons the collection of information for monitoring purposes is not easy to accomplish. However, despite the difficulties, monitoring of remands is a vital aspect of any attempt to work effectively with the remand process.

Similarly, and as far back as 1986, the Welsh Office (1986, p. 1) observed:

> We conclude that, extensive information is available about the final disposal of juveniles entering the formal justice system, there is usually a dearth of information about interim disposals such as bail and remand in care. We suggest that this information gap should be addressed at all levels.

With this in mind, CASA from its inception, has set out to ensure that in terms of promoting best practice, monitoring should be viewed as an essential feature in the development of any local authority remand management strategy. Furthermore, a fundamental priority for CASA is the development of an over-arching monitoring system drawing upon the information available from the 22 local authorities in order to establish a national picture of court trends and remand management practice across Wales.

The All Wales Monitoring of Remands: Towards the Development of Remand Management Strategies

The reorganisation of local government in Wales created 22 unitary authorities from an existing eight counties, the effect of which was not insubstantial. Although this was welcomed by some who saw it as an opportunity to establish new power bases and a chance to redefine agendas, largely it was regarded as an unnecessary step that would result in chaos. In the majority of instances the carving up of the county structure meant diminished budgets, fragmented expertise and a dramatic reduction in resources. Authorities with well-established multi-disciplinary approaches to the delivery of youth justice found themselves unable to sustain the same levels of commitment to these services. In a recent study which examined the youth justice element contained in Children's Services Plans in Wales it was stated that:

> Several plans identified that local government reorganisation has had an impact on the organisation or delivery of services. Key themes emerge as maintaining provision, developing new protocols between agencies and joint working arrangements (NACRO, 1998, p. 34).

Throughout Wales, in the aftermath of reorganisation, it has been very much a case of 'back to the drawing board' within a context of substantial root and branch change.

Clearly, effective consultation is imperative in undertaking CASA's primary task. It is absolutely necessary to communicate with representatives of all 22 Social Services departments in order to clarify the key aims of the exercise which are essentially fivefold. First, to identify what progress is being made in Wales in ending custodial remands for 15 and 16 year-old boys and to assist the Welsh Office to identify when the ending of custodial remands for this age group can take place. Second, to balance the demand for secure accommodation with the provision of community alternatives. Third, to examine the situation for those children and young people who are currently on remand in Wales (Where are they held? What is their status? How does the system operate?). Fourth, to identify particular trends which indicate the effectiveness or ineffectiveness of local provision and practice. Fifth, and finally, to inform the development of policy and practice within the pre-trial process across Wales.

It has to be said that the CASA initiative is taking place at a difficult time. Local authorities have not only been faced with local government reorganisation and its concomitant stresses and distractions, as discussed above, but youth justice services have had to contend with legislative change (the Criminal Justice and Public Order Act 1994 and the Crime and Disorder Bill 1997), a national audit (Audit Commission, 1996) and the looming reality of further structural change with the implementation of the youth offending teams. Equally, the variation between local authorities in relation to the management and delivery of youth justice services (particularly with respect to local agreements with the Probation Service concerning case management arrangements), and a range of quite different monitoring systems has created its own problems in terms of consistent data collection. Added to these structural issues are the practical problems in undertaking such an ambitious task, not least of which is the time it takes already busy practitioners to complete returns. Notwithstanding this rather challenging context, however, 'all Wales' monitoring is now taking place (albeit at an early stage) and initial findings drawing upon data collected from 18 of the 22 authorities are now available.

Some Initial Findings

Before reviewing the initial findings it is worthwhile recalling the Home Office guidance issued at the time of the implementation of the Criminal Justice Act 1991:

> Removing children and young people from home should be a course of last resort, and the Government believes that as many defendants under 17 as possible should be granted bail. In many areas bail information schemes are available. These provide detailed information which helps courts decide whether the general presumption in favour of bail should or should not be over-ruled. In some parts of the country community programmes, provided either by the voluntary sector or by local authorities, are available for work with defendants who might be at risk being refused bail without some kind of support. Such programmes offer a range of measures of support for, and work with, juvenile defendants. The approach is similar to that used to good effect in specified activities programmes for convicted juvenile offenders. The Government believes that such programmes have an important part to play in the arrangements for the remand of children and young persons (Home Office, 1992, para. 49).

The findings contained in the first report of the *All Wales Monitoring Agreement on Remands* relate to the period 1 April–31 July 1997 (NACRO Cymru, 1997). In particular the report focuses on the returns which relate to those young people who spent some period in custody defined as: held overnight in police custody; remanded into custody whilst awaiting sentence; and sentenced to custody. Of these 95 per cent were male, with young women constituting only 5 per cent of the sample. In all but one case (where there was no record) ethnicity was recorded as 'white'. From the outset it is important to say that the findings are based on limited information and, as such, cannot therefore be regarded as the definitive picture. Rather, at this point in time they represent an initial attempt at identifying trends in remand management practice in Wales. Notwithstanding this, the findings provide some interesting insights which have implications for practice. Of particular interest in the study were the 35 young people held overnight in police custody following a refusal of bail, and a further 35 young people remanded into custody during the same period.

In relation to those held overnight there were two 'subsets'. The first relates to 22 of the 35 young people who, although held overnight, were subsequently granted bail at a first court appearance. Within this group were eight young people who had been denied bail because matters against them were considered to be sufficiently serious or because they were adjudged to present a risk to public protection. In each instance all eight were granted bail when they appeared before a court. Furthermore, at the point of sentence none of these young people received custody. Potentially at least, there are issues of concern here. First, where a young person has been refused bail under the Police and Criminal Evidence Act 1984 S38 (1) there is a duty incumbent upon the police to ensure that, rather than detaining a young person overnight in police cells (which are widely regarded as inappropriate), the child concerned should be moved to local authority accommodation. The duty to transfer exists primarily in order to protect the safety of young people, as it is recognised that they have particular needs which might be difficult to meet in police custody (it is significant that for sometime prior to the introduction of the Police and Criminal Evidence Act 1984, young people were generally interviewed at home in the presence of their parents). Despite both the police and Social Services having a duty to ensure that juveniles are moved to local authority accommodation, the initial findings seem to suggest that in a number of cases this fails to happen. Equally worrying is the fact that in 22 of the 35 cases the young people detained overnight were granted bail at a first court appearance. This clearly raises questions as to why these children were denied police bail in the first instance.

The second 'subset' comprises the remaining 13 young people who were detained overnight, subsequently denied bail at court, and remanded into 'open' local authority accommodation. Again, at the point of sentence not one of these children was sent to custody. This begs a further fundamental question. Why, during the period in which they awaited sentence, were these children regarded as being in need of remand to local authority accommodation? Of particular concern in this category was the case of a 16 year-old boy who spent seven weeks in residential accommodation, only to have all matters against him dropped. Not only do arguments relating to the detrimental effects of removal from home and family and the severance of ties with education and community apply here, but also one would be hard pushed to justify such a case on grounds of sound financial management. Given that the current cost of residential accommodation is located in the region of some £1,800 per week, and that lack of funds is on occasion cited as justification for remanding 15 and 16 year-olds into custody instead of secure facilities, such cases are surely a matter of concern. Despite the limited numbers of young people in this group, their treatment within the 'justice' process nonetheless raises serious questions in relation to remand practice, especially when considered in the light of their ultimate sentences.

The second discrete category of 35 young people comprises children aged 15–17 years who spent part or all of their remand in custody. Within this group three were aged 15, 15 were aged 16, and 17 were aged 17. One 15 year-old had spent 13 days in custody but, at the point of sentence, he was made the subject of a Supervision Order. The two remaining 15 year-old boys both received custodial sentences. Nine of the 15 16 year-olds remanded into custody received custodial sentences. One of them, having spent a total of 210 days (the entire period of the remand) in prison service custody prior to sentence. The remaining six children in this age group all received community sentences (one had spent 59 days remanded in custody prior to being sentenced by way of a combination order). Ten of the 17 year-olds received custodial sentences, whilst five were sentenced by way of noncustodial penalties. Perhaps of most concern here were the cases of the two 17 year-olds (one male and one female) who each spent 28 days in custody (the entire period of their remands) only to receive discharges when sentenced.

Clearly there is evidence here of young people being subjected to significant periods of incarceration whilst awaiting sentence, at which point they are given noncustodial disposals. We know that Prison Service custody is a wholly unsuitable environment in which to place unconvicted, immature, vulnerable youngsters who may indeed be experiencing removal from home for the first time. Recent reports produced by the Howard League for example, have documented the bullying and intimidation that can occur in such institutions (Howard League, 1993, 1995, 1997, 1998). These reports have also drawn attention to the increase in incidents of self-harm and attempted suicides amongst teenagers within the prison system.

In addition to the issues raised above a further concern relates to the apparent inconsistency between local authorities in relation to the numbers of young people remanded. Indeed, there is evidence to suggest that in particular areas children in trouble face a disproportionately high risk of remand.

These early findings, although significant, are too limited to make any sweeping judgments regarding the overall effectiveness of remand management practice in Wales and some questions remain unanswered. Nonetheless we have enough data for the first report to conclude by raising a key issue:

> we can see from this first examination of statistics relating to young people awaiting trial in Wales, that there are some clear issues of concern. Although the study has shown up some problem areas, the numbers of 15 and 16 year old males being remanded in custody is not great, and so it should be possible for Wales to achieve the abolition of such remands, if both practice issues and the financing of the use of secure accommodation can be resolved. During the study period when eighteen 15 and 16 year olds spent some time remanded in custody, there were vacancies in secure accommodation and yet the use of such places does not appear to have been fully utilised (NACRO Cymru, 1997, p. 4).

Perhaps more surprising than the actual findings was the extent to which Social Services departments struggled with the process of completing the returns. Many departments appeared to have encountered real difficulty in providing what was regarded as reasonably routine in relation to those children with whom they worked. For some this appeared to be a case of too few staff working with heavy caseloads, with the result that monitoring was not regarded as a priority. For others, although integrated computerised client systems had been installed, there appeared to be a problem in mapping the complexities of the youth justice process onto those generic systems with the result that the detailed ongoing information required for effective youth justice monitoring was largely missing.

The authorities that appeared to fare best in terms of being able to easily access accurate information were those with dedicated youth justice packages, or those where manual procedures were administered by one key individual who was given specialist responsibility for coordinating that task. Whilst it is true that computerised systems have advantages in terms of the speedy collation of data the key learning point in relation to effective monitoring of the youth justice process appears to be about having a system, computerised or manual, that is specifically designed to monitor each of the key decision-making points of the process.

CASA has plans to increase the amount of information requested on individuals in the future in order to obtain a more complete picture of who these young people are, and what they do. The Audit Commission, in the influential report *Misspent Youth* (Audit Commission, 1996), identified a number of factors which contributed to youth crime. Poor school attendance and the use of drugs and alcohol were all identified as behaviours associated with delinquency. It is envisaged that at some point the scope of the monitoring could be broadened to include information relating to the number of offences that are committed by young people under the influence of alcohol or drugs. Information could also be gathered in relation to the number of offences that have been committed during the hours when that person should normally have been at school. In this respect the monitoring exercise might be expanded to consider the links that exist between offending behaviour and issues of truancy, school exclusion and the extent to which alcohol and substance misuse influence offending in specific areas of Wales. For the immediate future, however, it is intended that CASA will concentrate efforts on refining the standard of information received and closely monitor outcomes in relation to three particular groups: 12–14 year olds who, with the availability of Secure Training Orders, are now at risk of incarceration; 15 and 16 year-old boys remanded to custody; and 17 year-olds who remain uniquely disadvantaged within the youth justice system.

At the time of writing all these issues seem particularly pertinent. With the publication of the White Paper (Home Office, 1997), and the more recent draft guidance on the establishment of youth offending teams (Home Office, 1998), it is essential that those with responsibility for planning and developing the new arrangements possess accurate information regarding their services. With this in mind, then, the remainder of the chapter will focus upon the role that monitoring might have in informing strategic developments within the restructured youth justice system.

Future Developments

It is likely that the Crime and Disorder Bill will make it a statutory function of local authorities to provide both bail information and bail support services. If this is the case it will be essential that youth justice managers have a full understanding of the impact that such services will have on their resources, and an understanding of how the consistent application of approaches to structuring and delivering these services might reduce the need to remand 15 and 16 year-olds to prison service custody. As mentioned in the previous section, although the overall numbers of 15 and 16 year-olds remanded into custodial institutions may not be universally high, there are instances in some local authority areas where custodial remands are disproportionately high in comparison to areas of similar profile. It is necessary therefore to focus upon the factors that have led to such disparity, and to draw out lessons regarding the point at which specific interventions might be used to greatest effect. In so doing this could have an influential impact in ending custody for 15 and 16 year-olds in Wales.

Wales has four police authorities and eight Probation Services, and issues of co-terminosity will constitute an important element in the negotiations related to the establishment of youth offender teams. The coordination of establishing the new arrangements rests with the Chief Executives of the local authorities who also have responsibility for the creation of crime prevention strategies. Given that the Crime and Disorder Bill places a duty upon local authorities both to establish YOTs and, in so doing, to 'prevent offending by children and young people', it is essential that local strategies for the implementation of these new arrangements are well coordinated and based upon the most reliable information.

In all four police areas of Wales inter-agency fora exist and in order to establish a coordinated regional responses it would seem appropriate for these groups to take a lead in negotiating the viability and determining the structure of the joint working arrangements between the various authorities in their area. It is doubtful whether the existing 22 authorities could each sustain a YOT. For some, especially those in west and mid-Wales, the only realistic response might well involve the creation of a 'super team' that would cover a substantial geographical area. At the same time the authorities in these areas will need to address issues of rurality and the delivery of services in Welsh. Given the scale of the changes ahead, the key task for the CASA project will be to assist in the consistent application of the legislation across Wales, and through it's representation on inter-agency fora provide a national perspective and accurate information regarding best practice. The draft guidance on the establishment of YOTs recommends that youth justice steering groups be formed as a starting point for implementing change, to commission a local audit of existing services and gather evidence of local need (Home Office, 1998). It would seem appropriate for the fora organised in each of the police areas of Wales to assume these functions and CASA might assist in the task of compiling the statistical input to enable decision-makers to formulate plans for the development of services. In this sense, then, the 'all Wales' monitoring exercise may provide policy-makers and managers with information relating to trends in the way that the criminal justice process deals with young people, and the effectiveness of strategies to manage that process from a national and local perspective. In so doing it should give those charged with the responsibility of implementing the most radical overhaul of the youth justice system an advantage in coordinating their new local arrangements and delivering best practice for children in trouble.

Conclusion

This chapter has had two principal objectives. First, it has examined the development of a strategic national initiative and explored the issues and circumstances that led to its inception. Second, it has accounted for the role that the CASA project plays in helping to coordinate the policies and practices of local authority responses to the management of juvenile remands in Wales. The importance of systematic monitoring and the collation of accurate information has been emphasised as comprising a key element in the planning and structuring of services. Equally, effective inter-agency cooperation has been profiled.

The immediate future will undoubtedly be an interesting time in the youth justice arena. Local authorities, and those other agencies involved in the process of delivering services to young people in the criminal justice system, will have to grapple with the implications of new legislation as they implement local arrangements for the establishment of YOTs. Throughout this process the CASA project will aim to assist and influence negotiations through consultancy, training and in the dissemination of information regarding best practice. All this will occur against a backdrop where 15 and 16 year-old boys continue to be remanded to prison service custody many of whom, when sentenced, will not receive custodial disposals. At the same time younger children, those aged 12–14, will also become eligible for custodial disposals despite the fact that Secure Training Centres have been met by widespread disapproval and objection by child-care agencies and penal reform organisations. The liberal lobby continues to press the case for community alternatives and cites the failure of expensive and inhumane custodial regimes to curb offending. Even the tabloid press, whilst less concerned with issues of justice and welfare, has drawn public attention to cost. The current government line, in defence of proceeding with the Secure Training Centres, has been to claim that to renege on contractual obligations established by the previous administration would have been to incur punitive financial penalties. This justification, however, does little to explain why these centres will not be used in order to operationalise the enactment of Section 60 of the 1991 Criminal Justice Act and to secure the abolition of penal remands for 15 and 16 year-olds.

Within this challenging context the CASA project will continue to work with all agencies concerned in the youth justice process and aim to ensure that services at all points of the system are responsive to the needs of young people. In relation to pre-trial procedures, CASA will attempt to ensure that the principles contained in the *Code Of Practice For Juvenile Remand Proceedings* (Juvenile Remand Review Group, 1996) which provides a checklist for everyone involved at each stage of the juvenile remand process, are enshrined in the local protocols and Codes of Practice of all local authorities in Wales. These measures are essential in order to ensure that children and young people awaiting trial and sentence receive fair and just treatment from all agencies involved in the process.

Perhaps the principal difficulty for all those who work within the youth justice arena however, continues to be that as a society we seem unable to arrive at a point of consensus regarding the way in which we should respond to children and young people in trouble. In this respect successive governments have vacillated between 'welfarism' and punishment without resolving the key principles that should guide our interventions. As a society do we truly believe that youngsters who offend are 'children in need' as provided by the Children Act 1989. As Anderson (1994, p. 56) contends:

> it is possible to argue that children in the criminal justice system suffer the worst of both worlds. They are denied many of the rights and considerations extended to children in civil law, but lack the full rights of an adult in the criminal justice system. In short, there is no clear answer to the crucial question, 'Is a child who commits a criminal offence primarily to be regarded as a child or an offender'?

Recent government proposals do little to clarify this issue. It is crucial therefore, that the arguments advanced in favour of community alternatives are articulate, accurate and well evidenced. Monitoring has a crucial role to play in ensuring that this happens. It is only by systematically gathering information and subjecting it to analysis that local authorities can even hope to structure their services in a way that will maximise their potential to divert young people from spending lengthy periods in inappropriate institutional settings. The central aim of the CASA project, then, is to assist in developing and coordinating in the strategies and practices that might contribute to this happening in Wales first.

References

Anderson, B. (1995), 'The Criminal Justice Acts: "justice" by geography' in Franklin, R. (ed.), *The Handbook of Children's Rights: Comparative Policy and Practice*, London, Routledge.

Audit Commission (1996), *Misspent Youth: Young People and Crime*, London, Audit Commission.

Hill, G. (1992), *Managing Remands in the New Youth Justice System. A Handbook for Practice*, London, NACRO.

Home Office (1992), *Criminal Justice Act 1991: Young People and the Youth Court*, Circular 30/92, London, Home Office.

Home Office (1997), *No More Excuses – A New Approach to Tackling Youth Crime In England and Wales*, London, The Stationery Office.

Home Office (1998), *Draft Guidance for the Establishment of Youth Offending Teams*, London, Home Office.

Howard League (1993), *Dying Inside*, London, The Howard League for Penal Reform.

Howard League (1995), *Banged Up, Beaten Up, Cutting Up*, London, The Howard League for Penal Reform.

Howard League (1997), *Lost Inside – the imprisonment of teenage girls*, London, The Howard League for Penal Reform.

Howard League (1998), *Sentenced to Fail – Out of sight, out of mind: Compounding the problems of children in prison*, London, The Howard League for Penal Reform.

Juvenile Remand Review Group (1996), *Code of Practice for Juvenile Remand Proceedings*, London, NACRO.

NACRO (1993), *Survey of Juvenile Remands in Wales 1993*, London, NACRO.

NACRO Cymru (1997), *All Wales Monitoring Agreement, First Report: 1st April – 31st July 1997*, Swansea, NACRO Cymru.

NACRO Cymru (1998), *Plans for Youth Justice: An Evaluation of the Youth Justice Element in Children's Services Plans in Wales*, Swansea, NACRO Cymru.

Welsh Office (1986), *Handling Juvenile Crime in Wales*, Cardiff, Welsh Office, Social Services Inspectorate.

Welsh Office (1991), *The Review of Secure Care in Wales*, Cardiff, Welsh Office, Social Services Inspectorate.

7 Family Group Conferences and Youth Justice: The New Panacea?

SHIRLEY E. JACKSON

What are Family Group Conferences?

Family group conferences constitute a radically new way of working with young people and their families which originated in New Zealand as a response to the concerns expressed by Maori people about the over-representation of their young people in the care and justice systems. As an alternative to the Pakeha- (white settler-)instituted methods of dealing with young people in trouble, family group conferences are underpinned by traditional Maori practices which involve young people, their families, victims of crime and relevant communities in the decision-making process. These methods have been enthusiastically embraced and family group conferences are now enshrined in primary legislation as the principal way of tackling issues relating to the care, protection and offending behaviour of young people in New Zealand (Hassall, 1996; Stewart, 1996; Wilcox et al., 1991).

Family group conferences have attracted substantial international interest. Alongside other international developments, Australia has taken a lead in developing and applying the New Zealand model in youth justice. A police-led project in Wagga Wagga, New South Wales has used a modified form of family group conference for 'first offenders' alongside an improved diversionary policy. This approach, however, has differed in some significant philosophical and practical ways from the New Zealand model and has attempted to incorporate a practical expression of Braithwaite's *'theory of reintegrative shaming'* (Moore, 1995). Thereafter two essentially different approaches to family group conferences have developed internationally; those which centre around *a family empowerment model* and those which are shaped by a *victim offender restoration model*. Whilst the two models have common features, their fundamental purposes and priorities differ considerably.

Furthermore, whilst some practitioners are very concerned about such differences and their implications and have thus opted for one method or the other, others have either overlooked the fundamental differences in ethos or have opted for a hybrid approach (Hudson et al., 1996; Markiewicz, 1997).

The debates which have been played out in Australasia have also been repeated elsewhere in the world, as other countries have struggled to find the most suitable way of integrating family group conferences into the political context within which youth justice is located (McDonald, 1995; NACRO, 1996; Family Group Conference Interest Group; Jackson, 1998; Masters, 1998). Two critical views have surfaced in terms of the international development and application of family group conferences. First, the practical challenges created in terms of establishing and integrating a completely new form of practice. Second, debates in relation to the very purpose, philosophy and objectives of family group conferences (Blagg, 1997; Braithwaite, 1997; Family Group Conference Interest Group; Jackson, 1996; Marshall, 1997a and 1997b; Wright, 1997). There is a real danger, therefore, that a rather muddled approach will prevail (Markiewicz, 1997) which will raise fundamental questions in terms of whether or not family group conferences have really been implemented consistently, and whether or not they are working effectively.

I have outlined in detail elsewhere the differences between the two models identified above (Jackson, 1998). In essence the differences are as follows. The first model (see Figure 7.1) is underpinned by notions of *family empowerment* and is founded upon a belief that children and families have a right to be involved in making decisions that affect them (Wilcox et al., 1991; Hudson et al., 1996; Markiewicz, 1997). It is also grounded in a family strengths rather than family deficits approach and rests upon a belief that, given the mechanisms and resources to do so, families are capable of making effective decisions about their children's and young people's lives (Ryburn and Atherton, 1996; Hudson et al., 1996). In this sense, family group conferences may reverse conventional decision-making practice. Rather than the professionals (social workers, police officers, magistrates and judges) making decisions about young people in trouble, families (including wider kinship networks) take responsibility for the action to be taken. Within this *family empowerment model*, therefore, the family group conference process means that young people are directly confronted with their offending behaviour; are required to be accountable for their actions; are enabled to make appropriate reparation for their actions with the victim; and are involved in devising a plan with their wider family for tackling the underlying reasons for their offending.

Model 1:

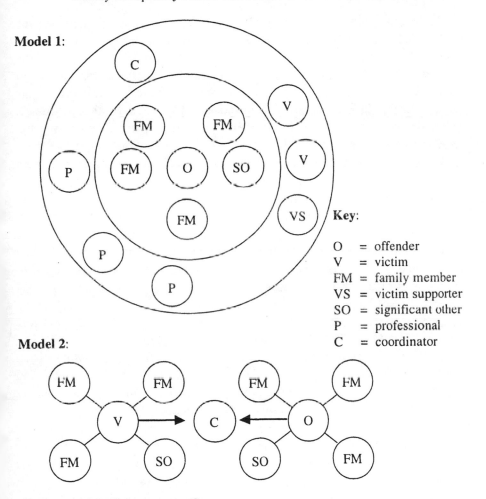

Key:

O = offender
V = victim
FM = family member
VS = victim supporter
SO = significant other
P = professional
C = coordinator

Model 2:

Models of family group conferences

The second model (see figure above) makes the *restorative* imperative the primary aim of the family group conference and by drawing together both sides of the 'conflict', it focuses on how to address the damage caused by the offence within a restorative (and in some schemes, a shaming) context. In this model both 'offender' and victim bring their families and community representatives to the conference, although the extent to which the wider family is involved in practice seems limited. This difference in emphasis appears to be giving rise to a change in terminology and the second model is increasingly being referred to as *restorative conferences* or *community conferences* (Thames Valley Police, 1997; Marshall, 1997a).

In practice, the role of the coordinator differs considerably between the two models. In the *family empowerment* model, the independence of the coordinator is increasingly an important consideration, whereas many of the *restorative model* initiatives have been police-led. This development has itself evoked considerable debate amongst those with an interest in children's rights (Blagg, 1997; Markiewicz, 1997; National Children's and Youth Law Centre, 1995). Furthermore, in the first model great care is taken in preparing the participants for the conference, which forms a vital part of the process, whereas in the second model the focus is almost exclusively on the conference itself (although I understand this practice may be changing in some areas, notably Thames Valley). In the first model, a central part of the plan which the family draws up indicates what measures are to be taken by both the family and the relevant public agencies to address the young person's needs, together with issues which have contributed to the offending behaviour. In the second model, the emphasis is placed on restorative priorities within the conference itself. Proponents of the *restorative* model have been influenced and informed by Maxwell's and Morris's (1993) research in which they discovered that victims of crime were not centrally involved in family group conferences in New Zealand and that as such they were not as satisfied with the conference itself as other participants. However, the involvement of victims in family group conferences in New Zealand subsequently improved (McElrea, 1995) and there is no clear evidence to suggest that victims cannot be successfully involved in family group conferences of either model. The differences within and between the two models are now sufficiently institutionalised that the generic term 'family group conference' has become misleading. For the remainder of this chapter, therefore, I shall refer to the first model (with its emphasis on family empowerment) as family group conferencing and the second (with its restorative/reparative justice focus) as restorative/community conferencing.

Recent Developments in England and Wales

Interest in family group conferences in England and Wales dates back to 1993, following their successful implementation in child welfare. The National Association for the Care and Resettlement of Offenders (NACRO), alongside the Family Rights Group, took a leading role in examining ways in which family group conferences might be developed in youth justice in England and Wales using a similar model of implementation to the one used in child welfare. Interested parties began meeting regularly and despite being unable to obtain specific funding to establish an overall coordinating body (as was the original aim), this national steering group has continued to meet in order to develop thinking and practice in relation to family group conferences in England and Wales. Pilot projects have been developed using local funding, notably in Kent, Hampshire, Kirklees and Sheffield, and such projects have applied family group conferences at various stages in the youth justice process, ranging from cautioning and diversion to release from custody (NACRO, 1998). Running in tandem with this initiative interest has also developed in England and Wales in the restorative/community conferencing model and some preliminary training was undertaken in Thames Valley Police Authority, where restorative conferencing has since been integrated as a component of interventions with 'offenders' (Thames Valley, 1997).

More recently, there has been considerable interest in the potential use of family group conferences by practitioners, policy-makers and politicians. Each of the major parties referred to family group conferences in their pre-general election literature in 1997 and the most recent government consultation papers in relation to the reforming and restructuring of the youth justice system and the recently published White Paper also make similar references (Home Office, 1997a; Home Office, 1997b).

Family Group Conferences and the Current Proposals for Reforming the Youth Justice System

In a number of ways, family group conferences are well-suited to New Labour's proposals for reforming the youth justice system. First, the government has offered some support to community-based initiatives which provide intensive offence-focused programmes of intervention (Labour Party, 1996). Second, the government is keen to replace what it has referred to as an 'excuse culture' with a system which actively confronts and challenges 'young offenders' and holds them directly accountable for their behaviour and actions. Third, the Home Secretary is intent on drawing those people whom he perceives to be marginal to the processing of 'young offenders' (particularly parents and victims of crime) more closely into the system. Within each of these new general policy priorities family group conferencing could clearly have a role. Similarly, and more specifically, the applicability of family group conferencing is evident in relation to the new proposals regarding final warnings; Action Plan Orders; Reparation Orders; Supervision Orders; Child Safety and Parenting Orders and finally, the Youth Panel.

Final Warnings

As an alternative to repeat cautioning, the government proposes to introduce a final warning system which

> [w]ill normally prompt an investigation of the young person's circumstances and behaviour, followed by a community-based intervention which will provide guidance and support to help prevent re-offending (Home Office, 1997a, p. 12).

Clearly a family group conference could be applied at this stage to enable the family and young person to be involved in this process. However, this is not without potential operational problems.

There may be some difficulties with implementing this system given the government's stated priority to 'avoid delay' and possibly issue the final warning before a detailed assessment is made. Preliminary observations in the Hampshire family group conference pilot project would suggest that issuing a caution before the family group conference plan has begun to be implemented may reduce the relevance and impact of the caution. An associated difficulty lies with the anomalous situation that might arise if a final warning were issued before an assessment had been made and the 'young offender' subsequently withdrew consent, as the warning would nonetheless have to stand (Home Office, 1997a). Thus, in such circumstances, where a young person is under no compunction to comply with any plan drawn up at a family group conference (or by a youth offender team for that matter!), the authority of the conference would inevitably be undermined, which could serve to compound any difficulties in family dynamics. Again, early evidence from the Hampshire pilot using family group conferences at a similar stage in the justice process is that the lack of sanctions may contribute to some young people failing to cooperate with the plan drawn up at the family group conference.

Finally, the government is proposing that the decision to issue a final warning would rest with the police (Home Office, 1997b). Therefore, to implement a family group conference project with inter-agency cooperation will require a very good working relationship between the police and other agencies to avoid premature warnings being given before a family group conference can be convened.

Action Plan Orders

The proposals for Action Plan Orders claim that they will be

[a]n intensive programme of community based activity combining reparation, punishment and rehabilitation. They will involve the offender's parents, and include action to tackle factors which may be associated with a young person's offending, such as truancy or drug or alcohol abuse (Home Office, 1997a, p. 3).

With the emphasis on including parents here, family group conferences could clearly be employed to determine the nature and extent of the action plan. Under current proposals, it is envisaged that the youth offender team (YOT) will have responsibility for writing a report to court outlining the specific nature of the action plan. This raises a further question in relation to the authority of the family group conference were it to be introduced at this stage of proceedings. If the YOT report writer has the power to overrule the decision of the conference, this would seriously undermine the effectiveness of the family group conference and/or the families' willingness to be involved. The undermining of families' decisions is a difficulty that has been noted in the use of family group conferences in other contexts (Maxwell and Morris, 1993; Thornton, 1993) and considered in relation to the use of family group conferences and pre-sentence reports in this country (Jackson, 1996).

Reparation Orders

Reparation is a central theme in family group conferencing. It is also a recurrent aspect of the government's youth justice proposals and specifically features in the new Reparation Order.

> The Reparation Order will help to show young offenders the harm which they have done to their victims and their communities, and will enable courts to impose punishments which make some amends to the victim (Home Office, 1997a, p. 8).

In relation to the Reparation Order, the Home Office consultation document referred to above goes on to state that the victim's views on whether such an order is appropriate and if so, what kind of activities it might comprise, are important. The court therefore will be required to consider information about the victim's views. The court could use established methods of obtaining victims' views, but a family group conference would provide a forum where the victim's perspective could be more comprehensively explored alongside that of the 'young offender' and his/her family. Equally, given that an 'apology' is one of the actions envisaged in a reparation plan, a family group conference would provide an appropriate context for agreeing and effecting that response.

Again, the government's proposals as they are presented at the time of writing are such that the responsibility for preparing and presenting the reparation plan to the court rests with the YOT. However, similar to the action plan above, the family group conference determined reparation plan could be presented to the court alongside or instead of this report.

Supervision Orders

Under the government proposals, Supervision Orders are to become more flexible and include elements of reparation in appropriate cases (Home Office, 1997a). Again, it may be pertinent to use a family group conference to determine the nature of the Supervision Order requirements, either at the court report stage or once the order has been made.

Child Safety and Parenting Orders

More controversial elements of the government's proposals for reforming the youth justice system are Child Safety and Parenting Orders. The government has stated its intention to introduce Child Safety Orders for children under the age of 10 who are adjudged to be at risk of developing offending behaviour patterns. Technically family group conferences could be employed once a child has been identified as 'at risk', in order to draw up a plan of support. This use of family group conferences might enhance the parent's capacities and access to family support from the wider family, the community and the relevant professional agencies in 'facing the problems of bringing up difficult and disorderly children', before having a Parenting Order imposed on them (Home Office, 1997b, p. 15).

Youth Panel

Finally, the government appears to recognise that adversarial court procedures may not be the most effective means of addressing youth crime and it is proposing to pilot the use of a Youth Panel as an alternative to court in order to

> set out clear requirements on the young offender and on others, such as his or her parents. These requirements would ensure the young person made amends to the victim or the community at large and would tackle the causes of the offending behaviour (Home Office, 1997b, p. 32).

A family group conference could be convened within the Youth Panel procedures to determine the steps that need to be taken by the young person and his/her parents in 'making amends to the victim' and in addressing 'the causes of the offending behaviour'.

It is apparent from this brief analysis that family group conferences offer wide-ranging potential for the reformed youth justice system. Indeed, they essentially constitute a means of decision-making rather than a discrete sentencing option and in this sense they could be employed at all stages of the youth justice process. However, it is of essential importance to remember (as many authors have now noted) that family group conferences are not just an expedient and convenient mechanism which (when routinely administered) necessarily yield the desired results (Hudson et al., 1996; Jackson and Nixon, 1998; Markiewicz, 1997; Ryburn and Atherton, 1996). Moreover, whilst it is clear that family group conferences could fit into the reformed youth justice system as outlined above, it is imperative that the underlying philosophy of family empowerment, which was the very *raison d'être* for their inception in New Zealand, does not get lost in a crude attempt to make them fit into a philosophical framework underpinned by punishment and retribution.

Potential Tensions and Contradictions

Young People and Responsibility

The very title of the White Paper published in November 1997, *No More Excuses: A New Approach to Tackling Youth Crime in England and Wales*, provides the first cause for concern. Whilst no one would wish to make lame excuses for youth crime, the title of the White Paper denotes a particular attitude to 'young offenders' and their families. The introduction claims that the current youth justice system 'too often excuses the young offender before it, implying that they cannot help their behaviour because of their social circumstances' (Home Office, 1997b, p. 1). Indeed, there has been an increasing move in recent years in England and Wales to treat children and young people in trouble in a similar way to adult offenders, and in so doing, to negate their specific needs as children in the criminal justice system (Allan, 1996; Goldson, 1997a).

This trend is explicitly evident in the government proposals to treat children more like adults by the removal of *doli incapax* and in the implication that there is little or no difference between a 10 year-old's and an adult's ability to comprehend the consequences of their actions. The central contention is that 'young offenders' must take more responsibility for their actions.

> We must stop making excuses for youth crime. Children above the age of criminal responsibilities are generally mature enough to be accountable for their actions and the law should recognise this (Home Office, 1997b, p. 1).

However, this touches upon a contested and contentious issue and it might be argued that we cannot assume that, in offending, children always exercise autonomy of responsibility for their actions.

> The fact that children are developing their capacities calls into question the extent to which they can properly be held responsible for their actions under the law and, even if they can, whether they can legitimately be blamed for them (Allan, 1996, p. 18).

Allan sets his comments in the context of the low age of criminal responsibility in England and Wales in comparison with other Western European countries and he demonstrates that the cognitive ability of children, including their capacity to make moral choices, is a developing process. To attribute the same level of culpability to a child 'offender' as to an adult is to deny the developmental processes of childhood. Allan concludes that there is a need to protect children in the criminal justice system because they are

> liable to be vulnerable and impressionable, lacking the maturity to weigh the longer term against the shorter, lacking the insight to know how they will react and the imagination to know how others will react in certain situations, lacking the experience to measure the probable against the possible (ibid., pp. 21–2).

This calls into question, therefore, the 'young offender's' capacity to be fully responsible for their actions at such an early age and raises a key issue in relation to the management of family group conferences. Indeed, the current emphasis on young people's responsibility for their actions could mean that family group conferences are located within an environment of hostility and blame. As I have argued, it is important that family group conferences are not conducted in this way. Whilst accepting responsibility for actions is clearly a part of the family group conference process, targeting and blaming children for something over which they have only partial control is likely to alienate them further and hence be counterproductive.

Parental Responsibility

The government proposals for reforming the youth justice system, as I have already noted, are based upon a clear position in relation to the responsibilities of parents.

> Parents of young offenders may not directly be to blame for the crimes of their children, but parents have to be responsible for providing their children with proper care and control (Home Office, 1997b, p. 12).

Despite the apparent inconsistency between making young people totally accountable for their actions whilst simultaneously also charging parents with a clear responsibility for such actions, the government undoubtedly wishes to raise the profile of parental responsibility in youth justice matters. Again, herein lies tension for family group conferencing. Indeed, employing conferences to make parents take responsibility for their children contradicts their primary tenets. The underlying message in the new proposals is one of parental failure which flies in the face of the family strengths and empowerment model inherent in family group conferencing. The tensions are primarily located along a continuum with help, support and welfare at one end and blame, condemnation and punishment at the other. There is a certain 'double speak' in the recent government documents in relation to assisting parents to assume responsibility.

> The government wants to *encourage* parents to accept their responsibilities for the behaviour of their children. Parents who *wilfully neglect* these responsibilities should be *answerable* to the courts, but *support* and *guidance* are also needed to *help* parents control children. The parenting *order* will *offer* parents training and *help* to change the offending behaviour of their children and may *direct* parents to exercise control over their children's behaviour (Home Office, 1997a, p. 9; my emphasis).

Whilst there is reference to 'support'; 'guidance' and 'help', the message is clear: either match up to expectations or be deemed irresponsible and be punished. This is in direct contradiction to the experiences of social work and criminal justice practitioners (and some magistrates) in relation to previous coercive measures to improve parental responsibility (bind-overs, court attendance, payment of fines). This experience provides evidence that such coercive measures are entirely counterproductive (Allan, 1996).

Research and professional experience in relation to family group conferences and other child welfare practice informs us that efforts to empower families are undermined by placing them in a 'straitjacket' of threats if they do not conform to the requirements (Jackson, 1993; Lupton and Stevens, 1997). Also, it is an imperative of the Children Act 1989 to try to work in partnership with parents. The new emphasis on parental responsibility without partnership is unhelpful and unnecessary, as the evidence shows that almost all families *are* able to construct effective plans using family group conferences (Maxwell and Morris, 1993; Thornton, 1993; Lupton et al., 1995; Marsh and Crow, 1998).

Additionally, it is not always the 'fault' of the families concerned when plans do not materialise. Graham and Bowling (1995) observed that most family support services are for parents of smaller children and the likely range of suitable assistance for parents experiencing difficulties with their teenagers is limited. There is a danger, therefore, that parents referred to unsuitable provision because of a lack of adequate alternatives will be penalised for their noncompliance. Research in relation to family group conferences, for example, has provided evidence that some family plans are not supported with the requested and agreed resources from the agencies concerned either due to miscommunication, unrealistic promises or a general lack of welfare provision (Lupton and Stevens, 1997).

All of this raises questions and judgement calls in relation to assessing parental cooperation and compliance. The first question to be considered is 'What if the parent's can't do it?' There is likely to be disagreement about the difference between 'can't' and 'won't', with both the previous and present government seemingly equally keen to take a firm line with those they deem 'won't' take responsibility. The Major government's proposals to consider breach of a parental control order as a criminal offence (Home Office, 1997c) are mirrored in the New Labour proposals regarding the imposition of a Parental Control Order and breach conditions (Home Office, 1997a). Therefore, it is conceivable that, some of the parents experiencing the most pressing difficulties in parenting their children effectively (those who are also likely to have the greatest social and financial needs) will be further penalised and criminalised by the youth justice system. This does not sit comfortably with attempts to introduce a mechanism for empowering families and working in partnership, and it flies in the face of the previously cited evidence that most families (given the encouragement of a coordinator) will agree to and participate successfully in a family group conference (Lupton et al., 1995; Marsh and Crow, 1998; Maxwell and Morris, 1993; Thornton, 1993).

Punishment, Welfare and Justice

Within contemporary developments in youth justice policy and practice, there seems to be a relentless drive to increase punishment, whatever the consequences of its application. Other jurisdictions have taken, and continue to take, a fundamentally different approach. For example in Canada, the rehabilitation of young people by addressing their welfare needs regarded to be the most effective means of reducing juvenile offending. Even in the USA, which has been witness to a marked 'get tough' approach in recent years, a young person's inexperience is often seen as mitigation in youth justice. Closer to home, in Scottish Children's Hearings, decisions can be made only to promote the child's welfare (Allan, 1996). Punishment is not the overriding consideration. Previously in England and Wales, welfare, rehabilitation and limited strategic intervention have directed youth justice policy and reaped practical benefits. Why is it that policy and practice now seem locked into an overarching paradigm of punishment?

Punishment may satisfy to a sense of moral indignation at youth crime and the desire for the culprit to be seen to pay, but how appropriate is that response in dealing with either crime reduction or the individual young person? Indeed, there is ample evidence to suggest that an exclusive reliance on punishment is not only ineffective, but also counterproductive in heightening the adolescent sense of disaffection and alienation and leading to further delinquency (Rutter and Giller, 1984; Rutherford, 1986; Allan, 1996). So what are the alternatives?

It has become rather 'infra dig' to speak of welfare in relation to youth offending and such considerations are now crudely conceptualised as 'making excuses' for criminal behaviour (Home Office, 1997b). However, the government seems confused in its attitude to welfare. Whilst it claims

> [c]oncerns about welfare of the young person have too often been seen as in conflict with the aims of protecting the public, punishing offences and preventing offending. This confusion creates real practical difficulties for practitioners and has contributed to the loss of public confidence in the youth justice system (Home Office, 1997b, p. 7).

It goes on to say

> [t]he Government does not accept that there is any conflict between protecting the welfare of a young person and preventing that individual from offending again (ibid., p. 7).

However, the government is reluctant to acknowledge the link between welfare and justice, preferring instead to see them as entirely separate concerns. Whilst there is little dispute that welfare needs should not entirely excuse offending, they certainly go a long way towards providing an explanation for it. It follows that addressing welfare needs effectively may be the best way of preventing the young person re-offending rather than simply turning to more and more punitive measures.

However, it also has to be acknowledged that there is some mileage in the argument that attending to a 'young offender's' welfare needs in themselves may not pay sufficient regard to the wrong they have committed and the needs of others, particularly their victims. There is therefore an underlying conflict between the condemnatory nature of criminal law and the primacy of the child's best interests in child welfare law. The very fact that 'young offenders' are still children in welfare law cannot be overlooked. There is certainly ample evidence to suggest that 'young offenders' are also 'children in need' (Goldson, 1997b). Hagell and Newburn (1994) found in their study of persistent offenders that half were already known to social workers and in most cases not for reasons of their offending. Allan (1996, p. 68) claims that

> [w]hile most of those children who do commit crime could be seen and dealt with as children in need, the shift towards punishment and deterrence has rendered such an approach increasingly out of step with popular and political expectation.

It is now well documented that 'young offenders' are more likely than others to fail at school, truant persistently, behave disruptively or be permanently excluded (Audit Commission 1996; Farrington, 1978; Graham and Bowling, 1995). In addition, figures for 1995 show that nearly 60 per cent of convicted 'young offenders' aged 16 or 17 were unemployed or not in training when sentenced compared with a national average of 12 per cent (Home Office, 1997d). Boswell (1995) also found that for some of the most serious offenders, 91 per cent had suffered some form of serious abuse or traumatic loss in childhood

Such findings give weight to the argument that family group conferences provide a good means to look at welfare needs *in addition to* offending behaviour. In this sense, the young person's needs are placed in a context of ensuring that he/she faces the consequences of his/her behaviour in tandem with addressing reparation to the victim. However, there may be welfare needs, which are out of the power of either the family or the social welfare agencies to alter. Farrington (1996) associates major risk of youth crime with low-income families, poor housing, and living in inner city deprivation. Indeed, some critics of family group conferences highlight the 'social exclusion' experienced by many of the families and communities within which 'young offenders' live and which are beyond the reach of the conference. Hence it is argued that family group conferences can result in 'victim blaming'

> where the families of offenders who lack structural power to overcome many of the deficiencies facing them and the young person, in systems such as unemployment, education and health, are held accountable for the solutions to these problems (Markiewicz, 1997, p. 32).

There is a clear risk here that implementing family group conferences within an overarching context of 'family-blaming' may even serve to compound the forms of exclusion and disadvantage that some young people and their families endure.

A further potential difficulty in relation to the application of family group conferences within the reformed youth justice system relates to the burgeoning move to early intervention programmes (Home Office, 1997a) and of 'nipping offending in the bud' (Home Office, 1997b). One consideration which militates against early intervention programmes is its potential cost. It is extremely difficult to identify those young people likely to move into a 'life of crime' without also including many who would not have offended (Hagell and Newburn, 1994). Hence there could be considerable costs if the 'net' is stretched too wide for these early intervention schemes. Early intermediate treatment schemes suffered from this 'net-widening' effect (Cohen, 1985) and inadvertently mixed 'offenders' with those deemed to be 'potential offenders' with crime-inducing results. The use of family group conferences at any early stage certainly has the potential to 'net-widen', especially if it is used at a first caution or 'risk of offending' stage. This concern has been raised by critics of family group conferences (Warner, 1994; National Children's and Youth Law Centre, 1995; Wundersitz, 1996). Equally, the issue of whether or not a young person admits guilt or appreciates the nuances of that admission, may get lost in a system in which they are not legally represented (Allan, 1996). It would be lamentable if a system designed to empower children and their families actually served to disavail them of some of their fundamental civil rights. It may be that an advocate should be provided to ensure that the young person's rights are not violated by the use of family group conferences, especially as it is proposed that legal representation is not included in the Youth Panels, which were considered earlier in this chapter (Home Office, 1997b).

Agency Priorities, Resources and Professional Power

The government has proposed the establishment of youth offender teams, comprising all the 'key players' in the youth justice system. Furthermore, it has declared that the principal aim of these teams will be to 'reduce offending' (Home Office, 1997b). However, despite the emphasis on the single-track approach, there is little acknowledgement of differing agency policies, practices, philosophies and priorities. It seems naïve to expect that such variation will be submerged under the 'common approach to youth justice focused on addressing offending behaviour' (Home Office, 1997b, p. 27). This has been a central problem encountered in implementing family group conferences and Markiewicz (1997, p. 117) notes that

> [e]ach advocate for the process may have different reasons for their support, and different priorities in relation to desired outcomes from the process. There may be agreement among the various stakeholders that group conferencing is a positive alternative model, but very different reasons for believing this to be so. The blurring of objectives can result in disagreement about outcomes.

It is not only at the level of agency priorities that difficulties may occur, however. Agency resources are also likely to be problematic. Under investment in welfare and justice provision for young people may mean that resources requested and agreed as part of a family group conference plan are simply not available. The tendency for promised resources to be unforthcoming was noted earlier and has been evidenced in research into the use of family group conferences in child welfare (Lupton and Stevens, 1997) and in youth justice (Maxwell and Morris, 1993). The government does not envisage additional funds being needed for the new youth justice proposals (Home Office, 1997b). However, research into the introduction of family group conferences in child welfare has shown that at least initially they are not a cost-saving mechanism and need to have sufficient pump-priming money for implementation to be effected properly (Lupton, 1995; Crow and Marsh, 1997). There is a danger that if under-resourced, and if the resources requested in plans are not made available, family group conferences themselves, and ultimately the families concerned could be set up to fail.

Finally, apart from agency priorities and resources the whole issue of professional power needs to be carefully considered. Wilcox et al. (1991, p. 8) found that in relation to implementing family group conferences

> [t]he major practice hurdle was to relinquish the power of final decision to the family. This had to be done in spite of personal or professional points of view. We needed to learn our role was information giving; we gathered and provided all information to the family group in order for them to make an informed decision ... the real movement came when we had committed ourselves to support and resource family decisions even when we did not personally agree with them.

New wide-ranging powers are to be allocated to the YOTs. In order to give the power of decision-making to families (as required by family group conferences), YOTs will need to be given the permission and have the professional will to make a major shift in thinking about fundamental power relations in youth justice. Whilst this has been one of the most pressing difficulties experienced by professionals in child welfare (Crow and Marsh, 1997; Jackson and Nixon, 1998), at least it was implemented within the positive legal framework of the Children Act 1989 with its emphasis on working in partnership with the immediate and wider family. There is no such practice mandate in youth justice; in fact the issues considered in this chapter and elsewhere in this volume present significant challenges if the youth justice system is to overcome the prevailing negative attitudes to children and young people in trouble and their families and to facilitate and support their capacity to make effective and valued decisions.

Conclusion

In this chapter, I have aimed to address many of the assumptions which are taking-hold in rhetoric and practice in relation to family group conferences in youth justice. I have outlined the differences between different models of conferencing and emphasised the *family empowerment* ethos which is fundamental to family group conferences. I have also shown how family group conferences could become part of the current proposals for reforming the youth justice system in England and Wales, but have set out a number of warnings about its wholesale and hasty adoption. Finally I have set out my concerns about the implementation of family group conferences without sufficient attention to the underlying philosophical bases especially family empowerment and a recognition of the social exclusion experienced by many families and young people who get into trouble.

I contend that we need to be careful not to 'jump onto the bandwagon' of family group conferences without clearly thinking through the underlying premises on which they are based. We need to think carefully about the implications of introducing a radically different way of working into an essentially punitive youth justice system.

However, I would not go so far as to discourage the introduction of family group conferences in England and Wales on the basis of these complexities and constraints. I would concur with Allan (1996, p. 82) when he summarises the potential and the warnings in the implementation of family group conferences.

> By involving a wider range of relatives, neighbours and other significant people than the conventional court process, the prospect of identifying successful measures is greatly increased. Moreover, the development of problem-solving strategies by young people, their families and neighbours themselves, rather than the imposition of measures from above, enshrines the participative ethos associated with lasting change. The difficulties involved in overcoming the accumulation of disadvantages faced by the majority of offenders should, nevertheless, not be underestimated. The Family Group Conference is no magic wand.

In summary, family group conferences have wide potential but should not be seen as the latest 'quick-fix' approach to youth justice. They are not, in themselves, the new panacea for the 'ills' in the youth justice system.

References

Allan, R. (1996), *Children and Crime: Taking Responsibility*, London, Institute for Public Policy Research.

Audit Commission (1996), *Misspent Youth*, London, Audit Commission.

Blagg, H. (1997), 'A Just Measure of Shame?: Aboriginal Youth and Conferencing in Australia', *British Journal of Criminology*, Vol. 37, No. 4, pp. 481–501.

Boswell, G. (1995), *Violent Lives*, London, The Princes Trust.

Braithwaite, J. (1997), 'Conferencing and Plurality: reply to Bragg', *British Journal of Criminology*, Vol. 37, No. 4, pp. 502–6.

Cohen, S. (1985), *Visions of Social Control*, Cambridge, Polity Press.

Crow, G. and Marsh, P. (1997), *Family Group Conferences, Partnership and Child Welfare*, Sheffield, University of Sheffield Partnership Research Programme.

Family Group Conference Interest Group, Family Group@Morgan.UCS.Mun.Ca.

Farrington, D. (1978), 'Human Development and Criminal Careers' in M. Maguire, R. Morgan, and R. Reiner (eds.), *The Oxford Book of Criminology*, Oxford, Clarendon Press.

Farrington, D. (1996), *Understanding and Preventing Youth Crime*, York, Joseph Rowntree Foundation.

Goldson, B. (1997a), 'Children, Crime, Policy and Practice: Neither Welfare nor Justice', *Children and Society*, Vol. 11, No. 2, pp. 77–88.

Goldson, B. (1997b), 'Locked Out and Locked Up: State Policy and the Systemic Exclusion of Children "In Need" in England and Wales', *Representing Children*, Vol. 10, No. 1, pp. 44–55.

Graham, J. and Bowling, B. (1995), *Young People and Crime*, London, Home Office Research and Statistics Directorate.

Hagell, A. and Newburn, T. (1994), *Persistent Young Offenders*, London, Policy Studies Institute.

Hassall, I. (1996), 'Origins and Development of Family Group Conferences' in J. Hudson et al., *Family Group Conferences: Perspectives on Policy and Practice*, Annandale, NSW, Australia: The Federation Press.

Home Office (1997a), *Tackling Youth Crime: a consultation paper*, London, Home Office.

Home Office (1997b), *No More Excuses – A New Approach to Tackling Youth Crime in England and Wales*, London, HMSO.

Home Office (1997c), *Preventing Children Offending: A Consultation Document*, London, HMSO.

Home Office (1997d), *Aspects of Crime: Young Offenders 1995*, London, HMSO.

Hudson, J. et al. (1996), *Family Group Conferences: Perspectives on Policy and Practice*, Annandale, NSW, Australia, Federation Press.

Jackson S.E. (1993), 'Partnership with Families' in A. Buchanan (ed.), *Partnership in Practice: Children Act 1989*, Aldershot, Avebury.

Jackson, S.E. (1996), *Family Group Conferencing in Youth Justice: The Issues for Implementation in the UK*, unpublished paper from the first national UK conference on Family Group Conferences, Solihull, October.

Jackson, S.E. (1998), 'Family Group Conferences in Youth Justice: the issues for implementation in England and Wales', *Howard Journal of Criminal Justice*, Vol. 37, No. 1, pp. 34–50.

Jackson, S.E. and Nixon, P. (forthcoming), 'Family Group Conferences: Challenging the Old Order?' in L. Dominelli (ed), *Community Approaches to Child Welfare*, Aldershot: Avebury.

Jackson, S.E. (forthcoming), *Family Justice?: an evaluation of a pilot project using Family Group Conferences in Youth Justice*, Southampton, University of Southampton Social Work Studies Department.

Labour Party (1997), *Tackling Youth Crime: Reforming Youth Justice – a consultation paper on an agenda for change*, London, Labour Party.

Lupton, C. et al. (1995), *Family Planning? An evaluation of the Family Group Conference Model*, Portsmouth, Social Services Research and Information Unit, Portsmouth University.

Lupton, C. and Stevens, M. (1997), *Family Outcomes: following through on Family Group Conferences*, Report No. 34, Portsmouth, Social Services Research and Information Unit, Portsmouth University.

Markiewicz, A. et al. (1997), *Juvenile Justice Group Conferencing in Victoria: an evaluation of a pilot program*, Melbourne, The Children, Young People and Families Research Unit, University of Melbourne.

Marsh, P. and Crow, G. (1998), *Family Group Conferences in Child Welfare*, Oxford: Blackwell.

Marshall, T. (1997a), 'Calls for Caution: Criminal Justice Conferencing', *Mediation*, Winter, pp. 10–11.

Marshall, T. (1997b), 'Criminal Justice Conferencing – calls for caution', *Mediation*, Spring, pp. 6–7.

Masters, G. (1998), Family Group Conference Interest Group: West Cheshire Conferencing Service 16 January 1998, G.Masters@Lancaster.ac.uk

Maxwell, G.M. and Morris, A. (1993), *Family, Victims and Culture: Youth Justice in New Zealand*, Wellington, New Zealand, Social Policy Agency.

Maxwell, G. and Morris, A. (1996), 'Research on Family Group Conferences with Young Offenders in New Zealand' in J. Hudson et al., *Family Group Conferences: Perspectives on Policy and Practice*, Annandale, NSW, Australia, The Federation Press.

McDonald, J. et al. (1995), *Real Justice Training Manual: Co-ordinating Family Group Conferences*, Pipersville, Pennsylvania, The Pipers Press.

McElrea, F.W.M. (1995), 'Accountability in the Community: Taking Responsibility For Offending', a paper prepared for the Legal Research Foundation Conference, Auckland New Zealand, May.

Moore, D. (1995), *A New Approach to Juvenile Justice: An Evaluation of Family Group Conferencing in Wagga Wagga*, Charles Sturt University, Wagga Wagga, NSW, Australia, Centre for Rural Social Research.

NACRO (1996), *Minutes of the Family Group Conference and Youth Justice Steering Group 19.07.96*, London, NACRO.

NACRO (1998), *Family Group Conferences and Youth Justice: a newsletter produced by the National Steering Group on Family Group Conferences and Youth Justice*, Issue 3, January.

National Children's and Youth Law Centre (1995), *Rights Now!*, Vol. 3, No. 4, Sydney, University of New South Wales, Australia.

Rutherford, A. (1986), *Growing out of Crime*, Harmondsworth, Penguin.

Rutter, M. and Giller, H. (1984), *Juvenile Delinquency: Trends and Perspectives*, Harmondsworth, Penguin.

Ryburn, M. and Atherton, C. (1996), 'Family Group Conferences: partnership in practice', *Adoption and Fostering*, Vol. 20, pp. 16–23.

Sandor, D. (1994), 'The Thickening Blue Wedge in Juvenile Justice' in C. Alder and J. Wundersitz (eds), *Family Conferencing and Juvenile Justice*, Canberra, Australian Institute of Criminology.

Stewart, T. (1996), 'Family Group Conferences with Young Offenders in New Zealand' in J. Hudson et al. (eds), *Family Group Conferences: Perspectives on Policy and Practice*, Annandale, NSW, Australia, The Federation Press.

Thames Valley Police (1997), *Restorative Justice: a balanced approach*, Kidlington, Oxford, Thames Valley Police.

Thornton, C. (1993), *Family Group Conferences: A Literature Review*, Lower Hutt, New Zealand, Practitioners Publishing.

Warner, K. (1994), 'The Rights of the Offender in Family Conferences' in C. Alder and J. Wundersitz (eds), *Family Conferencing and Juvenile Justice*, Canberra, Australian Institute of Criminology.

Wilcox, R. et al. (1991), *Family Decision Making: Family Group Conferences, Practitioners Views*, Lower Hutt, New Zealand, Practitioners Publishing.

Wright, M. (1997), *Victim/Offender Mediation in the United Kingdom: Legal Background and Practice*, paper to seminar on Mediation between juvenile offenders and their victims, organised by the Council of Europe and the Ministry of Justice (Institute of Justice) of Poland, Popowo, near Warsaw, 22–24 October .

Wundersitz, J. (1996), *The South Australian Juvenile Justice System*, Canberra, Australian Institute of Criminology.

8 Social Work with Young People in Trouble: Memory and Prospect

DAVID SMITH

How should the supervision of children and young people in trouble differ from that of adult offenders? According to the relevant National Standard for England and Wales (Home Office, 1995), not by very much. It is an instructive exercise to compare the requirements for Supervision Orders and for Probation Orders in the 1995 version of the most authoritative statement of official expectations. In general, the 1995 National Standards are much more concerned with procedures, including procedures for the enforcement of compliance with Orders, and much less concerned with the content of work, than the earlier version (Home Office, 1992), which contained various suggestions of good practice. The Standard for Supervision Orders is no exception, and the similarities of its prescriptions to those for Probation Orders are much more evident than the differences. In essence, the differences are sixfold.

First, Supervision Orders are to include an extra aim –

> to encourage and assist the child or young person in his or her development towards a responsible and law-abiding life, thereby promoting the welfare of the offender (Home Office, 1995, p. 24).

(note the slide within the sentence from 'child or young person' to 'young offender', which is the term most favoured in the Standard). Second, the 'young offender' is to be encouraged 'to understand and accept responsibility for his or her behaviour and its consequences', and an objective of supervision should be to ensure that he or she 'understands the difference between right and wrong' (ibid., pp. 24–5). Third, it is recognised that – apparently unlike adults – 'young offenders' may have 'personal difficulties'. Fourth, there are several references to the need to involve and inform the 'young offender's' parents or other carers, to ensure the involvement of other relevant agencies and coordination between probation and social services, to attend to educational

148

issues, and to take account of 'the welfare of the child or young person' (ibid., p. 30) in seeking to enforce the Order. Fifth, 'methods' of work might include 'activities designed to make reparation to the community' (ibid., p. 29). Finally, in a nod to the 1989 Children Act, there is a reference to working in partnership 'with the young offender and his or her parents or guardian' (ibid., p. 27).

Everything else, on commencement of Orders, their enforcement, their timing, content and desired outcomes, record keeping and breach procedures, is either identical to the Standard for adults or differs only in details of wording. Both include this warning:

> All ['planned and purposeful physical'] activities should be carefully assessed to ensure that *their location or nature could not give the impression of providing a reward for offending*. Offenders should never be sent abroad as part of supervision order [probation order in the adult version] supervision; and activities should amount to significantly more than recreation (Home Office, 1995, pp. 20 and 28; emphasis in original).

While it would not be true to claim that all concern with the welfare of children and young people in trouble has disappeared, it is clear that the National Standard envisages that they will be supervised in a style which is very close to that thought appropriate for adult offenders. Policy has travelled a very long way from the assumptions of the 1969 Children and Young Persons Act, and the movement is towards convergence of the systems of adult and youth justice – a process begun by the 1980 White Paper *Young Offenders* (Home Office, 1980) and the ensuing legislation. (As we will see later in the chapter, no such convergence has occurred in Scotland (Kelly, 1996), where very different – and arguably more positive – forms of supervision have remained possible.) The mention of overseas travel and the need to ensure that supervision is no fun reflects the peculiar preoccupations of the then Home Secretary Michael Howard and the dramatically punitive turn of policy over which he presided (see, for example, Cavadino and Dignan, 1997; Goldson, 1997a), but the guiding ideas of the National Standard – and in particular the idea that 'young offenders' are just that, before they are children in trouble or in need (see Johnson and Parker, 1996), or even young people with personal difficulties – go back further than that.

The main concern of this chapter is to suggest how workers in youth justice, faced with the expectations of the National Standard, can find ways of making the experience of community supervision positive, developmental and caring rather than restrictive, disciplinary and punitive, and adopt forms of practice which promote the social inclusion of the children and young people with whom they work, not their further stigmatisation and exclusion (Drakeford and Vanstone, 1996; Smith and Stewart, 1997). First, though, it seems important to trace briefly the course of events which made a document like *National Standards* possible. The main lines of policy development in youth justice are discussed elsewhere in this volume, and the discussion will not be repeated here. I want to stress, however, the contribution of practitioners to the emergence of certain themes in policy in the 1980s and early 1990s; to say something of the virtues and limitations of the youth justice practice which developed during that period; and to discuss some recent trends in the disposal of young people in trouble, arguing that while it is possible to exaggerate the extent to which the achievements of the recent past have been blown away by the chill political winds of the Howard (and Straw?) regimes, most of the recent trends are certainly alarming, and there may be worse to come.

'That is not it at all, / That is not what I meant, at all' (T.S. Eliot)

Bill Jordan (1983) observed in connection with the 1982 Criminal Justice Act that there was little force in complaints from probation officers that the Act would push them into a more controlling and less supportive style of work, since it merely legalised things which at least some officers had already shown themselves perfectly willing to do (for the background see Raynor (1985)). This is perhaps an extreme and unusually clear example of a recurring phenomenon: legislation – and the guidelines on implementation which often accompany it – reflect practice, but in a distorted or, so to speak, alienated form which makes it hard for practitioners to recognise in such texts their own image. Criminal Justice Acts, White and Green Papers, consultation documents, government circulars, statements of objectives, action plans and so on tend to use a language which social workers find antipathetic, and which encourages the view that these represent impositions from above, from a remote central government which neither knows nor cares about the day-to-day efforts and travails of practitioners. But practitioners are, or have been, among the most important influences on youth justice policy. Plainly, this influence will vary over time, and there will be periods when it is altogether absent – the punitive thrust of penal policy from 1993 to 1997 owed nothing to youth justice or any other social work practice, and a great deal to the blatant politicisation of law and order issues, a response, according to one observer who was well placed to know, to the 'internal difficulties of the Conservative Party at the time' (Faulkner, 1996, p. 17) (for the influence of David Faulkner's 'principled pragmatism' as senior civil servant see Rutherford, 1996). But, as Faulkner observed in an earlier comment (Faulkner, 1993), this imperviousness to 'expert' advice represented an abandonment of a well established pattern of policy development, and among the experts had been youth justice workers. Rock (1990) notes that civil servants attend conferences, read the papers that emerge from them, and are in contact with representatives of practitioners and with organisations, like NACRO, which have close contact with developments in the field. The influence of practitioners may not often have been direct, but this does not make it less real.

One example of particular importance for youth justice is Local Authority Circular 83(3), which appeared in January 1983 and announced that £15 million would be made available to voluntary organisations to develop what was then called 'intermediate treatment'. The circular encouraged the prioritisation of 'high tariff young offenders' at risk of care or, more often, of custody (Bottoms et al., 1990), and was a major influence on the development of youth justice practice in the 1980s: NACRO (1991) reported that 110 projects had been funded, and that all but 15 had continued after the initial central government money had run out (projects were funded for a maximum of three years). The hope, largely realised, was that local authorities would take over responsibility for the projects once the 'bridging' funds had enabled services in the community to be set up while residential institutions were closed down. The point here is that the civil servants who produced the circular were responding to emerging trends in practice: specialist youth justice (or 'intermediate treatment') teams and centres were being developed by local authorities keen to transfer resources from expensive and ineffective (or worse) 'community homes'; relevant skills, values and expertise were available (Thorpe et al., 1980); and the beginnings of what critics called the 'new orthodoxy' (Jones, 1984) were already evident. The circular was both a reaction to and an attempt to encourage these developments, and it was, of course, greeted with some suspicion by youth justice practitioners, always wary of Conservative governments bearing gifts (Blagg and Smith, 1989, p. 104), although they were themselves its main inspiration.

Later in the 1980s, youth justice practice was to have a wider influence on government policy, the clearest evidence of which was in the Green Paper (Home Office, 1988a) which introduced the term 'punishment in the community', and the associated 'Action Plan' for young adult offenders (Home Office, 1988b). In the view of the Home Office, youth justice workers had shown the way in developing the rigorous and intensive forms of supervision (including 'tracking', the low-tech forerunner of electronic tagging) which were essential if, as the Home Office hoped, community-based punishments were to become 'credible' as alternatives to custody. The gist of both these documents was that the probation service needed to shift its practice with adult offenders in the direction indicated by youth justice – towards closely defined offence-focused practice, with a commitment to monitoring and surveillance, and with prompt and consistent action when the conditions of supervision were breached; if it did not, organisations like the Save the Children Fund and National Children's Home (now NCH Action for Children) would be asked to do the job instead – as they had shown that they were both able and willing to do (Blagg and Smith, 1989, pp. 96–7). Again, government demands which many practitioners found threatening and alien to their sense of values were made possible by what practitioners themselves had done.

Youth Justice Practice in the 1980s: Some Virtues and Vices

The strategies which youth justice workers developed during the 1980s have had a few tenacious critics, notably John Pitts (1988; 1997), but commentators have generally agreed that they made a major contribution to the 'substantial decarceration' (Cavadino and Dignan, 1997, p. 242) of young offenders which took place during the decade. In 1981, 7,700 boys (aged 14–16) were sentenced to custody; in 1990–92 the figure was around 1,400. In percentage terms, the proportion of boys who received custodial sentences as a percentage of all those found guilty or cautioned declined from 8 per cent in 1981 to 2 per cent in the early 1990s (figures from Cavadino and Dignan, 1997, pp. 258, 267). The fall in absolute numbers shows that more than demographic forces were at work; and the percentage figures probably give the best indicator of the overall success of diversion, which was at the heart of the strategy, because they count both diversion from prosecution, through an increased use of cautioning, and diversion from custody, through persuasive interventions in court and the provision of credible community-based measures. In the pursuit of diversion, youth justice workers developed the idea of 'system management', which entailed negotiating with the police to encourage cautioning rather than prosecution, and 'minimum intervention' in the case of young people who were prosecuted. Sometimes, though not universally, on the grounds that help was necessarily harmful (Raynor, 1993), social work intervention was reserved as far as possible for young people whose offending clearly demanded some response, and who were liable to be sent to custody if a plausible alternative were not available.

Taking stock now of what was achieved, it seems clear that, as well as contributing to a genuine shift in penal practice away from custody, youth justice workers in the 1980s developed methods of face-to-face work with young people in trouble which were broadly in line with what subsequent research and analysis have suggested is likely to be most effective in reducing reoffending. This is in a sense paradoxical, since many of these practitioners were strongly influenced by the view that had prevailed since the mid-1970s, that 'nothing worked'. They developed their work without the benefit of the far more positive reports from effectiveness research which appeared from the late 1980s on (Raynor, 1988; McIvor, 1990; McGuire, 1995). Although it is important to avoid exaggerated claims of success (Raynor and Vanstone, 1996; Vennard et al., 1997), it is now reasonable to say that we know what kinds of approach are likely to be more, and less, effective, and the youth justice practice of the 1980s stands up well when it is judged by the criteria the recent research suggests. The 'risk principle' (Andrews et al., 1986) (that the intensity of intervention should be proportional to the risk of reoffending) implies exactly the kind of targeting which youth justice workers tried to maintain; their commitment to community-based rather than institutional measures is supported by the research; although they may not always have known it, the methods they used were cognitive-behavioural and focused on needs and problems relevant to offending, as the research recommends (Vennard et al., 1997); and their methods were also characteristically active and participatory, providing opportunities for the young people to develop their problem-solving skills (McGuire and Priestley, 1995). Though not entirely bereft of theoretical guidance (Denman, 1982), these workers arrived at the kind of practice which is known to be most strongly supported by research on the basis mainly of experience and intuition; and they did so with a confidence, clarity of purpose and coherence of thought which were unusual in social work then, and may be more unusual now.

Contemporary critics of this approach to youth justice, notably Pitts (1988), complained of its 'minimalism', its 'behaviourism', its neglect of aspects of young people's experience which were not directly related to their offending, its 'corporatism' (Pratt, 1989), and its tacit acquiescence in the anti-welfarism of the Thatcherite agenda. In retrospect, some of these charges had considerable force. Although in their actual practice many youth justice workers continued to behave as if something might work, and a focus on offending as the justification for intervention was in many cases compatible with genuine concern and care for children and young people (for an illustration see Smith, 1998), their conviction that nothing worked meant that some workers came to believe that it did not matter what they did, as long as they did little of it. Youth justice workers tended to reject all possibility of preventive or developmental work, on the grounds that this would simply draw more young people into an oppressive system, establishing a lasting institutional split between direct work with young people in trouble and crime prevention efforts (Pitts and Hope, 1997). Their leading value was 'anti-custodialism' (Nellis, 1995), and they succeeded in translating this into effective practice, but otherwise questions of values tended to be reinterpreted as questions of technical competence, leaving 'workers ill-equipped to argue on the basis of values, rather than of technical management, against the possibility of their being expected to take on a more overtly repressive, controlling role' (Smith, 1995, p. 85). The stress on offending as the focus for intervention did not inevitably entail neglect of everything else, but it was certainly compatible with the new stress on enforcement which appeared in the *National Standards*, and potentially compatible with the

> idea that individual moral responsibility exists within a vacuum ... Within this way of thinking 'offenders' clearly occupy so residual a category of citizenship as to endorse the spirit of moral superiority which suffuses the idea of one person 'confronting' or 'tackling' the behaviour of another (Drakeford and Vanstone, 1996, p. 3).

In this way, 'young offenders' become further marginalised and excluded (as, for example, the hyenas of a recent Home Office television crime prevention campaign), and youth justice workers risk becoming parties to their exclusion (Smith and Stewart, 1997).

Some Aspects of the Current Scene

Before suggesting what forms of practice might represent successful resistance to such a trend, and what ideas might underpin them, I want briefly to review some evidence of what the effects of the punitive rhetoric and legislation of the period since 1993 have actually been. First, it seems important to note that from the perspective of support for the decarceration and diversion which were achieved during the 1980s all is not lost. According to the latest full set of *Criminal Statistics* (Home Office, 1997a), a higher proportion of 'young offenders' were cautioned in 1996 than in 1986: the figures for males in 1996 were 86 per cent of 10–13 year-olds, and 54 per cent of 14–17 year-olds; for females the figures were 96 per cent and 76 per cent. The comparable figures for 1986 were 81 per cent and 44 per cent for males, and 94 per cent and 70 per cent for females. It is true that the proportional use of cautioning has declined since 1992 and 1993, when it reached its peak, particularly for 14–17 year-olds (the figure in these years was 63 per cent for males and 84 per cent for females), but there is no indication from these figures of an abandonment in practice of the principle that in general a caution is an appropriate and effective measure for most children and young people who have committed a criminal offence.

The latest *Criminal Statistics* (Home Office, 1997a) devote some space to research on the effectiveness of cautioning. Overall, only 19 per cent of 'young offenders' cautioned in 1994 were convicted of a standard list offence in the subsequent two years (22 per cent of males and 11 per cent of females), and there is no evidence that cautions have become less effective since the mid-1980s. There is, not surprisingly, evidence that conviction rates are higher among those who have received more than one caution (42 per cent with two or more previous cautions were convicted), but the numbers involved are not, and never have been, high: only 15 per cent of those cautioned in 1994 had been cautioned before). The conclusion most people would draw from these figures, that cautions are effective as well as quick and economical, is supported by the well-publicised report of the Audit Commission (1996; for a summary see Perfect and Renshaw, 1997), *Misspent Youth*, which suggests that cautions are the sensible option for first offences and that for subsequent offences the model of enhanced cautions developed by the Northamptonshire Diversion Unit (another practitioner initiative) is preferable to prosecution on grounds of cost, effectiveness and victim satisfaction (Perfect and Renshaw, 1997, p. 190). The principle of diversion by cautioning thus continues to receive authoritative support.

Lest we are induced by various moral and political panics to forget, it is also useful to remind ourselves that rates of known offending among young people have declined since the mid-1980s: successful decarceration was not accompanied by any increase in offending. For the younger (10–13) group, the rate of known (found guilty or cautioned) offenders per 100,000 in the population in 1986 was 2,527 for boys and 761 for girls; in 1996 the figures were 1,365 and 551. For the older group, the male figures are 7,148 and 6,164, and the female figures 1,578 and 1,647 (NACRO Youth Crime Section, 1998). Thus only among the older girls has there been a (small) increase, a trend not evident, incidentally, in the latest figures for young adult (18–20 year-old) women (so there is no basis for concern about a surge in female offending).

The most usual explanation of these figures is that there has been an increase in the use by the police of informal cautions; but only the most minor offences will be dealt with in this way, and it is quite reasonable to claim that these figures at the very least show no evidence of an overall increase in offending by young people. They leave open the possibility that serious – especially violent – offending by young people may have increased, and there are some grounds for thinking that this is so. Oliver James (1995; see also Downes, 1997) argues that violent crime among young people has increased as a consequence of growing relative deprivation and inequality in a 'winner-loser culture'; and Graham and Bowling (1995) suggest that young men at least may 'grow out' of crime rather less quickly than they used to. Rather than repeat the line of youth justice workers in the 1980s – essentially, that young people do grow out of crime and that there is no need to make such a fuss about their offending – I will argue later that practitioners should face these possibilities squarely, and use them to argue for socially inclusive forms of work aimed at reintegration and, in Anthony Giddens's (1994) terminology, the repair of 'damaged solidarities'.

Turning now to recent trends in sentencing, there is no doubt that the most recent figures show increases in numbers sentenced and in the use of custody, but the figures are still well below the level of the mid-1980s. Thus, for example, 36,500 14–17 year-old males and 4,900 females were sentenced for indictable offences in 1996, compared with 29,400 and 3,600 in 1993, but 63,400 and 6,900 in 1986 (Home Office, 1997a, ch. 7). The use of custody showed a similar pattern, being higher than in the early 1990s but lower than ten years before: the figures for Young Offender Institution sentences were 4,800 for males and 200 for females, compared with 3,300 and 100 in 1993, and 8,900 and 200 in 1986; at 13 per cent of sentences on males, the proportional use of YOI sentences was still lower than in 1986. The percentage use of community sentences increased fairly steadily for both males and females throughout the 10-year period, though the actual numbers involved have only risen since 1994; and the recent figures (Home Office, 1997a, Table 7.9) suggest that in the three years to 1996 community sentences were being used instead of fines, rather than instead of custody: this implies more diffuse targeting, and possibly a movement 'down tariff', of community sentences, which Raynor (1998) detects in the case of Probation Orders. This may also be reflected in the fact that the community sentence whose growth has been most rapid for 14–17 year-old males and females is the Supervision Order and not, as one might have expected, the more obviously disciplinarian sentences of Community Service or Attendance Centre Orders.

In summary, then, the most recent trends are towards greater punitiveness, measured by an increase in the use of custody and a decrease in the use of cautions; but the youth justice system overall was still nothing like as punitive in 1996 as it had been in 1986 – a year in which the efforts of youth justice workers described above must certainly have begun to have an impact. In optimistic mood, one could conclude that there is no reason to view the most recent trends as irreversible; they might even turn out to be a mere blip in the long-term trend towards diversion and decarceration; and, after all, Michael Howard is no longer the Home Secretary. Optimists can also point to those parts of the White Paper *No More Excuses* (Home Office, 1997b) and of the Crime and Disorder Bill, published in December 1997, which represent clear breaks with the recent past and (once again) suggest that practitioners are having some influence on policy. These include the provisions for integrated youth offending teams, coordinated local strategies on youth crime which give a central role to local authorities, a national Youth Justice Board to monitor the system, and the more tentative suggestion that the Youth Court might become more of a forum for dialogue and problem-solving – more, in fact, like a Children's Hearing in Scotland – and, some specific measures, like the Reparation Order and the support for 'caution plus' schemes, might also count as grounds for optimism. The White Paper (Home Office, 1997b) also cites with approval a number of practitioner initiatives in the areas of crime prevention, reparation and support for vulnerable young people and their carers; and, in the proposals to pilot various measures before full implementation, there is an indication of greater willingness than under the previous government to consider evidence and admit the possibility of error.

Unfortunately for optimists, however, the Crime and Disorder Bill also contains several provisions which suggest a continuation of repressive and punitive policies towards young people in difficulties, and certainly represent a considerable increase in the sheer scope of the criminal law. The abolition of the presumption of *doli incapax* for 10–13 year-olds will mean that in formal legal terms even the youngest children eligible to appear in criminal courts will be expected to participate in the legal process much as if they were adults (Ashford, 1998), and the clauses on Detention and Training Orders in effect allow for more custodial sentences to be imposed on children as young as 12, with a power held in reserve to extend this to 10 and 11 year-olds (something not apparently contemplated under the previous government). The replacement of the cautioning system by one of reprimands and final warnings may allow for the development of creative interventions at the second stage of warnings, but it must also raise fears of an increase in the number of young people who will needlessly acquire a criminal record. The Bill contains provisions for a remarkable number of new statutory Orders – Parenting Orders, Child Safety Orders, Antisocial Behaviour Orders, Action Plan Orders – which will drastically extend the powers of criminal courts in respect of young people and their carers; and child curfew schemes are among the measures to be piloted. Electronic monitoring of 10–15 year-olds, introduced by the Crime (Sentences) Act, 1997, is also due to be piloted in 1998, in a context in which this most overtly stigmatising of all community-based measures is now regarded as in many respects a success (Mortimer and May, 1997), and former opponents are beginning to be persuaded that they can at least live with it and may learn to like it (see McCullough (1997) and Whitfield (1997) for a sense of these developments among senior probation management). Overall, Butler and Drakeford (1997, p. 218) are surely right to argue that the Labour government's approach to youth justice is consistent with its predecessor's in maintaining an exaggerated sense of crisis and despair, and that 'the party's debate about juvenile crime is being set substantially in the terms developed and most commonly used by its political opponents'. In these circumstances, those who want to be optimistic about the possibilities of inclusionary and integrative youth justice practice will need to look elsewhere than to the government for support. In the remainder of this chapter I will try to outline some possibilities for youth justice workers seeking intellectual and practical resources which might make such optimism rational.

Making Connections: Restorative Justice, Social Theory and Community

In a recent lengthy draft article which tries to summarise what is known from research and practice in restorative justice, John Braithwaite (1997) argues that traditional rehabilitative approaches to work with offenders risk having stigmatising rather than reintegrative effects (cf. Braithwaite, 1989), and that empirically 'programs that strengthen community support for the offender outperform those that wrench offenders out of communities of care into the hands of professionals who offer individual treatment' (Braithwaite, 1997, section 1L; for supporting evidence see Cullen, 1994 and Raynor and Vanstone, 1996). He suggests, too, that restorative justice, as a form of nonviolent conflict-resolution and problem-solving, can contribute to the 'dialogic regulation of social life' (section 1I), as in family group conferencing or 'exit conferences' following inspections of nursing homes (see Makkai and Braithwaite, 1994). The two ideas here, that in 'supervision in the community'

'community' should mean something more than 'not in custody', and that dialogue about crime and conflict is a preferable approach in their resolution to coercion and violence, are central to the themes which I want to explore in what follows. Braithwaite (1997, Introduction) regards restorative justice as the 'unifying banner' behind which, during the 1990s, various related traditions of justice have united, among them the idea of 'making amends' (Wright, 1982), reconciliation (Dignan, 1992), relational justice (Burnside and Baker, 1994), and the 'peacemaking' tradition in criminology (Pepinsky and Quinney, 1991; Pepinsky, 1995), and I will follow this usage here, grouping all these lines of thought as versions of restorative justice. Braithwaite notes, too, the similar ideas developed in thinking about justice influenced by feminist ethics (Heidensohn, 1986; Harris, 1991; Braithwaite and Daly, 1994; Masters and Smith, 1998), and these will also be an important element in the argument below. Further, I will suggest that recent ideas in social and political theory, notably those advanced by Giddens (1994), can contribute to social work's (and youth justice's) understanding of the meaning of 'community', and to its understanding of itself.

I have argued elsewhere (Smith, 1997) that recent work on what makes some forms of community supervision more effective than others, while encouraging and suggestive as far as it goes, is based on a very narrow conception of what it is that should be evaluated. Essentially, it has concentrated on one kind of practice only – intensive group work with relatively serious or persistent offenders: it has insisted on the importance of delivering programmes which follow some manual of cognitive-behavioural methods to ensure that 'programme integrity' is maintained, and has castigated those who dare to deviate (Vennard et al., 1997, p. 51). It has been silent, or largely so, on what else might make a difference, or what 'works' in other aspects of practice. For instance, recent research by Sue Rex (1997) has confirmed what most of us have always intuitively assumed, that the quality of the worker-client relationship (the much-abused term 'client' seems less dehumanising in this context than 'offender') makes a difference to people's self-assessed likelihood of desistance from offending; but you would not guess this from the great bulk of mainstream effectiveness research.

It has been still more neglectful of a question of whose importance every practitioner is fully aware: what kinds of social support (or, in Braithwaite's terms, 'communities of care') do people need if they are to be helped to stop offending? Every study of the personal and social experiences of persistent known 'offenders' reveals that almost all of them have endured various kinds of abuse, neglect, deprivation and misfortune: they are far more likely than the general population to have been in local authority care, to have experienced family abuse, breakdown or loss, to have failed in, or been failed by, the school and training systems, to be homeless or insecurely housed, to suffer from some chronic illness (this applies even to younger people), to have problems with substance misuse, to be unemployed, and to be poor (for a summary of the evidence see Smith and Stewart, 1997). If anybody is genuinely to benefit from an offending-focused cognitive-behavioural programme, at least some of their most basic human needs must first be met; practitioners know this, of course, but, as we saw, there is very little acknowledgement of it in the National Standards by which they are supposed to abide; and the neglect of these issues in the effectiveness research is another symptom of the kind of thinking which sees children and young people in trouble as essentially offenders, marginalising or ignoring all other aspects of their experience. I suggested above that the pessimism which paradoxically underpinned the youth justice practice of the 1980s encouraged this abstraction of 'offending behaviour' from its relational and biographical context; I want to argue now that youth justice workers must re-establish the connection between the offending of young people and their broader social experiences, if they are not again to become complicit in the further marginalisation and exclusion of the already marginalised and excluded (Drakeford and Vanstone, 1996; Goldson, 1997b).

It may be, though, that before looking outwards youth justice workers will have to re-examine themselves. In principle and at its best, social work with offenders was protected from the urges, to which we are all susceptible, to moralise loftily about people who offend or to treat them as other than fellow citizens, by the emphasis in its own professional tradition on insight and self-understanding. This emphasis was exactly what the proponents of radical or 'new' social work in the 1970s objected to: it was argued that it encouraged an individualisation of what were in fact structural and economic problems, and left social work bereft of the possibility of developing a radical social critique (Bailey and Brake, 1975; Pearson, 1975). These critics, however, were in no position to foresee the authoritative transformation of social work's traditional concerns with the inner as well as the outer world into a set of behavioural competencies, and the concomitant development of managerialism, proceduralism and the values of bureaucratic conformity (Nellis, 1995). The American penal reformer Jerome Miller (cited in Pepinsky, 1991) has said that there are only two kinds of criminologists: those who think criminals are different from themselves, and those who don't. The stress on insight into oneself and one's motives which was among social work's traditional preoccupations, while liable to slide into amateur self-analysis or navel-gazing, at least encouraged practitioners, as practical criminologists, to align themselves firmly with the second group, making it harder for them to join in the chorus of condemnation, exclusion and rejection which has featured so strongly in recent political discourses about 'offenders' (Stern, 1996). If it continues to disown those parts of its heritage which cannot be fitted easily into a tidy managerialist model, social work with offenders will risk becoming incorporated into a response to crime problems framed by a discourse of coercion, exclusion and violence. It will also suffer intellectual isolation and impoverishment, because the importance of insight into oneself has recently been restated or rediscovered in criminology (Christie, 1997) and social theory:

> Individuals who have a good understanding of their own emotional makeup, and who are able to communicate effectively with others on a personal basis, are more likely to be well prepared for the wider tasks and responsibilities of citizenship (Giddens, 1994, p. 16).

The same theme is central to the successful nonviolent resolution of conflict sought by the peacemaking movement (Pepinsky, 1995) and by restorative justice as a whole (Masters and Smith, 1998). When criminologists and social theorists are starting to sound like old-fashioned social workers, is it inevitable that social workers should sound like newfangled bureaucrats?

If it is not, and youth justice workers can continue to treat young people who offend as fellow-members of the community, whose offending cannot be 'tackled' in isolation from the wider context of their experience, what are the implications for practice and its organisation? At the level of a social work agency, one can at least imagine what forms of practice might promote a more inclusionary, and less defensive and stigmatising, approach. They would include the decentralisation of agency resources, to make them more accessible and more authentically part of the communities they are supposed to serve; offices would become open and welcoming, offering a range of resources (advice, information, child care) rather than simply being sites for the delivery of cognitive-behavioural programmes; along with this, staff skills and interests would become more diverse, and the agency would be part of an open and productive network of resources including community and youth workers, employment advisers and trainers, and, in European terminology, 'social pedagogues'; and all members of the network would be actively concerned with the generation and dissemination of new knowledge and ideas, especially on those aspects of practice about which little is known at present. The aims of this kind of structure would be to maximise the non-stigmatic, developmental and positive elements of social work with 'offenders', thus reducing the likelihood that they will find contact with the agency inherently punitive and negative, and to bring about constructive changes in the social environment of young people who offend, recognising the moral unacceptability and the practical fatuity of insisting that they must change while their deprived and desolate circumstances do not. Such a structure would begin to bridge the present gap between those who work directly with young people and those concerned with neighbourhood crime prevention (Pitts and Hope, 1997); it would allow for the repair of 'damaged solidarities' (Giddens, 1994), including those of community and family life (see Farrington, 1996 for empirical support for working on family relationships); it would give young people access to local sources of support and help with personal development, thus promoting social inclusion and minimising stigmatisation; and it would allow for the emergence of a youth justice practice that would be less defensive, less limited, and more able to withstand incorporation into a repressive agenda than it is at present.

At this point some readers may well wish to say: (a) it's all right for you to talk; and (b) none of this is new anyway. Of course, resource constraints are a powerful material reality in the daily experience of youth justice workers, and the domination of cost-conscious managerialism in their organisations will often be felt as a heavily inhibiting presence. But it would be wilfully pessimistic to regard the proposals for a more coordinated local approach to youth justice (Home Office, 1997b) as devoid of positive potential, or (worse) as a sinister attempt to extend the coercive powers of the state (Sampson et al., 1988); and there are actually existing examples of strategic approaches to young people in trouble that go at least some way towards the ideal of an integrative and supportive network outlined above. The Freagarrach project in central Scotland (Smith, 1998) provides intensive (but flexible) help and support for the most persistent juvenile offenders in the region, but, rather than being isolated from other community resources, as has been the fate of many 'special' projects, it is, in intention and design, merely the tip of a much more extensive iceberg which involves support from the education department, the police, social work and the Reporters to the Children's Hearings. Educational resources include the provision of special places for young people attending the project, a coherent strategy to reduce school exclusions, and a commitment to joint work on reintegration into mainstream schools; the police support the project with information, ensuring that it can retain a focus on its intended target group; social workers are seconded to the project; the Reporters, discharging their statutory responsibilities for the care and welfare of young people, have supported the principle that attendance at the project should be voluntary, and have given the project time and space to achieve results. The project staff themselves provide an environment of care, comfort and safety for young people who in many cases have little experience of these human goods from elsewhere; they work on issues of offending, of course, but not in isolation from other aspects of the young people's experience; they promote their social reintegration into the worlds of education, training and employment; and they work, where possible, to heal the scars of many years of family conflict and despair. Of course, the project has its failures, and it is no more immune than any other from pressures on resources and the difficulty of maintaining commitment by all relevant parties (aggravated in this case by local government reorganisation); but it shows that it is possible to work with some highly stigmatised, vulnerable and in some cases very unhappy and damaged young people in a way which promotes their integration into a network of care, while not neglecting the reality of the harm done by their offending.

As for the complaint that the suggestions above are not new: in a sense, this is exactly my point. I am concerned with the recovery of forgotten possibilities, memories of social work's past which have been all but eradicated from practice today by managerial diktat and the rule-bound proceduralism of National Standards. Just as social work is at risk of losing touch with its sense of the importance of empathy and insight, so, in the focus of youth justice on the abstracted individual and his (much more rarely her) offending behaviour, it has lost a sense of how it might be mobilised to change social environments rather than personal behaviour. The question of social work's potential to influence the environments of young people in trouble was at the heart of one of the first research studies in this field (Davies, 1969; 1974); if the answers to the question proved clumsy and partial, as they did, that need not be taken as a reason for abandoning the effort for good.

More convincing answers are now emerging from the restorative justice movement (for example, Braithwaite, 1995; Braithwaite and Mugford, 1994), supported by arguments in broader social theory (Giddens, 1994), which are framed in terms not of the rehabilitation or quasi-medical treatment of young people who offend but on their moral education and their reintegration into communities of care. Instead of coercion, exclusion and violence, restorative justice seeks the resolution of conflicts through participatory dialogue; instead of condemning and outcasting 'offenders', it aims to condemn the act while conveying care and respect for the actor; instead of relying on universal, abstract rules (the ethic of justice), it stresses the importance of relationships, empathy, and common participation in problem-solving (the ethic of care) (Gilligan, 1982; Heidensohn, 1986; Masters and Smith, 1998). Instead of making war on 'offenders', it seeks to make peace. Stressing (once again) the centrality of insight into oneself, Pepinsky (1995) writes that the 'first step to peacemaking' is to 'pause to survey what you know and feel', and, in language reminiscent of Giddens (1994), tells us that:

> Peacemaking is the art and science of weaving and reweaving oneself with others into a social fabric of mutual love, respect and concern ... The other attitude is that of ... warmaking. We are all familiar with the art and science of warmaking. We all well know what deterrence is, for example (Pepinsky, 1995).

Giddens (1994) is among those who have associated warmaking, violence and aggression with culturally derived conceptions of masculinity (see also Newburn and Stanko, 1994); he suggests that as a result women have become 'the keepers ... of the moral fabric of social life' (ibid., p. 176), and asks 'will femininity, with its greater emphasis on interdependence, emotional understanding and care, increasingly be transferred to the public sphere?' (ibid., p. 190). The movement for restorative justice is arguably an example of exactly this movement of feminine values and concerns from the private sphere (especially that of the family) to the public domain. Masters and Smith (1998) suggest that Braithwaite's (1989) theory of reintegrative shaming, with its stress on mutually caring interdependent relationships, is the first full feminist theory in criminology; they note connections between restorative justice in practice and the feminine 'ethic of care' (Gilligan, 1982), personified in a criminal justice context by Heidensohn (1986) as 'Persephone', as opposed to 'Portia', the incarnation of the (masculine) ethic of justice. My point here is that there is much in restorative justice, conceived in this way, which social workers, if they can remember their own heritage, should find attractive. The skills (and the values) required for effective restorative justice in settings such as family group conferences are precisely those historically associated with social work: the capacity to convey acceptance, empathy, and 'non-possessive warmth' (Truax and Carkhuff, 1967), informed by respect and care for persons, and hope and belief in their ability to grow and change. In a broader context, that of local communities, the principles of restorative justice entail a commitment to the values of community cohesion and social justice (Bottoms and Stelman, 1988).

This last invocation of the term 'community' may also prompt an irritated response in some readers, even if they have not been irritated by its earlier appearances. It is a notoriously slippery and problematic concept, some of whose recent uses (for example, Etzioni, 1993) are far more about excluding the undesirable than including the vulnerable; and social workers have often struggled to make sense of it (Sampson and Smith, 1992). In this chapter I have sought to use 'community' not as a nostalgic or magical appeal to an imagined past of social harmony and homogeneity, but in ways which indicate the practical sense which it might acquire in the context of community supervision. Most fundamentally, this means recognising that 'young offenders' are, like the rest of us, members of some community; it means acknowledging that they have social rights and claims like the rest of us, which youth justice workers should encourage and enable them to exercise effectively, rather than seeing the task as over when the offending behaviour programme has been implemented in all its proper integrity. This is a matter of ethical obligation as well as of practical effectiveness. But restorative justice practice also allows for the active promotion by social workers of what Braithwaite (1995) calls 'micro-communities' of care. A family group conference may be the right model when family members are present, supportive, interested and capable; for young people without families in any conventional sense social workers may have to think more widely about who the relevant members of such a caring network might be (teachers, care workers, fellow-students, friends, employers, more distant relatives, local shopkeepers); very few young people are so isolated that there will be no-one to care, or no-one whose good opinion they value. Finally, restorative justice holds out the longer-term promise (Braithwaite, 1997, section 1J) of encouraging more democratic and participatory approaches to the maintenance of social order, by 'making the many dialogically responsible instead of the few criminally responsible', as retributive justice does. Just as whole-school approaches to bullying are more effective than those which rely solely on one-to-one mediation (for suggestive examples from Japan see Lewis, 1989 and Masters, 1997), the involvement of many people in responding to offending should be more effective in preventing crime than the involvement of a few. In the process, conflicts will be restored to those to whom they belong (Christie, 1977).

Conclusion

The main aim of this chapter has been to suggest how the practice of community supervision might be informed by ways of thinking drawn from the various traditions which have flowed into the movement for restorative justice. I am conscious that, despite my acknowledgement of the obstacles which recent penal developments in England and Wales (though less so in Scotland) present to the development of integrative and positive forms of practice, workers in the field may still have found the discussion naïvely optimistic and utopian. If one thinks of the immediate future only, there must be a great deal of force in such a charge; but there are also grounds for longer-term optimism in the emergence of a genuinely international movement for restorative justice, whose theoretical and empirical supports are far stronger than in the past. I have argued that the achievements of youth justice workers in the 1980s were substantial – indeed, the figures suggest that they were more influential in 1996 than in 1986 – but that they were also limited by a narrow set of theoretical assumptions and by an underlying pessimism about the possibility of doing good. Change in the 1980s did not happen overnight, nor will it in the late 1990s; but an approach to practice that is more rounded theoretically, better informed empirically, and above all more (but rationally) optimistic, should be better equipped to achieve more lasting and more fundamental change.

References

Andrews, D.A., Keissling, J.J., Robinson, D. and Michus, S. (1986), 'The risk principle of case classification: an outcome evaluation with young adult probationers', *Canadian Journal of Criminology*, Vol. 28, pp. 377–84.

Ashford, M. (1998), 'Making criminals out of children: abolishing the presumption of *doli incapax*', *Criminal Justice*, Vol. 16, No. 1, p. 16.

Audit Commission (1996), *Misspent Youth: Young People and Crime*, London, Audit Commission.

Bailey, R. and Brake, M. (eds) (1975), *Radical Social Work*, London, Edward Arnold.

Blagg, H. and Smith, D. (1989), *Crime, Penal Policy and Social Work*, Harlow, Longman.

Bottoms, A.E., Brown, P., McWilliams, B., McWilliams, W. and Nellis, M. (1990), *Intermediate Treatment and Juvenile Justice*, London, HMSO.

Bottoms, A.E. and Stelman, A. (1988), *Social Inquiry Reports*, Aldershot, Wildwood House.

Braithwaite, J. (1989), *Crime, Shame and Reintegration*, Cambridge, Cambridge University Press.

Braithwaite, J. (1995), 'Reintegrative shaming, republicanism and policy' in H.D. Barlow (ed.), *Crime and Public Policy: Putting Theory to Work*, Oxford, Westview Press, pp. 191–205.

Braithwaite, J. (1997), 'Restorative justice: assessing an immodest theory and a pessimistic theory' (http://www.aic.gov.au/links/braithwaite).

Braithwaite, J. and Daly, K. (1994), 'Masculinities, violence and community control' in T. Newburn and E.A. Stanko (eds), *Just Boys Doing Business? Men, Masculinities and Crime*, London, Routledge, pp. 189–213.

Braithwaite, J. and Mugford, S. (1994), 'Conditions of successful reintegration ceremonies: dealing with juvenile offenders', *British Journal of Criminology*, Vol. 34, No. 2, pp. 139–71.

Burnside, J. and Baker, N. (eds.) (1994), *Relational Justice: Repairing the Breach*, Winchester, Waterside Press.

Butler, I. and Drakeford, M. (1997), 'Tough guise: the politics of youth justice', *Probation Journal*, Vol. 44, No. 4, pp. 216–19.

Cavadino, M. and Dignan, J. (1997), *The Penal System: An Introduction*, 2nd edn, London, Sage.

Christie, N. (1977), 'Conflicts as property', *British Journal of Criminology*, Vol. 17, No. 1, pp. 1–17.

Christie, N. (1997), 'Four blocks against insight: notes on the oversocialization of criminologists', *Theoretical Criminology*, Vol. 1, No. 1, pp. 13–23.

Cullen, F.T. (1994), 'Social support as an organizing concept for criminology', *Justice Quarterly*, Vol. 11, No. 4, pp. 527–59.

Davies, M. (1969), *Probationers in their Social Environment*, London, HMSO.

Davies, M. (1974), *Social Work in the Environment*, London, HMSO.

Denman, G. (1982), *Intensive Intermediate Treatment with Juvenile Offenders: A Handbook of Assessment and Groupwork Practice*, Lancaster, Centre of Youth, Crime and Community, Lancaster University.

Dignan, J. (1992), 'Repairing the damage: can reparation work in the service of diversion?', *British Journal of Criminology*, Vol. 32, pp. 453–72.

Downes, D. (1997), 'What the next government should do about crime', *Howard Journal of Criminal Justice*, Vol. 36, No. 1, pp. 1–13.

Drakeford, M. and Vanstone, M. (eds.) (1996), *Beyond Offending Behaviour*, Aldershot, Arena.

Etzioni, A. (1993), *The Spirit of Community*, New York, Crown.

Farrington, D.P. (1996), *Understanding and Preventing Youth Crime*, York, Joseph Rowntree Foundation.

Faulkner, D. (1993), 'All flaws and disorder', *The Guardian*, 11 November.

Faulkner, D. (1996), *Darkness and Light: Crime, Justice and Management for Today*, London, Howard League for Penal Reform.

Giddens, A. (1994), *Beyond Left and Right: The Future of Radical Politics*, Cambridge, Polity Press.

Gilligan, C. (1982), *In a Different Voice: Psychological Theory and Women's Development*, Cambridge, Massachusetts, Harvard University Press.

Goldson, B. (1997a), 'Children in trouble: state responses to juvenile crime' in P. Scraton (ed.), *'Childhood' in 'Crisis'?*, London, UCL Press.

Goldson, B. (1997b), 'Children, crime, policy and practice: neither welfare nor justice', *Children and Society*, Vol. 11, No. 2, pp. 77–88.

Graham, J. and Bowling, B. (1995), *Young People and Crime*, London, Home Office.

Harris, M.K. (1991), 'Moving into the new millennium: towards a feminist vision of justice' in H.E. Pepinsky and R. Quinney (eds.), *Criminology as Peacemaking*, Bloomington and Indianapolis, Indiana University Press.

Heidensohn, F. (1986), 'Models of justice: Portia or Persephone? Some thoughts on equality, fairness and gender in the field of criminal justice', *International Journal of the Sociology of Law*, Vol. 14, pp. 287–98.

Home Office (1980), *Young Offenders*, Cmnd 8045, London, HMSO.

Home Office (1988a), *Punishment, Custody and the Community*, Cm 424, London, HMSO.
Home Office (1988b), *Tackling Offending: An Action Plan*, London, Home Office.
Home Office (1992), *National Standards for the Supervision of Offenders in the Community*, London, Home Office.
Home Office (1995), *National Standards for the Supervision of Offenders in the Community*, London, Home Office.
Home Office (1997a), *Criminal Statistics England and Wales 1996*, Cm 3764, London, The Stationery Office.
Home Office (1997b), *No More Excuses – A New Approach to Tackling Youth Crime in England and Wales*, Cm 3809, London, The Stationery Office.
James, O. (1995), *Juvenile Violence in a Winner-Loser Culture*, London, Free Association Books.
Johnson, T. and Parker, V. (1996), *Is a Persistent Young Offender a 'Child in Need'?*, London, Rainer Foundation.
Jones, R. (1984), 'Questioning the new orthodoxy', *Community Care*, October, pp. 15–17.
Jordan, B. (1983), 'Criminal justice and probation in the 1980s', *Probation Journal*, Vol. 30, No. 3, pp. 83–8.
Kelly, A. (1996), *Introduction to the Scottish Children's Panel*, Winchester, Waterside Press.
Lewis, C. (1989), 'Cooperation and control in Japanese nursery schools' in J.J. Shields (ed.), *Japanese Schooling: Patterns of Socialization, Equality and Political Control*, University Park and London, Pennsylvania State University Press.
Makkai, T. and Braithwaite, J. (1994), 'Reintegrative shaming and regulatory compliance', *Criminology*, Vol. 32, No. 3, pp. 361–85.
Masters, G. (1997), 'I conflitti e la mediazione nelle scuole in Giappone' in G. Pisapia and D. Antonucci (eds), *La Sfida della Mediazione*, Padova, CEDAM, pp. 133–46.
Masters, G. and Smith, D. (1998), 'Portia and Persephone revisited: thinking about feeling in criminal justice', *Theoretical Criminology*, Vol. 2, No. 1, pp. 5–27.
McCullough, C. (1997), 'Electronic monitoring of offenders: a task for probation?', *Vista*, Vol. 3, No. 1, pp. 12–19.
McGuire, J. (ed.) (1995), *What Works? Reducing Reoffending: Guidelines from Research and Practice*, Chichester, John Wiley and Sons.
McGuire, J. and Priestley, P. (1995), 'Reviewing "what works": past, present and future' in J. McGuire (ed.), *What Works? Reducing Reoffending: Guidelines from Research and Practice*, Chichester, John Wiley and Sons.
McIvor, G. (1990), *Sanctions for Serious or Persistent Offenders: A Review of the Literature*, Stirling, Social Work Research Centre, University of Stirling.
Mortimer, E. and May, C. (1997), *Electronic Monitoring in Practice: The Second Year of the Trials of Curfew Orders*, London, Home Office.
NACRO (1991), *Replacing Custody*, London, NACRO.
NACRO Youth Crime Section (1998), *Facts about Young Offenders in 1996*, London, NACRO.
Nellis, M. (1995), 'Towards a new view of probation values' in R. Hugman and D. Smith (eds), *Ethical Issues in Social Work*, London, Routledge.
Newburn, T. and Stanko, E.A. (1994), *Just Boys Doing Business? Men, Masculinities and Crime*, London, Routledge.
Pearson, G. (1975), *The Deviant Imagination*, London, Macmillan.
Pepinsky, H.E. (1995), *A Peacemaking Primer*, http://www.soci.niu.edu~critcrim/pepinsky/hal.primer.

Pepinsky, H.E. and Quinney, R. (eds.) (1991), *Criminology as Peacemaking*, Bloomington and Indianapolis, Indiana University Press.

Perfect, M. and Renshaw, J. (1997), 'Highlights of our misspent youth', *Vista*, Vol. 2, No. 3, pp. 188–96.

Pitts, J. (1988), *The Politics of Juvenile Crime*, London, Sage.

Pitts, J. (1997), 'Restorative justice: a better deal for the socially excluded?', *Social Work in Europe*, Vol. 4, No. 3, pp. 49–57.

Pitts, J. and Hope, T. (1997), 'The local politics of inclusion: the state and community safety', *Social policy and Administration*, Vol. 31, No. 5, pp. 37–58.

Pratt, J. (1989), 'Corporatism: the third model of juvenile justice', *British Journal of Criminology*, Vol. 29, No. 2, pp. 236–54.

Raynor, P. (1985), *Social Work, Justice and Control*, Oxford, Blackwell.

Raynor, P. (1988), *Probation as an Alternative to Custody*, Aldershot, Avebury.

Raynor, P. (1993), 'Systems purists, client refusal and gatekeeping: is help necessarily harmful?', *Social Action*, Vol. 1, pp. 4–8.

Raynor, P. (1998), 'Reading Probation Statistics: a critical comment', *Vista*, Vol. 3, No. 3, pp. 181–85.

Raynor, P. and Vanstone, M. (1996), 'Reasoning and Rehabilitation in Britain: the results of the Straight Thinking on Probation (STOP) programme', *International Journal of Offender Therapy and Comparative Criminology*, Vol. 40, No. 4, pp. 272–84.

Rex, S. (1997), 'Desistance from offending: experiences of probation', paper to British Criminology Conference, Belfast, July.

Rock, P. (1990), *Helping Victims of Crime: The Home Office and the Rise of Victim Support in England and Wales*, Oxford, Clarendon Press.

Rutherford, A. (1996), *Transforming Criminal Policy*, Winchester, Waterside Press.

Sampson, A. and Smith, D. (1992), 'Probation and community crime prevention', *Howard Journal of Criminal Justice*, Vol. 31, pp. 105–19.

Sampson, A., Stubbs, P., Smith, D., Pearson, G. and Blagg, H. (1988), 'Crime, localities and the multi-agency approach', *British Journal of Criminology*, Vol. 28, pp. 478–93.

Smith, D. (1995), *Criminology for Social Work*, Basingstoke, Macmillan.

Smith, D. (1997), 'How much do we really know about what really works?', in *Information: The Reality and the Potential*, proceedings of the 13th Annual Probation Information and Research Conference, Worcester, Midlands Probation Training Consortium, pp. 31–40.

Smith, D. (1998), 'Social work with offenders' in R. Adams, L. Dominelli and M. Payne (eds.), *Themes, Issues and Critical Debates*, Basingstoke, Macmillan.

Smith, D. and Stewart, J. (1997), 'Probation and social exclusion', *Social Policy and Administration*, Vol. 31, No. 5, pp. 96–115.

Stern, V. (1996), 'Let the ex-cons back in', *The Guardian*, 2 May, p. 15.

Thorpe, D.H., Smith, D., Green, C.J. and Paley, J.H. (1980), *Out of Care: The Community Support of Juvenile Offenders*, London, Allen and Unwin.

Truax, R.R. and Carkhuff, C.B. (1967), *Towards Effective Counselling and Psychotherapy*, Chicago, Aldine.

Vennard, J., Sugg, D. and Hedderman, C. (1997), *Changing Offenders' Attitudes and Behaviour: What Works?*, London, Home Office.

Whitfield, D. (1997), 'Electronic monitoring: what are the real issues?', *Vista*, Vol. 3, No. 1, pp. 20–27.

Wright, M. (1982), *Making Good: Prisons, Punishment and Beyond*, London, Hutchinson.

9   Institutional Troubleshooting: Lessons for Policy and Practice

JUSTINE ASHTON AND MARK GRINDROD

Introduction

The current orthodoxy amongst those developing youth justice policy and practice is inclined towards holistic and multi-agency approaches. This is all to the good, but there has been a tendency for those agencies working with children who are at risk of entering the penal system to regard their involvement as being at an end if a child is remanded or sentenced into prison custody. It is quite right that great efforts should be made to keep children out of prison but if this fails there is still much that can be done. Far from reducing the level of involvement when a child is sent to custody, it can be argued that it should actually be increased. Certainly the prison service and prison staff should be included in any inter-agency approach to working with young people in the criminal justice system. Preconceptions held one for the other of those working within and without the prison system are often wildly inaccurate and a barrier to effective cooperation. In this chapter we hope to show that agencies working outside the prison service can become involved in effective working with children and young people who are detained in custody. We will look at the background, methods, findings and case studies of the Howard League's *Troubleshooter Project* for 15 year-olds and the Children's Society *Remand Rescue Initiative*, both of which are, or have been, based directly in custodial institutions.

The Howard League has been active in the debate on youth justice, youth crime and the promotion of effective and humane alternatives to the use of prison service custody for children throughout the past decade (Howard League, 1989, 1993, 1994, 1995a, 1995b and 1997a). Through research, policy initiatives, briefings and conferences the League has continued to promote the use of community penalties and to oppose the increasing incarceration of

170

children and young people. In the 1990s the Howard League departed from its traditional role as commentator, critic and policy promoter to provide a 'hands on' service to children and young people within the prison estate. This *Troubleshooter Project* was a first for the Howard League and the experience and results of the project are discussed in the first part of this chapter. The latter part of the chapter will examine the Children's Society *Remand Rescue Initiative* which commenced in January 1997 and has developed and refined the previous work of the Howard League and applied it nationally.

Background

The *Troubleshooter Project* was launched on September 1993 with the specific goal of securing the release of 15 year-old children from prison custody. The project was a development of the body of work carried out by the Howard League which highlighted and condemned the costly and damaging practice of incarcerating children and young people in the prison system. With reconviction rates of 89 per cent within two years of release for 15 and 16 year-olds (Hansard 8 May 1998, Column 162) and alarming levels of self-injury (Howard League, 1995b), the need to divert young people from prison was clear. The suicides of three 15 year-old boys (Philip Knight, Jeffrey Horler and Craig Walsh) in prison in the course of 1990 and 1991 provided a tragic impetus to the development of the project.

At the time the project was being considered there were some 25 15 year-old boys and girls remanded in prison custody in England and Wales and Home Office policy was in favour of diversion (Home Office, 1994). Furthermore, Section 60 of the Criminal Justice Act 1991 provided for the abolition of the use of prison custody for the remand of 15 and 16 year-olds. Within a context in which the use of prison custody for children of this age appeared to be waning therefore, the direct involvement of *Troubleshooter* in individual cases was to be part of a last push to decarcerate 15 and 16 year-olds altogether.

The project and its specialist staff enjoyed the support and guidance of a dedicated advisory committee made up of members of the Prison, Police, Social and Probation Services, the magistracy, voluntary child care charities, youth justice organisations, academia, funding bodies and non-governmental organisations. This group met regularly throughout the lifetime of the project and was crucial to its successful establishment and running. Having the backing of such a strong multi-disciplinary committee gave the project both legitimacy and a degree of 'muscle' in negotiating with the various agencies involved in the youth justice system and the Home Office and the Department of Health were represented by observers at the group's meetings. The support for the project of the agencies and practitioner groups in the youth justice system was particularly welcome given the attention that youth crime was attracting at a political level. The period immediately preceding the inception of the project saw a dramatic about turn in the way that the criminal justice system deals with juveniles. Government and opposition parties vied with each other to sate a perceived desire amongst the populace for 'get tough' policies in dealing with young people in trouble. Long regarded as an area where consensus policies should prevail, youth justice became a political football punted between the parliamentary front benches to the hysterical urgings of an ill-informed but fanatical tabloid press (Graef, 1995; Goldson, 1994 and 1997). The result of this sea change in policy was a rapid rise in the number of juveniles remanded and sentenced into prison. On 30 June 1991, some 102 15 year-olds were held in prison service custody. On the same date in 1993 this figure had risen to 126 and by 1994 it stood at 167. A staggering 224 15 year-old children were held in English and Welsh prisons by June 1996 and at the end of June 1997 this had increased further to 278. By the end of March 1998 the figure had decreased slightly but it still stood at an alarming 251 (HM Prison Service, 1998)

Tough choices had to be made in the light of the drastically increased number of children being sent to prison and the project focused its initial attention on Feltham Young Offender Institution and HM Prison and Young Offender Institution Bullwood Hall.

The Principal Objectives and Strategy

The principal objectives of the *Troubleshooter* project were essentially fivefold. First, to rescue 15 year-olds from prison custody; second, to provide support and advocacy to such children during their time in prison custody; third, to advise and assist agencies working with juveniles in the criminal justice and penal systems; fourth, to monitor the circumstances of those children referred to the project and the factors leading to their being sent to prison; and, fifth, to disseminate the lessons learned by the project and to promote good practice in working with young people who are at risk in the criminal justice system. From the outset the aim was to be as pro active and directly involved in individual cases as possible. This meant establishing direct contact not only with children in custody but also with all those people and agencies exerting an influence in the process that led to their coming into prison. Youth justice teams and Social Services departments, parents and legal representatives were contacted as a matter of course, and the courts, Department of Health and Prison Service were consulted on a regular basis.

The project enjoyed and encouraged a multi-disciplinary approach to resolving the problems faced by 15 year-old children in prison and sought to forge improved contacts between all the agencies involved. To this end in addition to individual casework it brokered agreements between the various interested parties and brought them together in a series of workshops and seminars to foster a better understanding of the issues and problems in working with juveniles in prison, and to explore potential solutions to them.

Detailed information was gathered on each and all of the children referred to the project to determine who was sent to custody, from where, for what and for how long. Two detailed reports were written to disseminate good practice and to draw attention to the plight of the 15 year-olds being sent into prison custody (Howard League 1995c and 1997b). The reports made wide use of case studies to dispel stereotypical and often misleading images of the demonic 'juvenile offender' which were being used to justify the emphasis given to incarceration as a legitimate part of government youth justice policy (Davis and Bourhill, 1997; Graef, 1995; Goldson 1994 and 1997).

Project Implementation and Operation

The project could only function if high quality information was provided as soon as possible after a child was sent to prison. To this end the cooperation of both the Prison Service and the probation team at Feltham was sought and obtained to establish regular and reliable updates on 15 year-olds being received into the prison. A referral form for use at the induction stage in the prison was designed for use by prison staff. This was used to glean detailed information on the child, their home circumstances and any contact they may have had with statutory agencies. The form also served as a prompt to assess specific areas of concern such as vulnerability and risk of self-harm. Access to the prison's own records was granted and a daily list of 15 year-olds in Feltham was faxed through to the Howard League offices. This information allowed contact to be made with the relevant local authority youth justice team on the day following the young person's reception into Feltham in the vast majority of cases. As youth justice teams became familiar with the project's work a number increased the speed of operations still further by making referrals themselves on the day of remand or sentence into custody. Agreement was reached with particular teams or groups of teams to speed up and improve the provision of detailed information on the children coming in to custody. In the Inner London area a pro forma was designed and approved by the principal youth justice officers and the Probation Service for use in all cases where a young person was remanded or sentenced into prison. As well as containing all the child's details and any concerns regarding vulnerability or health problems the form also required youth justice teams to state the reasons that were given by the court for the custodial remand or sentence and any alternatives that had been available and proposed to the court. In this way the form could be used proactively to prompt the agencies to consider the legitimacy of such decisions and the adequacy or otherwise of the community alternatives put forward.

The *Troubleshooter* team was given free access to Feltham Young Offender Institution and Remand Centre to allow visits to children as soon as possible after their admission. A small office and access to a telephone was also provided by the prison service. Visits took place on the prison units themselves and not in the formal visits area. The flexibility of the prison management and staff in allowing access to the young people when and where project workers chose was an extremely important factor in the successful running of the project. Once initial contact had been made with the young person and the youth justice team responsible for them, the reasons and circumstances which led to their imprisonment could be established. Appropriate action could then be taken to remedy the situation, challenge the decision to place the child in custody, or investigate the possibility of an alternative community placement.

For those remanded to prison action may have involved no more than the very process of contacting the youth justice team and notifying them that a young person from their area was in custody. Over 11 per cent of the remanded children came into custody from adult magistrates courts and in a significant number of cases the youth justice team had neither been represented at court nor informed of the result. More commonly initial intervention involved liaising or advising on proposals to put forward bail support at the next court appearance, making an appeal to the Crown Court for bail or exploring the availability of a local authority secure accommodation placement and the funding to match it. In line with the pro-active approach employed elsewhere the project made direct contact with and representations to, Social Services management, the Department of Health, the Home Office, the Prison Service and the courts to promote the cases of individual children and to secure resources for alternative placements to prison custody.

In cases where the children were sentenced to prison the principal concerns revolved around the possibility of an appeal against the sentence and working with the young person and the staff within the prison to maintain as positive a service as possible. In a number of cases this extended to temporary release packages for young people to ameliorate the effects of prison, assist rehabilitation and allow the young person to obtain education or training to improve their chances of obtaining work on release. The use of temporary release as a useful tool in the planning of constructive regimes for juveniles under sentence has been endorsed by HM Chief Inspector of Prisons, Sir David Ramsbotham in recent reports on the YOI estate (HM Inspectorate of Prisons, 1997). Ramsbotham argues that the blanket restriction is not justified for those outside the high security prison units and he points with approval to the successful reintroduction at HMYOI Thorn Cross of the opportunities afforded by challenging community programmes outside the prison establishment (HM Inspectorate of Prisons, 1998).

Finally, the project was also heavily involved in the cases of children sentenced to periods of two years and more under the provisions of section 53(2) of the Children and Young Persons Act 1933. The Prison Service and Home Office were encouraged to expedite the allocation of these young people to local authority secure accommodation.

The Principal Findings from the Troubleshooter Project

When?

- 650 children were referred to the project between December 1993 and June 1996.
- 345 children were referred as remands to prison custody.
- 305 children were referred as sentenced to prison custody.
- There was a 280 per cent increase in remand referrals between the first and last six months of operation rising from 32 in January to June 1994 to 90 in the same period of 1996.
- There was a 205 per cent increase in sentenced referrals between the first and last six months.

Who?

- 97 per cent of the children referred to the project were male.

- 34 per cent of the children referred to the project were Black or Asian.
- 45 per cent of those referrals who were remanded to prison custody were Black or Asian.
- 26 per cent of those referrals sentenced to prison custody were Black or Asian.
- 55 per cent of those sentenced to over two years custody were Black or Asian.
- 25 per cent of the total group of children had no previous convictions.
- 80 per cent of the children were either excluded or were long term non-attenders at school.
- 31 per cent of the children had either been in care to or accommodated by Social Services.
- 29 per cent of the children were assessed as being particularly vulnerable to bullying, self-harm and suicide.

From Where?

- 75 per cent of children came into prison custody from the youth court.
- 11 per cent of children came into custody from the adult magistrate's court.
- 14 per cent of children came into custody from the Crown Court.
- 27 per cent of children came from Inner London boroughs.
- 29 per cent of children came from Outer London boroughs.
- 16.5 per cent of children came from the south and southeastern region.
- 22 per cent of children came from the Thames Anglia region.

For What?

- 29 per cent of children were sent to custody on burglary charges.
- 27 per cent of children were sent to custody on robbery charges.
- 17 per cent of children were sent to custody on violence charges.
- 11 per cent of children were sent to custody on motor related charges.
- 3 per cent of children were sent to custody on sex related charges.
- 58 per cent of children remanded to custody had a noncustodial outcome to their case.

For How Long?

- 50 per cent of custodial sentences were of two to four months duration.
- 14 per cent of custodial sentences were for over 12 months.

- The number sentenced to over 12 months custody rose by 300 per cent between 1994 and 1996.
- 30 per cent of children spent over one month in prison on remand.
- 9 per cent of children spent over three months in prison on remand.
- 34 per cent of remanded children were released within seven days.

A cursory examination of the statistics reveals a number of issues that are particularly startling and are of grave cause for concern. First, the huge leap in the number of children who were sent into prison custody was a particular cause for alarm. The number of 15 year-olds remanded to custody came close to tripling in the space of two years while the number sentenced more than doubled. Secondly, and related to this, was the fact that 58 per cent of those who were made the subject of a custodial remand did not receive a custodial sentence at the end of their court case. Clearly there were a large number of children who were being wrongly remanded to prison custody by the courts. Thirdly, there was a hugely disproportionate use of prison custody being made in respect of Black children. This was particularly marked in the case of those remanded to custody where the Black and Asian children accounted for 45 per cent of referrals to the project, and for those children sentenced to two years and over of which 55 per cent were from the minority ethnic groups. Fourthly, a large number of the children were being sent to prison from adult courts with no specialist training in, or knowledge of youth justice law and issues. Fifthly, the children entering prison custody were overwhelmingly from damaged and marginalised backgrounds. At the time they were sent to custody eight out of 10 had been out of school, one in three had been in the care of the local authority and another third were assessed as being particularly vulnerable and at risk of bullying or self-harm in the prison environment. Such issues pose discomforting questions in relation to both child-welfare and criminal justice.

The nature and degree of involvement of the *Troubleshooter* and the *Remand Rescue* teams in the case of each child coming in to custody was specific to the needs and circumstances of the individual. Indeed this 'tailored' approach is imperative. Notwithstanding the case by case method of working, however, particular themes have emerged which are best illustrated by reference to real cases.

In Prison by Default

The Absence of Appropriate Alternatives

Andrew was one of the most damaged and difficult young people with whom the *Troubleshooter* team worked in the course of the project. The subject of a Care Order, he was living with foster carers. There were allegations that he had been the subject of sexual abuse by an adult from outside the family and he was prone to acts of self-harm and was extremely confrontational with adults in general, and with representatives of social services in particular. The level of his offending was, however, unspectacular as he had only received two cautions before his arrival at Feltham on a six month sentence for an offence of attempted robbery. The offence had been committed when Andrew was 13 years of age. Andrew came into conflict with other inmates and staff within hours of his arrival at Feltham. He was placed in the hospital unit following a number of self-inflicted injuries including slashing of wrists and attempted hangings. He refused to see his social worker, youth justice officer or guardian ad litem and would only accept contact and communicate with the staff from *Troubleshooter*. We visited whenever we were in the prison, provided him with a radio and his favourite comics, and kept him supplied with pencils, crayons and paper as he enjoyed drawing. We acted as the contact between Andrew, his solicitor and social services and built up enough trust for case conferences involving Andrew to be set up in the prison to discuss and plan for the future. Supported by the prison staff, we negotiated a package whereby Andrew would be released on license by the governor, to be placed into a local authority secure unit on welfare grounds. In this way he would spend his sentence in a more appropriate environment where his psychological problems could begin to be addressed. The process was delayed, despite the goodwill of all involved, because of the difficulty in getting a psychiatric assessment of Andrew in the prison. Feltham's health centre is a national resource for the Prison Service but it is not provided with a full time psychiatrist. Ironically perhaps, the proposed transfer to secure accommodation fell through when it was vetoed by Andrew himself. He feared that he would be kept in the secure environment beyond the date on which he was due to be released from prison and was not prepared to countenance this. The relationship with social services had dramatically improved, however, and a detailed post-custody plan was drawn up including Andrew and his parents. Without the *Troubleshooter's* involvement it is unlikely that any such rapprochement could have been reached.

Another damaged child, **Bill** was both a risk to himself and to others as a result of being sexually abused. He was physically immature for his age, excruciatingly thin and very nervous. Numerous placements had been tried and had broken down as Bill absconded from local authority accommodation or came into violent conflict with those charged with his care. Bail having been refused, no specialist secure or therapeutic place was available as an alternative to prison custody. At Feltham he was placed on the hospital wing as he was unable to cope even on the 'vulnerable persons unit'. *Troubleshooter* liaised with the youth justice team to organise daily visits and supplied him with a radio and comics in an attempt to keep his spirits up. The priority was to ensure that he survived until sentence when Social Services hoped to have an intensive supervision package to put before the court. This succeeded and Bill was eventually sentenced to two years supervision. The pre-sentence and psychiatric reports indicated that prison would only make Bill more damaged and potentially abusive.

The lack of resources in the health and child care systems leads to the incarceration of damaged children in prisons which are neither designed nor equipped to deal with such vulnerable youngsters. Perversely, those most in need of intensive therapeutic treatment find themselves in the institutions which are least able to provide it, and where their problems are exacerbated rather than solved (Howard League, 1995b).

Deficits in Mental Health Provision

Chris was arrested having failed to attend court on charges of theft and robbery. He was found by the police sitting in the lotus position on top of a phone box. Clearly in need of psychiatric care, there was no placement available for a child in an appropriate hospital. As a result Chris was remanded to Feltham by the magistrates where he was placed in the health care centre. The court wrongly assumed that the Prison Service had the resources to assess Chris prior to his second court appearance. As no legal aid had been granted for the purpose, no psychiatrist was instructed to prepare the required report on Chris in the first week of his stay in prison. He was clearly confused and distressed and was too ill to communicate coherently with anyone. *Troubleshooter* worked with the prison staff to meet his physical needs and try and ensure his safety. He was finally assessed and transferred to receive inpatient psychiatric treatment after two weeks on prison remand.

Dan's case was one of the most difficult and protracted with which the project was concerned. He was physically big, even intimidating, but had a child-like view of life which revolved around clothes, music and attending raves. As we got to know him well it became clear that he spent much of his time in a fantasy world. Unable to read, he would spend hours studying the pictures in fashion and music magazines. We were heavily committed in supporting Dan and also in brokering between the agencies involved with him to find a solution to his predicament. Initially remanded for offences of violence committed in the children's homes he had been living in, his situation deteriorated following his assaulting his social worker in court, the stabbing of a fellow inmate and the slashing of a prison officer with a home-made knife. His behaviour was bizarre, violent, unpredictable and dangerous. Because of the nature of his offences it was impossible to find a vacancy in local authority accommodation or to generate much sympathy for his case amongst his local Social Services and youth justice teams. He remained in Feltham for 17 months. Part of this time was under sentence for the original offences but the larger part was spent on remand or awaiting sentence for those offences committed while in custody!! It was clear to all who dealt with Dan that there was something 'wrong'. In all, some 11 psychiatric assessments were made on him. It was agreed that he suffered from a personality disorder but as this did not amount to a mental illness it did not merit admission to hospital. There was a marked and understandable reluctance to label a 15 year-old as a psychopath, and in any event there was no secure hospital unit for someone of his age and with his level of violence. No one wanted to see a juvenile admitted to Broadmoor. No one believed that prison was the place for him either, but the outside agencies were less than dynamic in seeking or providing alternatives. The turning point came for Dan when a psychometric test, carried out by the psychology team in Feltham, showed him to have an IQ of 47. This suggested a significant mental impairment which had never previously been identified. Further enquiry suggested it was possibly because of physical damage to the brain when he was nine. It is a mystery as to why this profound disability had not been spotted in the educational system. The isolation of the problem pointed to an explanation for Dan's reliance on violence rather than verbal communication, and opened new avenues to his future care and treatment. A final medical report led to Dan's placement under mental health legislation by the sentencing court in a privately run specialist unit in East Anglia which was prepared to address his behavioural problems.

The Failure of Legal Safeguards

Illegal Remands to Prison Custody

Frank and Grant are examples of 15 year-olds being placed in prison inappropriately and illegally because of a failure to follow basic legal principles. Grant was charged with a commercial burglary. He was remanded into custody by the Youth Court in the belief that, in the words of the presiding magistrate, this would 'teach him a lesson'. We pressed his lawyers to refer the case back to court and informed them of the grounds of appeal against the courts' decision. Notwithstanding the Crown Prosecution Service's decision to raise no objections to bail, Frank was remanded to custody by the Magistrates Court on a charge of taking and driving away a motor vehicle. The bench considered that, despite the fact that he had not been involved in any accident or been apprehended while speeding, Frank posed a risk to the public by virtue of driving whilst disqualified. Quite apart from the bench's incorrect interpretation and application of the criteria for a remand to custody, of greatest concern was the reluctance of the solicitor to appeal the decision despite Frank's explicit instructions to do so. When contacted by *Remand Rescue* project workers he cited a concern that to lodge an appeal on behalf of so prolific an offender might damage his credibility!!

Juveniles may not be sent to prison on remand save where the offence is sexual or violent in nature, or bears a sentence on conviction of 14 years or more, *and* the public would be at risk of serious harm if the placement was anywhere else (Section 23(5) Children and Young Persons Act 1969). The courts in both these cases were clearly ignorant of the basic legal protections put in place to keep all but the most serious juvenile offenders out of prison. The consequences for Grant were nearly fatal, and fortunately his attempt to hang himself failed. He was released on bail at his next court appearance. After a month on remand in Doncaster Remand Centre Frank was placed on supervision for 12 months.

Initially granted bail subject to a residence requirement, **Henry** was found at a neighbour's flat playing video games half an hour after curfew. He was arrested, brought to Lewisham Youth Court the next day and remanded to Feltham for breaching his bail conditions. Henry had no convictions. Tiny in stature, he looked nearer 10 than 15 years old. Despite accurate legal advice from an experienced youth justice officer, the court wrongly presumed that a breach of a bail condition was a criminal offence and compounded the error by remanding him to prison rather than to local authority accommodation.

We visited and supported Henry while his youth justice team organised a swift return to court on appeal. Henry was released from custody by a different youth court six days later and granted unconditional bail.

Illegal Sentences to Prison Custody

Both **Liam and Mark** were sentenced to prison custody by two different courts in the same region within a matter of days. A basic error was made in each of their cases which led to them being imprisoned illegally. In each case guilty pleas were entered to the charges against the children when they were 14 years old. The court then sentenced them following their 15th birthdays. At the time YOI custody was not available to magistrates as a sentence for those under the age of 15. The relevant date for the court in determining the age of the defendant is the date on which a plea of guilty or a finding of guilt is made. For sentencing purposes both Liam and Mark should have been dealt with as 14 year-olds, therefore. The illegality of the sentences was only picked up when the *Troubleshooter* met Liam and Mark in Feltham. As soon as the error was detected the youth justice teams and solicitors were contacted and the boys were released the same day. In Mark's case the youth justice worker had queried the legality of the sentence with the court clerk but had been assured it was correct. In Liam's case his solicitor, who was candid as to his inexperience of youth court work, had questioned the sentence and was again assured of its correctness. It is profoundly disturbing that such a fundamental error could have passed unnoticed by magistrates, court clerks, lawyers and youth justice practitioners. If the Howard League project had not picked up the courts' mistakes it is extremely likely that the boys would have served out their illegal sentences in prison.

Whilst members of the Youth Court bench undertake regular training on the specific (and constantly changing) provisions relating to children, it is significant that there are no specific training or certification requirements for those lawyers who represent children in the criminal courts. This is an anomaly that must be addressed, particularly given the extremely serious consequences for the child that can result from a lawyer's failure to keep abreast of this complex area of the law. It is unacceptable that juveniles find their way into prison because the courts and lawyers are ignorant of the legal protections introduced in recognition of the need to keep them out. The Judicial Studies Board, the Law Society and the Bar Council must improve the standard of legal training on the law as it applies to juveniles for all those who practice in the youth justice system. This training should include all magistrates and court clerks and not simply those on the Youth Court panel.

Agencies in Conflict: The Client in the Lurch

A Failure to Take Responsibility

Oscar was an Irish traveller arrested in Kent and remanded to Feltham. A dispute arose as to whether he was 14 or 16 years of age. If he were 14 then the remand would be unlawful by virtue of his age. A further complication arose when it was discovered that Oscar was known to one London borough and had given an address in yet another. For a considerable amount of time the dispute as to which of the three Social Services departments had responsibility for Oscar diverted attention away from the priority issue of removing an underage child from prison. He was finally released following the *Troubleshooter's* intervention.

The Conflicting Criteria for Custody

Scott was remanded to custody for an offence of kidnapping. He had no previous convictions and was not known to Social Services. The Youth Court was satisfied that the offence was so grave that bail was not appropriate and that a security requirement was necessary to protect the public from serious harm. The offence had been committed with another boy who, while a year younger than Scott, was well known to the courts. The co-defendant was also denied bail and was placed in local authority secure accommodation. He could not be remanded to prison by virtue of his age. Despite vigorous representations the local authority did not look for a secure accommodation placement for Scott, on the basis that he did not satisfy the Children Act 1989 criteria for such a placement. Caught between the devil and the deep blue sea, Scott spent five months in Feltham on remand. His predicament is not uncommon. The reluctance of local authorities to allow the use of secure accommodation except as a last resort is understandable because of competing pressures on social services budgets. It is the child in prison, however, who pays if the court insists on custody.

    Dean was remanded into prison custody for burglary. Some months previously he had allegedly verbally threatened a residential care worker, leading to a charge of common assault. He experienced a number of difficulties in custody, culminating in an attempt to hang himself. Dean's youth justice worker contacted several secure units, all but one of which declined to accept him, citing the risk posed to staff. On other occasions, evidence has emerged of units informing other homes about a child's behavioural difficulties. Whilst such information can be helpful in developing a care plan once the child has successfully been placed, it frequently results in the recipient unit declining to accept the child in the first place. It is difficult to understand how units designed and licensed to accommodate the most damaged and damaging young people can justify such selectivity. This often results in needy children suffering still greater harm through remaining in prison custody.

Prejudging the Issues and Prejudicing the Case

Geoff was remanded to custody by an adult magistrate's court on an extremely serious charge which had attracted a great deal of media attention. He had never been in trouble with the law before and was unknown to Social Services. The Youth Court wanted to place Geoff in secure accommodation but initial approval for funding was overruled by social services senior management. Geoff's case was prejudged on the basis that he was likely to receive a lengthy sentence in prison at the outcome of the case and that the cost of a placement in secure accommodation while on remand would be a waste of money. At a time of intense pressure on resources Geoff was not a priority.

It was clear on visiting Geoff that he was in an intense state of shock. He was withdrawn, introspective, frightened and tearful. All those who had dealings with Geoff in Feltham agreed the appropriate place for him was in the child care system. Despite the best efforts of the Prison Service, which provided a special regime, extra unit visits, round the clock monitoring and counselling Geoff made a serious attempt to hang himself. We wrote directly to the Director of Social Services to voice our very real concern that Geoff would not survive if he stayed in prison. As a result he reassessed the case and reversed the decision on funding and Geoff was moved four days later. Because of the exceptional circumstances of the case an 18 month Supervision Order was the sentence handed down by the Crown Court.

Delay and the Damage Caused

Remanded to prison custody on a serious charge, 11 months passed before **Ivor's** case was finally disposed of by way of a custodial sentence from the Crown Court. On his arrival in prison Ivor was already a volatile, demanding and difficult young person. He was completely isolated in Feltham as contact with his family and, with the passage of time, his Social Services department dwindled to the occasional letter. We provided his only regular source of visits and support. No funding for a secure accommodation placement was forthcoming from the local authority. The lengthy remand, the attendant isolation and uncertainty as to what the future held, led to a marked deterioration in Ivor's mental state and behaviour, and he spent some three months on the segregation unit. Although a difficult case, the delay in getting it to court directly contributed to the problems in looking after Ivor, and frustrated the commencement of any treatment to address his challenging behaviour.

Post-custody Priorities

Appeals: The Need for Speed

Never previously in trouble with the courts, **Melvin** was sentenced to four months for an assault. Because of a breakdown in communications it was the *Troubleshooter* who alerted Melvin's Social Services team to his being sentenced into custody. We advised Melvin to lodge an appeal against sentence in the Crown Court as soon as possible but he was reluctant to do so as he feared an increase in his sentence. We spent some time discussing the possible outcomes of an appeal and pointed out that it was very unusual for the Crown Court to increase a sentence. After liaison with his parents, youth justice worker and social worker the decision was made to appeal. The final bar to appeal presented itself in the form of an unenthusiastic solicitor but once he had been replaced, the appeal went ahead and a supervision order was substituted for the original sentence.

Isolation

Sentenced on a burglary matter to detention in a Young Offender Institution **Vernon** was transferred from Feltham to Portland Young Offender Institution in Dorset within four days of his arrival. Neither his mother nor his youth justice team knew of this until contacted by the *Troubleshooter*. The reason for the transfer was the chronic lack of space in Feltham. The result was Vernon's complete isolation from his family who could not afford to make the six hour round trip from Surrey to visit him. **William** was also transferred to Portland after a few days in Feltham. His situation was even more acute, as he lived in Norfolk. For his family to visit Feltham would have posed problems, for them to travel a further 150 miles to Dorset proved impossible. What was more William had been assessed by Social Services as someone who was particularly vulnerable to bullying and self-harm. In both cases we lent our support to applications on behalf of the young people to have them transferred back to within reach of their families. Vernon was moved back to Feltham within a few weeks but William remained in Portland for the duration of his sentence.

Remand Rescue – Consolidating and Focusing Decarcerative Practice

The *Troubleshooter* project was intended from its inception to have a limited duration. From the outset, the objective was to rescue individual children and to develop models for good practice. Following the project's scheduled conclusion in December 1996, therefore, the Children's Society *Remand Rescue Initiative* consolidated *Troubleshooter's* impact and focused its remit. Taking as its starting point the commitment, in the form of Section 60 of the Criminal Justice Act 1991, to end custodial remands of juveniles, the *Initiative* has concentrated exclusively upon unconvicted children and those awaiting sentence.

Illegal and Unnecessary Custody

Interestingly, given that five years have elapsed since the Howard League began publicising factors contributing to the overuse of custody for children, recently emerging themes have again echoed those highlighted during *Troubleshooter's* life span.

Lack of understanding of the remand criteria on the part of defence lawyers or magistrates continues to contribute to the significant number of remands classified as 'illegal' by project workers. In the majority of instances, our ability to interview the child within a couple of days of their remand and to appraise their solicitor of the issues lead to release at the second remand hearing. Most significantly, many local authorities simply lack the resources such as remand foster carers, remand homes and comprehensive bail support. In a third of the 430 cases dealt with between January and December 1997, no offer of bail support was made to the court at the child's first appearance. Whilst many children had been assessed as unsuitable for available services, in 52 (12 per cent) of cases, the local authority was simply unable to provide any remand services for this age group.

The imposition by the Crime and Disorder Act of a statutory duty upon local authorities to provide bail support for children and young people is to be welcomed, but no additional funds will be available to finance the creation of such schemes. It remains to be seen whether local authorities, beset by the inevitable expense of establishing young offender teams, and of supervising the new range of sentences, will be in a position to offer the comprehensive support required to keep children out of custody.

Not Vulnerable Enough?

The Children's Society has serious reservations about locking up children (The Children's Society, 1993). Local authority secure accommodation is not regarded as a panacea and project workers will argue for a community based remand in every appropriate instance. Where children are charged with grave offences, however, and face a refusal of bail, the focus of 'rescue' attempts inevitably shifts to local authority secure accommodation as a 'lesser evil' than prison custody. In the *Initiative's* first year, of the 143 children released prior to sentence, 22 were moved into secure accommodation. Where no secure order was sought, the reasons given ranged from a lack of places (22 cases) or of funds (34), to a failure to anticipate a custodial remand (86). In an alarming 124 cases, the child was assessed by youth justice workers as being unsuitable for placement in secure accommodation. In some instances, age was the obstacle. In others, however, the child had had considerable input in the past leading to an understandable, but nonetheless inappropriate, assessment by social services that they had 'had his chances'.

Operating from a prison base is fundamental to assessing children at particular risk. Observing a child in the environment in which they are suffering can reveal more than any amount of contact in a visits hall. Particularly valuable is the easy access to the establishments' other professionals. The insight of prison officers, teachers, probation officers and psychologists into children's welfare has proved invaluable in securing the release of many damaged or disturbed young people previously thought to be capable of 'coping' with custody. Of the 430 children in 1997 project workers identified 368 instances of 'risk' (some children where included in more than one category of 'risk'). These included a propensity to self-harm, drug dependency, victimisation and a general inability to cope.

The Future for Remanded Children

The Criminal Justice Act, 1991, recognising the inherent vulnerability of all remanded juveniles, empowered the courts to remand direct to secure accommodation. Implementation was postponed pending the creation of sufficient secure places. At the time, an additional 35 places were estimated to be required, a total number of between 690 and 710 secure accommodation places are now felt to be necessary (Home Office, 1998). The juvenile remand population at the end of December 1997 stood at 224 (HM Prison Service, 1997).

In the light of this, the Crime and Disorder Act provides for the partial implementation of section 60 of the 1991 Criminal Justice Act. In future, 15 and 16 year-old boys who '*by reason of* [their] *physical or emotional immaturity or a propensity ... to harm* (themselves) (Clause 81(5A), Crime and Disorder Bill 1997) may be remanded direct to secure units. Any attempt to impose a definition of vulnerability is fraught with difficulties. Inevitably larger children, or those whose difficulties which, whilst considerable, do not easily fit the categories listed in the Act will be disadvantaged. Moreover, it is unclear whether a child's classification will be revisited and reassessed at subsequent appearances, to take account of problems that arise whilst in custody. Most alarmingly, the Act implies that a child's vulnerability is to be assessed by reference not only to his or her personal characteristics but also with regard to the availability of secure unit vacancies. With remanded 12 to 14 year-old boys and 15 and 16 year-old girls 'competing' for the same supply of vacancies, extremely damaged and vulnerable children will inevitably continue to be condemned to prison custody.

Future Troubleshooting

It is hard to conceive how the enhanced regimes currently envisaged by the Home Office are to be developed and resourced by a prison service already compelled (by substantial cuts) to restrict positive regimes for a soaring population. Further the needs of developing and vulnerable adolescents and the security and disciplinary requirements of an environment designed for the most serious and dangerous adult offenders are fundamentally incompatible. No amount of adaptation will ever be adequate to transform prisons into acceptable homes for children.

The youth justice system is currently characterised by widespread change.

All the indications are, however, that despite the diversionary focus of the early 1990s, the need for working with children in a custodial setting will be significantly greater in the years immediately ahead. Court-ordered secure remands for 12 to 14 year-olds and 15 and 16 year-old girls are on the point of introduction. The first child prisoners have been admitted to Medway Secure Training Centre in Kent and the irresistible rise in the juvenile prison population has led to gross overcrowding in prisons and the 'doubling up' of children in single cells.

It now seems ironic that when the *Troubleshooter* project was established it was hoped that it would make itself redundant within two years by securing the release of those few 15 and 16 year-olds who remained within the prison system. Now, more than ever, there is a need for committed focused intervention and advocacy on behalf of the marginalised children who are being sent into prison custody. The Howard League and the Children's Society have been tenacious and courageous in challenging the dogmatic 'get tough' policy approach to children who fall foul of the law. The *Troubleshooter Project* and the *Remand Rescue Initiative* have proved to offer practical, effective and much needed interventions within prisons themselves. While the medium-term goal must be to end the imprisonment of children altogether we hope that the example afforded by these two projects will encourage other agencies to commit themselves to working directly with children in prison.

References

The Children's Society (1993), *A False Sense of Security: The Case Against Locking Up More Children*, London, The Children's Society.

Davis, H. and Bourhill, M. (1997), '"Crisis": The Demonisation of Children and Young People' in P. Scraton (ed.), *'Childhood' in 'Crisis'*, London, University College London Press.

Goldson, B. (1994), 'The Changing Face of Youth Justice', *Childright*, 105, pp. 4–5, London, Children's Legal Centre.

Goldson, B. (1997), 'Children in Trouble: State Responses to Juvenile Crime' in P. Scraton (ed.), *'Childhood' in 'Crisis'*, London, University College London Press.

Graef, R. (1995), 'Media and Political Interest in Youth Crime in the UK in The Howard League', *Child Offenders: UK and International Practice*, pp. 1–4, London, The Howard League for Penal Reform.

HM Inspectorate of Prisons (1997), *Young Prisoners: A Thematic Review by HM Chief Inspector of Prisons for England and Wales*, London, Her Majesty's Inspectorate of Prisons for England and Wales.

HM Inspectorate of Prisons (1998), *HMYOI Stoke Heath: Report of an Unannounced Short Inspection 14–15th October 1997*, London, Her Majesty's Inspectorate of Prisons for England and Wales.

HM Prison Service (1997), *HM Prison Service Strategic Planning Group Statistics December 1997*, London, HM Prison Service.

HM Prison Service (1998), *HM Prison Service Strategic Planning Group Statistics March 1998*, London, HM Prison Service.

Home Office (1994,) *Prison Statistics England and Wales*, Cm. 3087, London, HMSO.

Home Office (1998), news release 12 January 1998, London, Home Office.

Howard League (1989), *Suicides at Leeds Prison: An Enquiry into the Deaths of Five Teenagers 1988/89*, London, The Howard League for Penal Reform.

Howard League (1993), *Suicides at Feltham. Report of an Inquiry into Suicides of Four Young Men Between August 1991 and March 1992*, London, The Howard League for Penal Reform.

Howard League (1994), *Good Practice Guide in Working with Young Offenders*, London, The Howard League for Penal Reform.

Howard League (1995a), *Child Offenders: UK and International Practice*, London, The Howard League for Penal Reform.

Howard League (1995b), *Banged Up, Beaten Up, Cutting Up. Report of the Howard League Commission of Inquiry into Violence in Penal Institutions for Teenagers under 18*, London, The Howard League for Penal Reform.

Howard League (1995c), *Troubleshooter: A Project to Rescue 15 Year Olds from Prison*, London, The Howard League for Penal Reform.

Howard League (1997a), *Lost Inside – The Imprisonment of Teenage Girls. Report of the Howard League Inquiry into the Use of Prison Custody for Girls aged under 18*, London, The Howard League for Penal Reform.

Howard League (1997b), *The Howard League Troubleshooter Project: Lessons for Policy and Practice*, London, The Howard League for Penal Reform.

10 Appealing for Justice for Children and Young People: A Critical Analysis of the Crime and Disorder Bill 1998

CHARLES BELL

Introduction

We are witness to a time of major upheaval both within and outside of the formal youth justice system. The Crime and Disorder Bill is, at the time of writing this chapter, under consideration by the House of Commons. The references to clauses that follow should be taken by the reader to reflect the structure of the Crime and Disorder Bill as passed by the House of Lords and introduced in the House of Commons on 1 April 1998. The Bill was presented to the House of Lords for its first reading on 2 December 1997 and was preceded by the government's White Paper *No More Excuses – A New Approach to Tackling Youth Crime in England and Wales* published on 27 November 1997 (Home Office, 1997a). Whilst much of the content of the White Paper and the Bill had been open to consultation beforehand (Home Office, 1997b, 1997c and 1997d) some of the more contentious proposals and provisions were conspicuously absent, for example, giving the Secretary of State power to introduce custody for children as young as 10 (Clause 69), came as a complete surprise, unjustified by the evidence and at loggerheads with 90 years of criminal justice policy in England and Wales. In addition to this caveat there were clauses in the Bill when presented to parliament which purported to give the Secretary of State power to make *regulations* or to provide *guidance* in relation to certain provisions which, at the time of writing and whilst the Bill remains the subject of initial Parliamentary scrutiny, are unpublished – even in draft form. It is only possible to speculate (on the basis of from the series of consultation papers referred to above) what such guidance might comprise. Ministers have divulged little, consistently rebutting requests for clarification and referring instead to the government's plans to 'pilot' many of its provisions in order to inform the detail of guidance and regulations. Legislation which develops in this way can only undermine the integrity of the legislature in taking authority from it and transferring it to the executive, that is – the government. This process comprises a worrying dilution of the fundamental principles of a liberal democracy.

The youth justice system is on the verge of a new horizon: a system that is to be driven by electoral commitments on the part of the Labour Party to halve the time that it takes to process cases through the Youth Court and to reduce the burden of legal aid (see for example, Labour Party, 1996). Taken together these two commitments will inevitably lead to greater injustice for children than is currently the case. Coupled with these pledges is a belief, not supported by research on the youth justice system, that *doing something* to children, young people and their parent(s) will prevent further offending. Indeed that belief is so pronounced that Clause 34 of the Bill states:

34 (1) It shall be the principal aim of the youth justice system to prevent offending by children and young persons.

(2) In addition to any other duty to which they are subject. It shall be the duty of all persons and bodies carrying out functions in relation to the youth justice system to have regard to that aim.

Similarly, despite the acknowledgement within the influential Audit Commission report *Misspent Youth* (Audit Commission, 1996), acknowledging that the conditional discharge has consistently been the most effective disposal available to the Youth Court in terms of preventing reoffending, Clause 62 of the Crime and Disorder Bill provides that such a disposal should only be available in *exceptional circumstances* where a child or young person has been given a final warning by the police within the preceding two years.

This chapter is therefore intended to 'appeal' for justice for children in its widest sense in the hope that it can assist those directly engaged within the new youth justice system, to recognise and avoid the inequities that may arise as the government's flagship legislation is brought into effect. 'Flagship' it certainly is, given that it comes after five years where the politicians of both main parties have attempted to 'outgun' each other on issues of law and order. The background is one where children in trouble and their parents have constantly been the target – caught in the crossfire of two political parties seeking to oust each other into the political wilderness. As it is the Labour Party have apparently gained the ascendancy through adopting what were hitherto regarded to be Conservative policies, repackaging them and marketing their message in a manner which they perceive to be acceptable to the electorate.

This 'hijacking' of Conservative policies is exemplified by a number of provisions in the legislation. Clause 34 will establish the prevention of offending as being the principal aim of the youth justice system. Clauses 12 and 13 will establish child safety orders in relation to children under 10, and Clause 15 will give local authorities power to make child curfew schemes. Clause 36 requires local authorities to establish, in partnership with other agencies, youth offending teams. Clause 9 will introduce the Parenting Order. All these new and contentious powers are subject to 'piloting'. Prior to the general election in May 1997, the Conservative government published a consultation paper entitled *Preventing Children Offending* (Home Office, 1997e). The government of the day intended to give courts the power to impose a Parental Control Order where a child had demonstrated behaviour which was likely to lead to offending or had resulted in conviction for an offence. It proposed establishing child crime teams comprising police officers, probation officers, teachers, social workers and a Health Service representative. This was to be overseen by the local authority chief executive and the Chief Officers of the representative agencies. Criteria for referral to the team would include evidence or strong indications of behaviour by a child under 10 which, but for his/her age, would be criminal or the existence of a number of factors known to be associated with criminal activity by children. Unlike the Labour government, the previous administration took the view that new legislation was not necessary to introduce such ideas:

> The Children Act 1989 requires local authorities to plan services for children in need. Under Schedule 2, they must take reasonable steps to reduce the need to bring criminal proceedings ... and to encourage children in their area not to commit criminal offences. Also, section 17 of the Act empowers the Secretary of State to add further duties and powers to those already conferred on local authorities. The effect of these provisions is that it would not be necessary to legislate simply to establish the proposed teams (Home Office, 1997e, ch. 3, para. 58).

The new youth justice system created by the Labour government goes considerably further down the road of repressive intervention than that proposed by the Conservatives. The concept of *doli incapax*, the presumption in law that a child under the age of 14 years does not necessarily know at the time that the act which prima facie constitutes an offence in law was *seriously* wrong, is to be abolished and the Secretary of State will have power to introduce custody for children as young as 10. Such policies were not even on the Conservative agenda. In that sense, the Home Office under the stewardship of Jack Straw has not only endorsed Conservative policies but has taken the process of demonising children in trouble several stages further than those proposed by his predecessor Michael Howard. It is also interesting to note that the recommendations arising from the Narey report, *Review of Delay in the Criminal Justice System* (Home Office, 1997f), commissioned by the previous Conservative administration but acted upon by the new Labour government have, with few exceptions, been endorsed and inform government policy in this area. One such exception was the recommendation to do nothing to the youth justice system at the present time other than to have a separate and informed review encompassing the purpose of the Youth Court, the range of penalties available to it, and the role of agencies other than the police. An opportunity for cool reflection informed by both academic research and practice experience has thus been lost in favour of reactionary political imperatives.

The outcome of all this is of course that the new government, having an unchallengeable majority in the House of Commons, is currently so powerful to ensure that what is in the Bill is fated to become statute with little meaningful challenge. This overbearing majority may be perceived as reflecting the 'will of the people' (though as suggested above this has arisen for negative reasons rather than any identifiable distinction between the policies of the two major political parties) but in itself it is going to contribute to injustices within the new youth justice system. Justice is not a concept ordinarily associated with political expedience and the manner in which this legislation has passed through the parliamentary process to date has not allowed for objectivity or impartiality. Justice is something that arises out of the division of powers within our constitution where notionally there is separation between the executive, the legislature and the judiciary. In theory it is the legislature that is required to review and where necessary curb the authority of Her Majesty's Government and it is for the courts to protect the citizen from any misuse of power thereafter. In practice, parliament endorses the authority of government and it is left to the judiciary to regulate and rebuke government. This was demonstrated under the previous administration where the then Home Secretary, Michael Howard, regularly found himself on the losing side when actions were taken against him in the courts both in this country and in Europe. The Crime and Disorder Bill, and future proposals concerning the reform of the Youth Court outlined in skeleton within the most recent White Paper (Home

Office, 1997a), will impact upon that constitutional balance in a number of respects. That the present composition of parliament has such a hefty government majority coupled with the fact that the Labour Party has chosen to sustain youth crime as a high profile political issue (it could easily have placed it above populist politics and subject to informed consensus as was the case in the 1980s when Douglas Hurd was Home Secretary with John Patten as his Minister of State) does in itself suggest that unjust legislation will find itself onto the statute book without recourse to meaningful review or revision. In consequence there will be considerable scope for both judicial interpretation of provisions within the Crime and Disorder Act and review of the guidance and regulations that are made by the Secretary of State.

Throughout the 1980s both legislation and practice within the field of youth justice was characterised by principles of *decriminalisation, diversion* from the formal criminal justice system and the *decarceration* of children and young people from custodial institutions. These guiding principles were underpinned by the concept that responses to offending behaviour should be proportionate to the seriousness of the offence taking full account of mitigating factors and therefore reflecting minimum necessary intervention. This process was seen as being so successful that the government of the day encouraged increased cautioning of young adult and adult offenders (Home Office Circulars, 1985 and 1990) and imposed statutory limitations on the scope of the courts to impose custodial sentences to all offenders by virtue of the Criminal Justice Act 1991 (Goldson, 1997). That same Act also removed, in the case of 14 year-olds, the sanction of detention in a Young Offender Institution. Six years on the Crime and Disorder Bill takes us in exactly the opposite direction! The government's decisions to proceed with implementation of Secure Training Orders and to extend the availability of electronically monitored curfew orders to children as young as 10 (at present in pilot areas only), coupled with many of the provisions in the Crime and Disorder Bill concerning children in trouble are likely to cause an international outcry when the UK government reports on its implementation of the United Nations Convention on the Rights of the Child in January 1999. The Committee, which has responsibility to monitor implementation and to make recommendations, has consistently emphasised that implementation should be guided and informed by the United Nations Standard Minimum Rules for Juvenile Justice – the Beijing Rules (Resolution 40/33, United Nations, 1985). When the UK government presented its Initial Report to the UN Committee in 1995 (Department of Health, 1994) the Committee recommended, amongst other things:

that serious consideration be given to raising the age of criminal responsibility throughout the areas of the United Kingdom (and that there should be an) introduction of careful monitoring of the new Criminal Justice and Public Order Act 1994 with a view to ensuring full respect for the Convention on the Rights of the Child. In particular, the provisions of the Act which allow for, *inter alia*, placement of secure training orders on children aged between 12 and 14, indeterminate detention, and the doubling of sentences which may be imposed on 15–17 year old children should be reviewed with respect to their compatibility with the principles and provisions of the Convention (United Nations Committee on the Rights of the Child, 1995).

Despite the UN Committee's scathing indictment of youth justice policy and practice in England and Wales, the Crime and Disorder Bill threatens to perpetuate, and even intensify, the very issues over which the Committee confesses concern. Indeed, the principles of decriminalisation, diversion, and decarceration which so effectively steered youth justice throughout the 1980s and early 1990s have been abandoned and the new legislation will only serve to criminalise children, promote their prosecution and condemn them to incarcerative regimes.

Criminalisation

Clause 31 of the Crime and Disorder Bill places children aged 10–14 on an equal footing with adults by virtue of abolishing the concept of *doli incapax* which had previously required the prosecution to prove that a child under the age of 14 knew that what he or she was doing was seriously wrong. The government, when in opposition, had mooted simply reversing the burden of proof by laying it on the defence to prove that a child did not know that what s/he was doing was seriously wrong. On 3 March 1997 Jack Straw, when launching the Labour Party's election manifesto, stated that 'it would be open to the defence in a particular case to argue that the child did not know the difference between right and wrong (for example, if the child had serious learning handicaps)' (Labour Party Press Release, 1997). But now the government is determined to go further than that and remove what in practice is a little-used protective mechanism. This cuts across one of the very concerns raised by the UN Committee in 1995. Rule 4 of the Beijing Rules states:

In those legal systems recognising the concept of the age of criminal responsibility for juveniles, the beginning of that age shall not be set at too low an age level, bearing in mind the facts of emotional, mental and intellectual maturity (United Nations, 1995).

Clause 12 Crime and Disorder will, when implemented, effectively criminalise those *below* the age of criminal responsibility by creating the Child Safety Order. If such an order is breached, behaviour which, but for a child's age, would be deemed criminal, may result in a deprivation of liberty coupled with a suspension of parental responsibility. The fact that the Order is to be made in a Family Proceedings Court is not an expression of the government's concern with the welfare of such children. If that was the case the Crime and Disorder Bill would have inserted the new power into the Children Act 1989 which would have required the court to consider the child's welfare as paramount as provided by Section 1(1) of the Children Act. Moreover the court would also need to take into account the other considerations required by the Children Act by way of the 'welfare checklist'. The real reason behind this arrangement is that the standard of proof required will be 'on the balance of probabilities' which is less strict than that of the Youth Court where the 'offence condition' would have had to be proved 'beyond a reasonable doubt'. Where a child is found to be in breach of a requirement made under a Child Safety Order a court will be empowered to deprive the parent of care and control and make a care order perhaps coupled with a secure accommodation order. The 7(7) Care Order (which was available in criminal proceedings by virtue of the Children and Young Persons Act 1969 (until its abolition under the Children Act 1989) is effectively reinvested albeit in relation to children below the formal age of criminal responsibility! The UN Beijing Rules anticipate such quasi-criminal legislation. Rule 3 states:

(1)   The relevant provisions of the Rules shall be applied not only to juvenile offenders but also to juveniles who may be proceeded against for any specific behaviour that would not be punishable if committed by an adult.

(2)   Efforts shall be made to extend the principles embodied in the Rules to all juveniles who are dealt with in welfare and care proceedings.

Interestingly Rule 3 continues:

(3)   Efforts shall be made to extend the principles embodied in the Rules to young adult offenders (United Nations, 1985).

The Crime and Disorder Bill will create further quasi-criminal orders to which Rule 3 above has relevance. The Antisocial Behaviour Order introduced by Clause 2 of the Crime and Disorder Bill will apply to children aged 10 or over, and will simply require a court to form the opinion that the child acted in a manner likely to cause harassment, alarm or distress. The Order is prohibitory in nature over a minimum of two years duration. Breach of prohibitions will amount to a conviction which may, in the case of a young person, result in a fine or six months imprisonment. The Sex Offender Order that will be borne from Clause 3 of the Bill, is similar in terms of consequences but may be made in respect of a child or young person who has not necessarily been convicted of a sexual offence but has simply been reprimanded or warned for an alleged sexual offence.

Local authorities will be empowered under Clause 15 of the Bill to introduce curfews in relation to children below the age of 10. Where such a curfew is in force children will be excluded from a public place after 9.00 p.m. except when accompanied by a responsible adult. Curfews may be made for 'the purpose of maintaining order'. It is instructive to consider this new power in relation to the European Convention on Human Rights. Article 8 provides:

(1)   Everyone has the right to respect for his private and family life, his home and his correspondence.

(2)   There shall be no interference by a public authority with the exercise of this right except such as is in accordance with the law and is *necessary* in a democratic society in the interests of national security, public safety or the economic well-being of the county, *for the prevention of disorder or crime*, for the protection of health or morals, or for the protection of the rights and freedoms of others (Council of Europe, 1950).

Imposing curfews for *the purpose of maintaining order* gives considerable scope for state interference, and goes well beyond justifying that such restrictions are necessary for the *purpose of preventing disorder or crime*. Moreover, there must be some question as to whether a genuine and serious threat to the maintenance of order can be demonstrated by local authorities. It must be the case that they will have to demonstrate first, that there is a serious and genuine threat to public order and, second that they have been unable to maintain order amongst children below the age of 10 despite having fulfilled their duties and exercised their powers under the Children Act 1989. Additionally the Crime and Disorder Bill requires local authorities to consult with the police and 'such other persons or bodies as it considers appropriate' before making a curfew. There is good case law (*W v UK*, 1987 10 EHRR 48) to suggest that before parental rights are infringed as will be the case where a curfew is in force their views and interests must be considered. There is therefore a serious question mark over whether the introduction of child curfew schemes are realistically operational and, more importantly, whether they are compatible with the government's obligations under the European Convention on Human Rights.

When making a Child Safety Order on a child under the age of criminal responsibility, an Antisocial Behaviour Order, a Sex Offender Order, or where a parent is convicted of an offence for failing to secure school attendance of a pupil, a court will also have a discretionary power to make a Parenting Order when Clause 9 Crime and Disorder Bill is enacted. A court *must* do so where a child or young person under the age of 16 is convicted of an offence unless it states why the making of an order would not be desirable in preventing the commission of a further offence. Clause 9 (7) provides that where a court finds that a parent has failed to comply with a requirement of such an Order s/he shall be liable on conviction to a fine. The Parenting Order is likely to be discriminatory in practice and made in most cases against the mother of a child or young person if only because it is the mother who is most likely to attend court with their child. There is no provision for separate legal representation of parents and the single parent mother will fall to be the subject of the majority of such orders. There is no provision to address estranged or absent parents whose behaviour and conduct is so often the root cause of adolescent behaviour that leads children into trouble. The Crime and Disorder Bill will not only criminalise children below the age of criminal responsibility and those of that age where evidence does not have to be 'beyond a reasonable doubt', but it also provides for the same in relation to their parent(s) (and for 'parent' read woman). Where is the justice in that?

Promoting Prosecution

The Audit Commission (1996, p. 105) recommended a transfer of resources from the court system into pre-court intervention thereby decriminalising children and diverting them from the formal criminal justice system which is, as the audit demonstrates, inordinately expensive, slow in response and ineffective. The report considered that after three cautions it was unlikely that a child or young person would desist from offending if made subject to further pre-court disposals. In place of cautioning, Clauses 61 and 62 of the Crime and Disorder Bill will establish, on a statutory basis, a system of reprimands and warnings. The reprimand is intended for first time offenders who have not committed a serious offence whilst the warning (which is a 'one-off' disposal unless at least two years have elapsed from the date of an earlier warning) is reserved for second time offenders and those who are alleged to have committed an offence which is not considered so serious that a charge must result. It falls to the Secretary of State to publish 'guidance' on the levels of seriousness and other criteria to be applied in determining whether to reprimand, warn or charge a child or young person. Where a warning is to be administered by a police officer s/he will be required to refer the child or young person to the local youth offending team for assessment for a programme of rehabilitation. Again it is for the Secretary of State to define the category of police officer who will undertake this. There has been no suggestion to date that persons who will make such decisions will receive special training to enable them to do so consistently and effectively. In this respect it is relevant to note that the United Nations Committee on the Rights of the Child has consistently recommended that all those involved with children in the juvenile justice system receive adequate training with particular reference to the provisions of the Convention and related United Nations Minimum Standards. Rule 12 of the Beijing Rules (United Nations, 1985) states:

> (1) In order to best fulfil their functions, police officers who frequently or exclusively deal with juveniles ... shall be specially instructed and trained.

The rigidity of the reprimand and warning scheme also gives cause for alarm when international law and rules are considered. Article 40(3) of the UN Convention on the Rights of the Child requires that:

> State Parties shall seek to promote the establishment of laws procedures, authorities and institutions specifically applicable to children alleged as, accused of, or recognised as having infringed the penal law and, in particular:
>
> (a) the establishment of a minimum age below which children shall be presumed not to have capacity to infringe the penal law;
>
> (b) whenever appropriate and desirable, measures for dealing with such children without resort to judicial proceedings, providing that human rights and *legal safeguards* are fully respected (United Nations, 1989).

Furthermore, Rule 11 of the Beijing Rules elaborates and makes some important points:

(2) The police, the prosecution or other agencies dealing with juvenile cases shall be empowered to deal with such cases, *at their discretion*, without recourse to formal hearings, in accordance with the criteria laid down for that purpose in the respective legal system and in accordance with the principles laid down in these Rules.

(3) Any diversion involving referral to appropriate community or other services shall require *the consent of the juvenile* ... provided that such decision to refer a case shall be *subject to review* by a competent authority upon application (United Nations, 1985).

There are five principal problems with this new system of reprimands and warnings, both of which must be administered in the case of children and young people in the *presence* of an 'appropriate adult' though as the Crime and Disorder Bill is presently drafted there is no provision requiring the consent of either the child or the 'appropriate adult'. First, given the political imperative to avoid delay in the youth justice system, it is likely that the decision to reprimand, warn or charge will fall to be made with undue haste perhaps immediately after a child or young person has been interviewed by the police. Second, the child interviewed may not have had a solicitor present or may have been in police detention for an inordinate amount of time. Third, the person acting as an 'appropriate adult' may be a parent or some other person who is neither qualified nor able to give the detained child appropriate advice or may not wish to seek it for fear of increasing delay. Fourth, there is considerable research which points to the injustices of current arrangements and they are unlikely to improve under the proposed changes (Evans, 1993; Home Office, 1995). Fifth, there is no transparency, no oversight and no review of the manner in which decisions will be made. This is a serious matter given that both reprimands and warnings are to be citable at any future court or youth panel appearance, as is any failure to comply with an associated programme of rehabilitation.

Indeed these new police disposals are to be citable at court where a child or young person subsequently reoffends. Under current arrangements magistrates generally consider a caution as a 'ticking off'. However how will they, over time, come to view a failure to comply with a programme of rehabilitation? Is it likely that it will come to be viewed as an unwillingness to respond to a previous disposal? How is programme of rehabilitation to be distinguished from those sanctions available to the court – the new Action Plan Order being the most obvious example? Will prompt and recent failure to comply with a rehabilitation programme coupled with the commission of a fresh offence during its currency, lead sentencers to conclude that there would be little purpose in dealing with an offence by a Supervision or Action Plan Order? The very fact that 'diversionary' disposals have been placed on statute diminishes their diversionary value and promotes a proclivity to prosecute.

In the case of either diversionary disposal *the police* will have to satisfy themselves that there is evidence that the child or young person has committed an offence and that there is a realistic prospect of them being convicted. As a fundamental principle of any system aspiring to deliver justice no person should be a judge in their own cause. Yet this is precisely what the new arrangements promote. In addition the evidential test falls well short of being 'beyond a reasonable doubt'. It will of course also be necessary for the child or young person to admit the offence, though this does not address the problem of the police perceiving a set of facts as amounting to an offence when in law they do not, nor of the detained child admitting to facts constituting an offence either to take the blame for someone else or to secure their prompt release from police detention. All cases that previously went to court did so on the basis of the police believing there to be a realistic prospect of securing a conviction – yet year in and year out it is consistently the case that approximately one third of all such alleged offences do not come to that. In fact, the police are particularly poor judges of the quality of their own evidence. This in itself is one of the principal reasons why the Crown Prosecution Service was established in the first place! Furthermore, where the police consider the above criteria to be met the officer concerned must also be satisfied that it would not be in the 'public interest' for the child or young person to be prosecuted. The 'public interest' is not defined in the Crime and Disorder Bill but doubtless will be addressed in 'guidance' to be published by the Secretary of State. Whatever form this guidance will take, it is unlikely that it will include any overbearing requirement to take into account, as a mitigating factor, issues concerning the child or young person's welfare. The emphasis of the new scheme is to avoid delay and it would take time to gather the information necessary for an informed decision to be made which takes into account such factors.

Thus the new diversionary system to be established under Clauses 61 and 62 of the Crime and Disorder Bill places all decision making in the hands of a single agency, *the police*, other than the requirement that an 'appropriate adult' must be present when a reprimand or warning is administered. Neither the consent of the 'appropriate adult' and/or the parent is required according to statute. It will be the police who both investigate and adjudicate upon an offence assuming the role of investigator, prosecutor, judge and jury under the new diversionary arrangements. It will then fall to the new multi-agency youth offending team, unless they consider it unnecessary to do so, to devise a programme of *rehabilitation* the content of which is to be subject to guidance drawn up by the Secretary of State. According to the consultation paper *Tackling Youth Crime* (Home Office, 1997b) such programmes are always likely to include an element of *reparation* to the victim or to the community at large. The Bill fails to establish a framework for rehabilitation other than defining its purpose as preventing a person from reoffending. There is no principle established within the legislation itself that it should be proportionate to the seriousness of the offence or take account of other principles of sentencing that would apply in a court setting. What justice is there in parliament considering legislation that gives the Secretary of State power to publish guidance that is itself not available for consideration and examination even in draft consultative form? It is also conceivable – no inevitable – that the concept of proportionality will be stood on its head with more intrusive interventions being provided on the basis of pre-court warnings for less serious offences than those disposals that are the sole prerogative of the court. It is quite clear that the new system of reprimands and warnings (effectively a 'two strikes and you're in court' rule) will lead to a significant increase in the number of children and young people appearing before the Youth Court in many cases for alleged minor infringements of the criminal law.

In due course the government intends to introduce yet further legislation in order to establish the 'youth panel' in anticipation of a substantial reduction in diversionary activity on the part of the police and in recognition of the rigidity of the final warning scheme. The recent White Paper (Home Office, 1997a) suggests that for those children and young people who cease to be eligible for diversion and who plead guilty at court on their first appearance, a referral to a youth panel would be an option for the court. The panel would then negotiate a 'contract' with the child or young person ostensibly within a framework of restorative justice. Failure to comply with the contract would result in a return to court. Such a system of quasi-diversion holds out many dangers of injustice not least the perverse incentive to enter a guilty plea promptly possibly without the benefit of adequate and competent legal advice.

Incarceration

The Children and Young Persons Act 1969 was the last piece of legislation placed on the statute book by a Labour government that sought to reform the youth justice system. As with the Crime and Disorder Bill, the 1969 Act aimed to further the development of preventive work with children. What happened over the following decade resulted in an explosion of child custody. Thousands of children were subjected to local authority care and Prison Service custody, many spending their adolescence trapped in a revolving door between the two (Thorpe et al., 1980). The prevalent sentencing scenario that was typical of the juvenile court in the 1970s and early 1980s often meant that a first court appearance resulted in a Supervision Order being imposed (particularly where there was an inkling of a welfare problem) regardless of the seriousness of the offence. Often such sSupervision Orders included a condition giving social workers discretion to require the supervised child to take part in Intermediate Treatment for up to 90 days. A second offence was seen as a failure – not of supervision, but of a child's parents to exert proper care and control over him or her. As a consequence the child would be dealt with by the making of a Care Order usually entailing removal from home and placement in a residential establishment. A third offence would all too frequently result in a Detention Centre Order, and a fourth in a Borstal Training Order being imposed.

There is a danger – if not an inevitability – that the Crime and Disorder Bill will achieve the same result as the 1969 Act because it is built upon many of the same foundations. For Intermediate Treatment read programme of rehabilitation/contract/Action Plan Order; for Care Order read Supervision Order with a residence requirement; for Detention Centre and Borstal read Detention and Training Order. It is not inconceivable that sentencers, when faced with a child or young person who has not responded in the required way to a police warning supplemented by a programme of rehabilitation, has similarly been unable to comply with a contract negotiated by the youth panel and has continued to offend despite a Supervision or Action Plan Order being imposed, will resort to a custodial sentence that has a training element to it. Clause 69 of the Crime and Disorder Bill will create a new single custodial sentence to be known as a Detention and Training Order. As with the old Borstal order a child's date of release from such a sentence will to some extent be determined by his or her response to it. Such a sentence will be served in 'secure accommodation' which may be a young offender institution, a secure training centre or local authority accommodation for the purpose of restricting liberty. Clause 35 of the Crime and Disorder Bill will permit the Secretary of State to delegate to youth offending teams the decision as to what type of secure accommodation a Detention and Training Order will be served in thereby opening up the possibility that incarceration will be seen as some sort of secure Care Order. Coupled with the government's response to Sir David Ramsbotham's recommendations arising from the *Thematic Review of Young Prisoners* (HM Inspectorate of Prisons, 1997), child custody will inevitably be viewed by many as an inherently attractive option where children and young people can receive 'treatment' and 'rehabilitation' in a secure and safe environment. It will be safe to incarcerate children, and safer for the public too. The risk here is that 'custody with curtains' will be viewed favourably and its perceived inherent attraction will in turn fuel its use.

Unlike the Children and Young Persons Act 1969, which in its original form sought to ultimately abolish Detention Centre and Borstal sentences, the Crime and Disorder Bill threatens to incarcerate even younger children than is currently the case. It is too easily forgotten that in 1990 there was all-party agreement to repeal legislation permitting the sentence of detention in a young offender institution being imposed on 14 year-olds. Within two years of implementing the Criminal Justice Act 1991 (in October 1992) the Conservative government placed on statute the Criminal Justice and Public Order Act 1994 which created the Secure Training)rder for 12–14 year-olds which the Crime and Disorder Bill now incorporates within the new single custodial sentence – the Detention and Training Order. In addition to meeting the statutory restrictions on the use of custody, in the case of a 12–14 year-old the court will only be able to impose a Detention and Training Order where it is of the opinion that the child is a 'persistent offender'. The term 'persistent offender' is not defined for this purpose, though under the to-be-repealed criteria for a Secure Training Order, the child has to have accumulated three previous convictions and be in breach of, or offended whilst subject to, a supervision order. There is a clear danger in this failure to provide a statutory definition that goes beyond the inevitability of variable interpretation in different areas of the country. It is one of transference.

Clause 41 of the Bill will give the Secretary of State power to make regulations that create additional time limits in the case of defendants aged under 18. It is likely that such regulations, when published, will include a definition of a 'persistent offender'. Paragraph 7.17 of the recent White Paper, in discussing the fast-tracking of persistent young offenders, suggests that they will be defined as:

> someone aged 10–17 who has been sentenced for one or more recordable offences on three or more separate occasions and is arrested again (or has an information laid against him or her) within three years of last being sentenced. In practice, the Government would expect others who do not fit this exact profile

– in particular 'spree offenders' who commit multiple offences over a short period – to be fast tracked ... (Home Office, 1997a).

Such a definition is very broad, particularly given that it applies to those processed by the youth justice system over a three year period and also invites the inclusion of those referred to as 'spree offenders'. Is such a definition going to be borrowed from regulations to be made under Clause 41 and applied in relation to the imposition of child custody under Clause 69? Or perhaps that is too restrictive in the potential interpretation of the phrase 'persistent offender'? Will courts deem offending to be persistent where they are faced with a child who has reoffended in spite of a warning and programme of rehabilitation or in spite of being the subject of a contract drawn up by the youth panel? We should not forget the general scenario in response to the 1969 Act – three strikes and you go to jail. An appropriate definition of 'persistence' will hopefully be addressed at an early stage after implementation of the legislation by means of judicial review. The High Court could consider resurrecting the custodial criteria that was one of the original restrictions on the use of custody in the long since repealed section 1(2) Criminal Justice Act 1982 – *having a history of failure to respond to noncustodial penalties and is unable or unwilling to respond to them.* Youth offending teams need to encourage the acceptance of such a definition too.

The Crime and Disorder Bill was preceded by an array of consultation, policy and manifesto documents issued by the Labour Party whilst in Opposition dating back to 1993. Since coming to power in May 1997 a further range of consultation papers emanated from the Home Office (Home Office 1997b, 1997c and 1997d). At no point was there any suggestion whatsoever of making a custodial sanction available for children below the age of 12. Clause 69 Crime and Disorder Bill will give the Secretary of State power to make custody available for 10 year-olds. In addition to meeting the 'persistent offender' criterion the court will have to form the opinion that only a custodial sentence would be adequate to protect the public from further offending by him. There is no suggestion that where further offending is likely it must be of such a nature as to place the public at risk of serious harm. Thus the prison gates are potentially opened up to receive the child who is a persistent Teletubby thief!

The fact that there was no consultation on the extension of custody to children of that age (other than one week before the Bill's publication when the possibility was mooted in the White Paper) (Home Office, 1997a)) undermines the usual democratic process which requires there to be a problem or issue requiring action followed by informed discussion as to how it should be addressed. There would be little point in placing custody for 10–12 year-olds on the statute book unless there was an intention to use it.

Conclusion

So where is the justice in all this? It seems that the multi-agency constitution of youth offending teams will make it increasingly difficult to sustain principles of minimum intervention in the face of a philosophy that demands for something to be done to children in trouble at every stage of the youth justice system. Things are going to be done to children and to their parent(s). These interventions are probably not going to work in terms of preventing offending and there is no evidence that they will be any more effective than sanctions currently available. More interventions will mean more breaches of orders which in turn will ratchet up the case for custody. The lessons of the 1969 Act will not have been learnt.

For those children and young people who fall to be sentenced for their wrongdoings far better be it for that disposal to be determined in accordance with principles of proportionality and without undue intervention arising to address welfare concerns unconnected with the offence itself. For those who choose to avoid the warning scheme a conditional discharge will remain an option available to the court on all occasions. The right to legal representation will remain thereby allowing full mitigation to be argued on behalf of the child in trouble and his or her parent. In determining the most appropriate

Justice is something to be found in the courts. It is not something to be delivered by the police, the local authority or the probation service. Justice is obtained through the services of the legal profession. Whilst this view may not prevail amongst those who support restorative justice, it seems that it will fall to lawyers to obtain justice for children. Their advice to clients should be to accept at most a police reprimand but avoid the pitfalls of the warning and the associated programme of rehabilitation (which courts may view as a previous conviction and sentence) the availability of which may, in any case, be determined not by need but by resource demands placed upon youth offending teams. Better be it for a child to go before a court where an alleged offence can be reviewed by an independent Crown Prosecution Service and the issue of guilt or innocence determined if need be by an independent tribunal versed in law who must satisfy themselves that a case is made out beyond reasonable doubt.

method of dealing with a child the court can continue to be informed by a pre-sentence report written by a probation officer or social worker from a youth offending team who, by virtue of the potential workload arising for such teams as much as anything else, will have an interest in minimum intervention. Remember both the failure of the 1969 Act and the success of the legislation of the 1980s.

A further advantage in retaining jurisdiction within a judicial forum is that it will allow for critical scrutiny of decisions and interventions made by the police and youth offending teams. At present police cautions can exceptionally be the subject of judicial review. Given that current diversionary arrangements are to be replaced by a statutory scheme where reprimands, warnings and failures to comply with programmes of rehabilitation will be citable at court, lawyers must in all cases evaluate the efficacy of these in light of both the statutory provisions and the guidance that will be issued by the Secretary of State. The same will apply where a contract agreed by the youth panel has been breached. Just as lawyers scrutinise the conduct of investigation and detention under the Police and Criminal Evidence Act 1984 they will need to do the same in relation to the new youth 'justice' system.

Some issues concerning the new system will have to be addressed by judicial review thereby establishing precedent which lower courts will be obliged to follow. There should be no reluctance in pursuing this route to justice particularly in relation to some of the issues discussed in this chapter. Some matters, the child curfew order is the most obvious example, may infringe European law and International Convention, necessitating recourse to the European Court of Human Rights. So too those elements of the Crime and Disorder Bill that have criminalising consequences for parents (when the behaviour of their children which led to the making of non-criminal orders in the first place) look distinctly suspect in relation to fundamental principles of law.

The youth panel (if the government proceeds with its plans in this respect) holds out dangers for children and young people not least the lack of representation. The government's proposals in this respect offend international law and Convention. For example, Article 15.1 of the Beijing Rules deals with adjudication and disposition in stating:

> Throughout the proceedings the juvenile shall have the right to be represented by a legal adviser or to apply for free legal aid where there is provision for such aid in the country (United Nations, 1995).

Referral to the Youth Panel is an option (assuming that defendants will have a choice in the matter) to be avoided given that the proposed contract will be enforceable for up to a year. In essence the Panel will be able to impose a programme of intervention equivalent to a 12 month Supervision Order with reparation. The proposed involvement of victims in the Panel system simply does nothing for the child in trouble. It is about naming and shaming: the denunciation of the child and nothing else. Reparation, given the potential numbers involved, is likely to focus on reparation to the community at large through participation in schemes (assuming enough suitable work can be identified) that will be little different to junior community service, contrary to child employment and health and safety laws and undertaken primarily at weekends. Such schemes will not be restorative; they will be retributive in nature. We should not be fooled by this sham that is restorative justice. Sensitive issues concerning the family or the child's upbringing or history in care will not be openly shared. It is the welfare of the child or young person that should be a paramount consideration not the perceived need of society to extract a pound of flesh. Increasing the transparency of the arena in which children who offend are dealt with, ostensibly at least, has an inverse effect upon the quality of information available to inform the most appropriate decision.

If justice for children in trouble is to remain the primary objective of those charged with assisting them it will not be found within the three Rs: responsibility, restoration and reintegration – which is apparently becoming increasingly fashionable (NACRO, 1997). Justice is found in a system that is characterised by impartiality, objectivity and competency and which is moulded by checks and balances to prevent abuse of power. Responses to delinquent behaviour should be proportionate to its gravity and relevant to the child or young person. The Crime and Disorder Bill aims to establish an interventionist approach to preventing youth crime when all the evidence suggests that what is required is a long term universal preventive strategy aimed at all children, not just those who offend. It is society that needs rehabilitative action through bringing social justice to families and their children who have been increasingly marginalised over the past 15 years or so (Joseph Rowntree Foundation, 1995). That used to be what the Labour Party was about, but is it now a wolf in sheep's clothing?

References

Audit Commission (1996), *Misspent Youth*, London, Audit Commission.

Council of Europe (1950), *The European Convention on Human Rights*.

Department of Health (1994), *The UN Convention on the Rights of the Child : The UK's First Report to the UN Committee on the Rights of the Child*, London, HMSO.

Evans, R. (1993), *The Conduct of Police Interviews with Juveniles*, London, HMSO.

Goldson, B. (1997), 'Children in Trouble: State Responses to Juvenile Crime' in P. Scraton (ed.), *'Childhood' in 'Crisis'?*, London, UCL Press.

Her Majesty's Inspectorate of Prisons (1997), *Young Prisoners: A Thematic Review by HM Chief Inspector of Prisons for England and Wales*, London, Home Office.

Home Office (1985), *Circular 14/85: The Cautioning of Offenders*, London, Home Office.

Home Office (1990), *Circular 59/90: The Cautioning of Offenders*, London, Home Office.

Home Office (1995), *Appropriate Adults: Report of the Review Group*, London, HMSO.

Home Office (1997a), *No More Excuses – A New Approach to Tackling Youth Crime in England and Wales*, London, Home Office.

Home Office (1997b), *Tackling Youth Crime: A Consultation Paper*, London, Home Office.

Home Office (1997c), *New National and Local Focus on Youth Crime: A Consultation Paper*, London, Home Office.

Home Office (1997d), *Tackling Delays in the Youth Justice System: A Consultation Paper*, London, Home Office.

Home Office (1997e), *Preventing Children Offending*, London, Home Office.

Home Office (1997f), *Review of Delay in the Criminal Justice System* (The Narey Report), London, Home Office.

Joseph Rowntree Foundation (1995), *Inquiry into Income and Wealth*, Vols 1 and 2, York, Joseph Rowntree Foundation.

Labour Party (1996), *Tackling Youth Crime: Reforming Youth Justice*, London, Labour Party.

Labour Party (1997), *Labour's Six Point Policy Plan for Juvenile Crime and Disorder*, London, Labour Party Press Office.

NACRO (1997), *The New Three Rs for Young Offenders – Responsibility, Restoration and Reintegration: Towards a New Strategy for Children who Offend*, London, NACRO.

Thorpe, D., Smith, D., Green, C. and Paley, J. (1980), *Out of Care*, London, Allen and Unwin.

United Nations (1985), *The Beijing Rules: The United Nations Standard Minimum Rules for the Administration of Juvenile Justice*, New York, United Nations.

United Nations (1989), *The United Nations Convention on the Rights of the Child*, New York, United Nations.

United Nations Committee on the Rights of the Child (1995), *Eighth Session. Consideration of Reports Submitted by States Under Article 44 of the Convention*, New York, United Nations.

Index

Thompson, Robert 42
Tonry, M. 8–9
training, lawyers 182–3
Triseliotis, J. 21
Troubleshooter Project 170–86, 189

unemployment, ethnicity 54–5, 58–9
United Nations Committee on the Rights of
    the Child 195–6, 200
United Nations Convention on the Rights of
    the Child xii, 1–2, 195
  age of criminal responsibility 18
  critique of UK policy 3–4
  girls 34
  incarceration 11, 20
  prosecution 200
United Nations Guidelines for the
    Prevention of Juvenile Delinquency
    (Riyadh Guidelines) 11
United Nations Rules for the Protection of
    Juveniles Deprived of their Liberty
    (Havana Rules) 11
United Nations Standard Minimum Rules
    for the Administration of Juvenile
    Justice (Beijing Rules) 11, 18, 20, 195,
    196–7, 200–1, 208
United States
  CtC programme 85–6
  curfews 16, 17
  ethnicity 70
  welfare needs 139
urban neighbourhoods *see* inner cities
Utting, D. 84

Vanstone, M. 154
Venables, Jon 42
victim offender restoration model 127,
    129–30, 131

victims
  Reparation Orders 133
  restorative justice 98, 100–1, 102–3, 106–
    7, 127, 129–30
violence
  girls 29, 30–1
  increase of 156
  racial 68
vulnerability 187, 188

Waddington, David 79
Wales 110–25
Walsh, Craig 171
warnings 104–5, 106, 131–2, 157–8, 200–3,
    207
welfare 139–41, 197
'welfare model' 91
Welsh Office 110, 111–14, 116
West, D.J. 12, 83–4
Westergaard, J. 57
Wilcox, R. 143
women xii, 6
Wootton, Barbara 41
World Summit for Children 1990 1
Worrall, Anne xii, 28–47

YOTs *see* youth offending teams
Young Offenders (White Paper 1980) 149
Young, P. 15
youth offending teams (YOTs) 37, 117, 142,
    204, 207
  Action Plan Orders 133
  crime prevention 88
  decision-making 143
  monitoring 122, 123, 124
Youth Panel 134–5, 142, 203, 208–9
youth training programmes 59